India between Tradition and Modernity

INDIA between Tradition and Modernity

Edited by

JOANNA KURCZEWSKA
ISHWAR MODI
JANUSZ MUCHA

RAWAT PUBLICATIONS
Jaipur • New Delhi • Bangalore • Hyderabad • Guwahati • Kolkata

ISBN 978-81-316-0625-4

This volume draws upon articles published in the special issue of *Polish Sociological Review*, Vol 2 (178), 2012.

Published by
Prem Rawat for **Rawat Publications**
Satyam Apts, Sector 3, Jawahar Nagar, Jaipur 302 004 (India)
Phone: 0141 265 1748 / 7006 Fax: 0141 265 1748
E-mail: info@rawatbooks.com
Website: www.rawatbooks.com

New Delhi Office
4858/24, Ansari Road, Daryaganj, New Delhi 110 002
Phone: 011 2326 3290

Also at *Bangalore, Hyderabad, Guwahati* and *Kolkata*

Typeset by Rawat Computers, Jaipur
Printed at Chaman Enterprises, New Delhi

Contents

Contributors

Joanna Kurczewska is Professor of Sociology at the Institute of Philosophy and Sociology, Polish Academy of Sciences. Editor-in-chief of the *Polish Sociological Review*. E-mail: jkurczew@ifispan.waw.pl

Ishwar Modi is Professor of Sociology, and a pioneer of leisure studies in India. Director of the India International Institute of Social Sciences, President of the Indian Sociological Society. E-mail: iiiss2005modi@yahoo.co.in

Janusz Mucha is Professor of Sociology. He heads the Department of Sociology and Social Anthropology at AGH University of Science and Technology in Kraków, Poland. His interests cover minority studies, social theory, Central and Eastern Europe, social aspects of technology and intergenerational relations. Author of many books and articles on these subjects. E-mail: jmucha@post.pl

Yogendra Singh is a noted Indian sociologist. He is one of the founders of the Centre for the Study of Social Systems, Jawaharlal Nehru University, New Delhi, India, where he is a professor emeritus of Sociology, and where he has been a professor since 1971. An alumnus of Department of Sociology, Lucknow University, he has been the President of the Indian Sociological Society, and received the 'Indian Sociological Society Lifetime Achievement Award' in 2007, apart from Best Social Scientist Award of the Government of Madhya Pradesh. Author of many books and articles. E-mail: yogendrasinghjnu@hotmail.com

M. Krzysztof Byrski, Professor of Indian Studies, University of Warsaw. Director of Eurasian Research Centre, Collegium Civitas. Specialist on Indian history and affairs. From 1993–1996, Ambassador of the Republic of Poland to India. Graduate of Indology at Warsaw University (1960). He completed his Ph.D. research at Banaras Hindu University (1966) and his post-doctoral studies in 1978 at Warsaw University. Author of more than a hundred publications, including a number of books, such as *The Concept of Ancient Indian Theatre* (New Delhi, 1973), and *Methodology of the Analysis of Sanskrit Drama* (New Delhi, 1997) and the Polish translation of the *Manusmriti* (Warszawa, 1985).
Byrski has been awarded several prestigious prizes in India bequeathed upon him in the name of different organizations among others by the President and the Prime Minister of India. Research interests cover classical indology, history of classical Indian culture and literature and Indian axiology, Hindi. E-mail: m.k.byrski@uw.edu.pl

Dhruv Raina is Professor of History and Philosophy of Science and Education at Zakir Husain Centre for Educational Studies, School of Social Sciences Jawaharlal Nehru University, New Delhi. His research has focused upon the politics and cultures of scientific knowledge in South Asia. He has co-edited *Situating the History of Science: Dialogues with Joseph Needham* (1999) and *Social History of Sciences in Colonial India* (2007), and more recently *Science between Europe and Asia* (2010). *Images and Contexts: the Historiography of Science and Modernity* (2003) was a collection of papers contextualizing science and its modernity in India. S. Irfan Habib and he co-authored *Domesticating Modern Science* (2004) which again addressed the encounter between modern science and the so-called 'traditional sciences' in colonial India. He has published papers on related subjects in journals of the history and philosophy of science, social studies of science and social and political history. Over the last couple of years he has been working on cultures of history and science policy in post-colonial South Asia, and the social theory of science, technology and mathematics. A forthcoming work deals with transnational academic networks and the formation of academic disciplines. E-mail: d_raina@yahoo.com

Pratap Bhanu Mehta is currently the President, Centre for Policy Research Delhi. He previously taught political theory at Harvard

University and has published widely in political theory and Indian politics. His recent publications include *The Burden of Democracy* and *The Oxford Companion to Politics in India* (co-edited with Niraja Jayal). He is the recipient of the Infosys Prize and the Malcom S. Adhisehiah Prize for Social Sciences. E-mail: pratapbmehta@yahoo.co.in

Ananta Kumar Giri is Associate Professor at the Madras Institute of Development Studies, Chennai. His interests cover New Horizons of Human Development and Social Transformations in India and the World: Dialogues, Dignity and Responsibility; Religion, Spiritual Mobilizations and Social Transformations; Social Theory and Social Movements: Criticism, Creativity and the Contemporary Dialectics of Transformations; Creative Transformations in Education, Philosophy and Literature.
E-mails: aumkr-ishna@yahoo.com/aumkrishna@gmail.com

K.L. Sharma, Professor of Sociology is currently Vice Chancellor of Jaipur National University, Jaipur (India). Formerly, he was Rector at Jawaharlal Nehru University, New Delhi. Sharma was also Vice Chancellor of Rajasthan University, Jaipur (India). Between 1991–2006, he was a visiting professor for five times at College de France, Paris. Sharma has also lectured at various universities in Holland, England and Germany. The University Grants Commission of India honoured him with Swami Pranavanand Saraswati Award in 2002 for his contributions to sociology and social anthropology. Sharma has twenty-three books and eighty papers to his credit. E-mail: klsharma@hotmail.com

Paramjit S. Judge is Professor of Sociology and Coordinator, Centre for the Study of Social Exclusion and Inclusive Policy at Guru Nanak Dev University, Amritsar, Punjab, India. He has worked and published in the areas of social movements, diaspora studies and sociology of dalits. Some of acclaimed works are: *Insurrection to Agitation: The Naxalite Movement in Punjab* (1992), *Terrorism in Punjab: Understanding Reality at Grass-roots Level* (co-authored) (1999), *Religion, Identity and Nationhood: The Khalistan Movement* (2005), *Mapping Dalits: Contemporary Reality and Future Prospects* (2009), and *Changing Dalits: Exploration Across Time* (2010). He is also an accomplished novelist in Punjabi. E-mail: paramjit.judge@gmail.com

Maitrayee Chaudhuri has been teaching sociology at the Centre for the Study of Social Systems, School of Social Sciences, Jawaharlal Nehru University (JNU), New Delhi since 1990. She was the Director of the Women's Studies Programme (WSP), JNU (2006–2008). She has published widely in the area of gender, culture, media and pedagogy. Her work includes (ed.) *Sociology in India: Intellectual and Institutional, The Indian Women's Movement: Reform and Revival,* (ed.), *The Practice of Sociology,* (ed.), *Feminism in India.* She has been the Advisor and author for Sociology School Textbooks, National Council for Education, Research and Training, NCERT, India. She has been Visiting DAAD Guest Professor, Albert Ludwigs University, Freiburg, Germany, 2003, Visiting Fellow, Committee on Degrees in Women's Studies, Harvard University, Cambridge, USA, 1995–1996, Visiting Fellow, Institute of Asian American Studies, University of Massachusetts, Boston, 1995–1996. She has lectured widely both within India and outside. E-mail: maitrayeec@gmail.com

Duru Arun Kumar is a faculty in Sociology of Science at Netaji Subhas Institute of Technology, New Delhi, India. Her areas of interest are Higher Technical Education, Globalization, and Science and Technology Research.
E-mail: duruarun@rediffmail.com

Piotr Kłodkowski specializes in international affairs with focus on Indo-European political, social and cultural relations. He is a professor of University of Information Technology and Management in Rzeszów, and is currently (since 2009) the Ambassador of Poland to India. E-mail: pklodkowski@interia.pl

Binay Kumar Pattnaik, Professor of Sociology, currently working at the Department of Humanities and Social Sciences, Indian Institute of Technology Kanpur, India. With more than 26 years of experience in teaching and research, he has contributed handsomely to the area of Sociology of Science and Technology and Sociology of Social Movements. More particularly, he has contributed to the studies on the effects of globalization and liberalization process on science and technology regimes in developing countries. His recent contributions include papers in *People's Science Movement in India and Appropriate Technology Movement in India* (JSST). His scholarly contributions include more than thirty research papers in refereed journals of repute, and half a dozen books (both edited and written). He has been Guest Editor to couple of international journals too. E-mail: binay@iitk.ac.in

From the Editors

An Invitation to Debates

JOANNA KURCZEWSKA
ISHWAR MODI
JANUSZ MUCHA

This book, which is the outcome of the special issue of the *Polish Sociological Review*, is primarily a self-presentation of Indian sociologists and their recent theoretical and empirical research achievements. The suggestion to prepare this issue and, in turn, this book came from the Indian Sociological Society with which the Polish Sociological Association cooperates. Except for two articles by Polish diplomats and academics, who specialize in the cultural and political problems of India, this entire volume was conceived by Ishwar Modi, a sociologist of international renown and *spiritus movens* of several valuable publishing endeavours.

The volume includes essays, expert opinions and articles by sociologists from various research centres in India, selected as markers of the most important fields of research in contemporary Indian sociology and testimonies of significant contributions to the development of our discipline.

Not only does this book attests to the successful cooperation between our two sociological associations, it also testifies to the well-meaning of Asian sociologists and their interest in sociological institutions in Central and Eastern Europe, recently dubbed 'The Younger Europe'.

We are happy that our Editorial Board applauded the initiative of the Indian sociologists and that the 'Indian issue' of our journal could go on. On behalf of the Editorial Board we wish to thank our colleagues in India and hope that we can also speak on behalf of our readers when expressing our gratitude to them for offering both a very heterogeneous picture of contemporary Indian society and a multidimensional picture of Indian sociology, its role and place in the structure of science and scientific institutions, and in the public sphere of a society which is moving towards democracy, spurred on by many external and internal factors.

The first 'editorial reading' of this volume suggests that European readers have received a significant intellectual proposal. Rather than painting a celebratory portrait of 'the largest and most populated democracy in the world' and 'a serious partner in new global geopolitics', the contributions offer several insightful and mutually complementary diagnoses of what Indian sociologists have identified as the most important issues for various types of social communities—issues which stimulate the most intense emotions and cognitive interest.

First and foremost this book is a cultural gift, an attempt to create a space for intellectual contact with what is going on in the Indian modernization and—more generally—social change in Asiatic context with its economic, social and political mechanisms and its mental and technological dimensions. We have been given an opportunity to take a closer look at new social diversities, new social movements, mass consumption, and the legacy of colonialism. This is also a space in which we find significant clashes between ancient Indian religious and philosophical traditions, and the universality and rationality of modern technology.

The articles, written by specialists in different fields of sociology, variously engaged in public life, not only create an opportunity for diagnosis, as mentioned earlier, but also can help us to reproduce the idiomatic interpretation of modernization in the colonial, and above all post-colonial, context. Last but not least, they offer a convenient point of departure for reflection on Western Europe and its international role-modelling function. Thanks to the authors of these articles that we could take a different look at Western Europe which perceives itself in many 'grand narratives' of capitalist transformation as the primary source and model of modernization in Eastern Europe and the world. In other words, the articles contained in this volume expose the intellectual strength and weakness of Western Europe, encompassed in sociology, with its assumptions of historicism, nationalism or individualism, its categories of time, rationality, sovereignty or gender. They also pave the way for debate on the patterns of capitalist modernization in Western and non-Western Europe and the so-called Third World as relicts, for discussions on the transition to capitalism in the post-colonial and post-communist era, for the analysis of this transition which civilization under development has automatically rendered incomplete or deformed. We think this issue may inspire us to come to terms with the European language of modernism, with its weaknesses and ingenuity expressed in sociological categories pertaining to the market, democracy and the nation state.

These articles deserve to be read carefully, not only because they provide an excellent review of universality, rationality and diversity in post-colonial India but also because they show that it makes sense to translate the western world of modernization into the categories and images of Indian capitalist modernization. By approaching the determinants, mechanisms and consequences of this translation in contemporary India so comprehensively and insightfully, they direct our attention towards European modernization rationale and help us to take reliable stock of European sociological achievements.

Also—and this is particularly valuable for Polish sociology and Polish sociologists—they help us to get a better view of our Western European case of translation of capitalist models of transformation vis-à-vis the European context and the global context. When Polish sociologists focused on the issues of political and economic transformation 'in the Polish mode', seeking its uniqueness in Polish history rather than analysing its Eastern or Western European context, new research options were uncovered. They were created by, for example, the theories of multiculturalism, globalization and post-colonialism. These languages, we assure you, took root in social sciences in India a long time ago, so we can count on the support of 'these sciences' in the formation of the Polish contribution to the debate on the future of Europe after globalization. Indian research pursuits could greatly help to further our understanding of Poland's place in Europe or the place of post-Communist Europe in the worldwide modernization process. Could it perhaps help us to revise our visions of social transformation? Or inspire us to take a different perspective on the legacy of Marxism, official and unofficial, for the Polish transformation, and above all encourage us to reconstruct the role of solidarity as a self-organizing, peaceful social and cultural revolution? To conclude, we wish to thank our colleagues from India for their inspiration and for their interesting suggestions concerning the cultural and social interpretation of Poland and Europe.

1

Society and Sociology in India

Some Reflections

ISHWAR MODI

It is a matter of great pleasure for me that this particular issue of the prestigious and internationally acclaimed *Polish Sociological Review (PSR)* is entirely devoted to some of the important aspects of Indian society. The aspects covered in this special issue are important not only historically but also in the contemporary context. Whatever has been included in this volume will certainly provide a window to the world, and more so to European sociologists to have a glimpse of the contemporary Indian society. This would provide better understanding of society and sociology in India, and also generate further interest among overseas scholars, particularly the Polish sociologists and social scientists to study Indian society. The very fact that the Polish Sociological Association and the *PSR* invited me to guest edit this special issue on India, when I was not President of the Indian Sociological Society, speaks of the interest that the Polish sociologists already had for understanding Indian society. It is not only a matter of honour for me to be associated with *PSR* but also a matter of satisfaction and pride that India is drawing renewed attention of the international community of sociologists and other scholars.

It can be mentioned that India being an old society faced contradictions, has several socio-political turmoils, not only due to internal but also because of foreign onslaughts and invasions. As a consequence, in the past, it went through many socio-structural changes and transformations which naturally were reflected in its socio-cultural fabric (Modi 1985). Each period of major socio-structural change in Indian society had its nuances and impact, altering and creating a set of new social hierarchies and social formations. These hierarchies and social structures have presented in one or, the other form, and have shaped and reshaped the nature and character of Indian society and its various institutions, be it marriage, family, *jāti*, caste, community, kinship, religious practices, rural/urban/tribal communities, state, etc.

As such, socio-cultural and economic and political institutions had been at the centre of indigenous intellectual traditions and discourses in India. A tradition of reflection on socio-cultural and politico-economic institutions had persisted in different philosophical and scholarly texts. A large number of these classical texts authored and compiled by eminent sages and scholars over the millennia contain valuable insights on different aspects of Indian society.

Some of the early pioneers of sociology in India subscribed to an indological approach which rested on the assumption that historically Indian society and culture were unique and that this 'contextual' specificity of Indian social realities could be grasped better through 'texts' (Mukherjee 1977).

However, one of the most eminent sociologists in India, namely, Yogendra Singh (1967) observed a few decades ago that the contemporary sociological literature in India from the point of theoretical orientation could be classified into five major types: (1) the comparative-historical approach, (2) philosophico-sociological approach, (3) logico-philosophical approach, (4) structural-functional approach, and (5) statistical-positivistic approach. Besides these major approaches, Indian sociology has also shown some evidence of psychological and psycho-analytical approaches.

The above classification of theoretical orientations in Indian sociology still holds true to considerable extent. However, several new approaches and orientations have been in vogue in recent researches and writings. The prominent ones pertain to the domains of justice, feminism, cultural identity and civil society.

As on today, Indian sociology is passing through a critical phase. On the one hand, it is still dominated by the paradigms and methodologies of Western sociology and, on the other, Indian sociologists are becoming increasingly conscious of the persisting inequalities. They are trying to understand the nature of social inequality. Social justice and distributive shares have become key concerns today. Thus, for example, many sociologists are engaged in understanding the dynamics of the reservation policy (affirmative action). However, these studies are descriptive or at best analytical, but in most cases bereft of a sound theoretical foundation (Modi 2010).

The emergence of sociology in India as a formal discipline in the year 1919 coincided with several critical phases of history, both in India and in the West. By 1919, Mahatma Gandhi had already returned from South Africa. The scars of the First World War (1914–1918) were still vivid and were haunting mankind. The post-war reconstruction was underway everywhere. Gandhi's presence not only galvanized the freedom movement but also inspired several pioneering sociologists to study the problems of the common man, besides the study of day-to-day institutions, such as marriage, family, caste, community and kinship (ibid.).

Since the 1950s, the Indian sociologists have remained preoccupied with the issues of social change, social development and modernization. These issues are still important for Indian society as is apparent from the paper of Yogendra Singh in this issue of the *PSR*. Similarly, caste in Indian society still continues as a major concern. Caste constantly reinvents itself and appears in myriad forms contrary to the wishful thinking of many for its disappearance. Its economic and political gains keep strengthening it. A thorough and analytical discussion on caste in contemporary India has been undertaken by K.L. Sharma. Debates on caste have continued for long. Many Western scholars have seen and interpreted caste from their own perspective and mindset. As such, most Indian sociologists would be amused to see when M. Christopher Byrski has equated *jāti* with nation. Exclusion of dalits as a consequence of the rigid hierarchy in the caste system is one of the most debatable issues in Indian society today. Alternative strategies adopted by the lowest caste groups known by the generic term dalits to improve their social status in Indian society has been taken up by Paramjit S. Judge. India is also often seen as a land of contrast where tradition and modernity coexist and Indian women are often showcased as emblematic of this coexistence. Paper by Maitrayee Chaudhuri presents a more historicized account of India's modernity from the vantage point of gender, offering a feminist critique, which is a new trend in Indian sociology. Indian society cannot be properly visualized without taking cognizance of the place of religion and secularism in contemporary India. Susan Visvanathan's paper examines such aspects where the secular and the religious domains intertwine. Besides the above, one of the central challenges confronting post-colonial India in its march toward decolonization is the intellectual challenge posed by the idea of modernity. Dhruv Raina has examined this challenge through the works of historians of science and philosophy.

No account of the Indian society and polity can be completed without taking cognizance of the nature of the state and democracy in India. Pratap Bhanu Mehta examines the obstacles in the path of accountable government even in well-established democracies more so in the face of social inequality, making a politics of common citizenship difficult to achieve. The question of common citizenship leads to the issues of civil society. Civil society as on today has become a globally valorized discourse. Anant Kumar Giri explores pathways of Indian modernities and its implication for rethinking civil society and public sphere globally. As on today, sociological picturization of any society cannot be completed without examining and exploring the impact of the globalization induced ICT revolution on socio-cultural aspects of society. India cannot be an exception in this regard. The impact of the ICT revolution on different sections of the Indian society and how it is creating new social classes in the era of globalization has been taken up by Binay Kumar Pattnaik.

The issues that have been taken up in this issue of the *PSR* would certainly motivate people to form and create a particular image of India. The image building of a nation by the nationals of some other country also depends not only on what they are reading about that country at a particular moment, but also, what they had been seeing and reading about it for a long time and as such, it is always possible to construct clashing images of a country or a nation. Piotr Kłodkowski in his paper attempts to figure out such factors that provide clashing images of India both at home and in Poland. The themes that have been included in this issue of the *PSR* are of utmost significance in the context of contemporary Indian society, but these are certainly not exhaustive. There are several other equally significant issues, which may be taken up in another issue of the journal.

Among the many challenges that sociology is facing in India, while some pertain to the quality of students—since the brightest or even the brighter of them are not coming to sociology under the current market forces—others pertain to the paucity of facilities and funding due to neglect on the part of State. The role of sociologists in public life is shrinking, particularly in the planning bodies of the country. The community of Indian sociologists has not been quite conscious about its role to contribute to theory building and conceptualization (Modi 2010).

REFERENCES

Modi, Ishwar. 1985. *Leisure, Mass Media and Social Structure*. Jaipur: Rawat Publications.

——. 2010. 'Indian Sociology Faces the World', in Michael Burawoy, Mau-kuei Chang and Michelle Fei-you Hsieh (eds), *Facing an Unequal World: Challenges for a Global Sociology*. Taipei: Institute of Sociology at Academia Sinica, Taiwan and Council of National Association of the ISA.

Mukherjee, R. 1977. 'Trends in Indian Sociology', *Current Sociology*, Vol. 25, No. 3.

Singh, Yogendra. 1967. 'The Scope and Method of Sociology in India', in T.K.N. Unnithan et al. (eds), *Sociology for India*. New Delhi: Prentice Hall of India.

2

Sociology of India, Sociology in India, Indian Sociology[1]

JANUSZ MUCHA

Indian natural and social scientists play an increasingly significant role in the field of research and education. Bearing in mind the traditional Western visions of the world, we must be aware of the global transformations. It is true that modern universities emerged as the Western-style research and education institutions; science, in the contemporary sense of the term, is a relatively recent enterprise originating in the Western world; sociology and social anthropology (the latter is very relevant here) emerged in Western Europe. All the universities, modern science and sociology and social anthropology, under the influence of colonialism, imperialism and globalization, have since expanded and become a significant part of the global culture. Not only are economic and political processes and institutions constantly shifting, but so also are cultural and scholarly centres. What was believed to belong to the peripheries and/or semi-peripheries is no longer at the 'margins'. Moreover, with the increase in domestic and international migrations, many people raised and educated in one culture, work (not necessarily permanently) in another and thus contribute to the 'universal' culture. The 'margins' have ceased to be only the mines of interesting (sometimes 'exotic') empirical data elaborated by social scientists in the metropolitan areas. The interest in the non-Western, non-metropolitan social sciences and their achievements seems to be growing in today's sociological community (see, e.g., Connell 2007; Burawoy et al. 2010; Patel 2010). Our engagement is not only with the Western style 'sociology of India', but also with 'sociology as such' being developed in India and with the attempts to build 'Indian sociology', in the sense of systematic research of structural and cultural issues based on conceptual models of society closer to Indian rather than to Western experiences and philosophies, based on India's own indigenous perspectives (see, e.g., Mukherjee 1989; Modi 2010; Patel 2010). Sociology[2] as practised in India is very important for international sociology. We not only learn *about* the Indian subcontinent, but also learn *from* it. What is important in 'southern sociology' is not necessarily the discovering of alternative 'founding fathers' of the same social sciences but rather the fact that 'peripheral' societies can 'produce social thought about the modern world which has as much intellectual power as metropolitan social thought, and more political relevance' (Connell 2007: viii, xii).

The teaching of 'sociology' (actually, at that time as social anthropology) started in India in 1919, at the University of Bombay (today's Mumbai), but was preceded by systematic empirical research devoted to satisfy the colonial government's needs to classify, categorize and document the life of people under its rule. During the pre-independence period,[3] the most important topics of social research were the caste system, tribal communities, family, marriage and kinship, rural and urban communities. The colonial administration had been aware of the inadequate and often inaccurate commonsense understanding of local customs, traditions and misjudgements about different institutional arrangements. Selection of research topics was based at that time on Western values and normative principles of Christianity, was ideologically biased and according to today's Indian scholars, it exaggerated segmentary cleavages in Indian society. In 1947, sociology and/or social anthropology was taught at three universities: Bombay, Calcutta and Lucknow, as well as in smaller colleges in Poona, Mysore and Hyderabad. In the early years, most units of sociology and social anthropology were located within departments of Economics. The expansion of Indian social anthropology and sociology began in 1952. At the end of the 1970s, fifty universities and colleges offered MA programmes in sociology. By 2000, sociology was taught in almost one hundred (out of about two hundred) Indian institutions of higher education. More than ten thousand teachers conduct sociology lectures at all levels of education (including high schools) in India today (Patel 2010: 280; Modi 2010: 316–318). The Jawaharlal Nehru University of New Delhi is a very strong centre of sociological research and teaching. Four out of eight of our Indian authors come from this institution.

According to Sujata Patel, sociology in India faces, since the last decades, at least two distinct challenges. The first relates to the growth of the higher education system and the demands of the regional (in states and territories) elites to establish local colleges and universities. In these institutions, instruction is provided in local languages, but very often without the support of textbooks published in these languages. Infrastructure is usually poor in these institutions. Moreover, sociology practice often represents regional interests, mostly those of local elites. New generations of students, coming from previously excluded and uneducated communities are faced with sociology teachers unprepared for new students' needs. According to Patel, sociology came about in these local colleges to acquire the status of a non-professional and commonsensical subject of low prestige. The second challenge is actually a variation or consequence of the former. Social movements of different kinds, representing excluded and discriminated groups (landless people, peasants, working class, slum dwellers, middle and lower castes, tribal communities, religious groups and women being examples) emerged and became strong. Social inequalities have grown in the country. The poverty level reached 40 per cent of the total population and the number of urban poor is increasing rapidly due to migration from villages. Since the 1980s, some sociologists have made efforts to integrate the formerly unheard voices into the discipline, often engaging with other intellectual currents such as subaltern studies, post-colonial studies, and feminist studies. Simultaneously, older areas of mainstream sociology have become reconstituted and new specializations have developed (Patel 2010: 288–289; Modi 2010: 319–321).

In December of 1951, with the initiative of G.S. Ghurye, head of the Department of Sociology in Bombay, the Indian Sociological Society (ISS) was formally registered. Ghurye served as its president until 1966. In 1952, the Society started its biannual periodical, *Sociological Bulletin* (from 2004—three issues a year). It publishes a biannual *Newsletter* as well. Regional sociological associations publish their own periodicals. Since 1955, the All-India

Sociological Conference (AISC) was established, concentrating on workshops and seminars, which were organized in various parts of the country. In 1967, AISC merged with the ISS. M.N. Srinivas was elected the new president. Today, Ishwar Modi from the India International Institute of Social Sciences (in Jaipur) is the president of the ISS. When we look at the titles of the research committees of the ISS, we could put the topics of articles in this issue of the *Polish Sociological Review (PSR)* into a perspective of current interests of Indian sociologists, as well as in the ways of Indian categorization of the social: (1) theory, concepts and methodology; (2) family, kinship and marriage; (3) economy, polity and society; (4) migration and diasporic studies; (5) education and society; (6) religion and religious communities; (7) rural, peasant and tribal communities; (8) social stratification, professions and social mobility; (9) dalits and backward classes; (10) gender studies; (11) sociology and environment; (12) population, health and society; (13) science, technology and society; (14) culture and communication; (15) social change and development; (16) urban and industrial studies; (17) social movements; (18) sociology of crime and deviance; (19) age and social structure; (20) leisure and tourism; (21) social problems and marginalized groups; and (22) military sociology, armed forces and conflict resolution (see, *Indian Sociological Society*). Ishwar Modi is of the opinion that while comparing the structure of the ISS with the structure of the International Sociological Association (ISA), some of the specialized research areas missing in his country are: future research, language and society, sociology of sports, sociology of work, sociology of youth, sociology of arts, biography and society, sociology of disasters, sociology of childhood, sociology of global-local relations, and sociology of the body. On the other hand, according to this scholar, areas such as backward and marginalized groups, tribal communities which face the problems of poverty, inequality and injustice, are studied very successfully in India. He believes that the fast growth of the NGO sector is highly contributing to the development of applied and action sociology (Modi 2010: 324).

When looking at the history of social sciences (social anthropology and sociology) in India, Sujata Patel discusses two important phases. What was significant in the first phase was the role played by the discourse of colonial modernity in defining the disciplines' identities and the propagation of the use of social anthropology's theories and methods to reproduce the upper caste and class colonial discourse of sociability. During this stage, we can observe the challenge to traditional anthropology from the emerging indigenous sociology rooted in 'Indian values'. It is interesting that at that time anybody who studied the 'East' or 'South' was defined as an anthropologist while those studying the 'West' were labelled sociologists. Patel distinguishes between the Ghurye's Bombay-based practice of sociology identified as social anthropology, reflecting concepts and categories having been framed in Europe, and the Lucknow's 'genuine' sociological perspective, oriented to the present and future, and not to the past. Lucknow's sociology was to be focused on social practice, like social work and social policy, or political intervention. It recognized that India was overburdened with poverty and backwardness and that on the other hand, these facts were determined by colonial exploitation. What I would like to stress here, due to the content of this issue of the *PSR*, is the difference between 'castes' and 'tribes', as conceptualized by the Ghurye's school.

> Castes were defined in the context of Hinduism as groups who cultivated land, had better technology and a high civilization attribute, while tribes were defined in contrast to castes as those who practised primitive technology, lived in inferior jungles and were animistic in religious practices. In the process, caste and tribe were hierarchically placed and made out to be far more pervasive, totalizing and uniform as concepts than ever before and defined in terms of religious order, which it was not always so. These perceptions consolidated and hegemonized an upper caste view of sociabilities in India. (Patel 2010: 282)

The second phase, according to Patel, was dominated first by M.N. Srinivas and later by A.R. Desai. Srinivas based his sociology on the British functionalist social anthropology. In his opinion, the defining attribute of Indian society was its caste system. Focusing first on the villages, he stressed the integration of this system. Later, he moved to the analysis of the general social change of the whole society and the adaptation of the caste system to the overall economic and political transformations of the homogenized Indian nation. Modernity and modernization were not, as such, a topic of his analysis. He also neglected the analysis of colonialism as a force and process of societal and cultural destruction. His sociology, says Patel, did not provide Indians with concepts and hypotheses needed in order to allow the understanding of contemporary processes of change and conflict in society. Opposition to Srinivas' sociology came from a Marxist, A.R. Desai. He underlined not the homogeneity of the Indian nation but its inequalities, power and property relations and the perspective of the excluded, who engaged in new social movements (Patel 2010: 283–287). The more contemporary challenges to sociology in India were already discussed in this text.

Indian scholars are very active in the international arena. T.K. Oommen served as the President of the ISA during the 1990–1994 term, and D.P. Mukerji and Sujata Patel served as Vice Presidents in 1959–1962 and 2002–2006 respectively; nine Indian scholars were members of the ISA's Executive Committee until 1997 (see, Platt 1998). With regards to its own annual conferences, the ISS regularly organizes a North-South dialogue between Indian and foreign sociologists. Particularly close relations link Indian with Brazilian and South African social scientists (Modi 2010: 323).

At the end of this introduction, I would like to address some of the themes elaborated in this issue of the *Polish Sociological Review*. Naturally, this collection of Indian contributions is a very small and therefore limited sample of short texts on selected aspects of modernizing Indian society. In my opinion, however, this selection addresses the crucial issues. Two Polish articles were authored by well-known scholars in the field of orientalism (not necessarily in the Edward Said [1978] sense of the term) who also had served as Polish ambassadors to India. Self-reflection of modernizing Indian society during and after the painful colonial period is a topic in one and the concept of the *yati*, as a very problematic equivalent of the modern Western concept of nation, is an issue debated in the second. India consists of numerous castes, tribes, ethnic and religious groups, and an umbrella concept helping to understand what keeps this variety together seems to be of the utmost importance. The Indian-authored articles deal with what have been the crucial problems of the authors' highly diversified society. I would divide these eight articles into the following categories. One is the colonial legacy and decolonization in the field of broadly understood culture. The second is modernization of the country, including various contradictions and aspects of the complicated and painful process. The third is the modern public domain, including the state organization, democratic process as well as the civil society. The fourth is the problem of ethnic, in a very broad sense, composition of India—in particular the transformations of the Indian caste system.

There are topics which could not have been covered in this issue of the *PSR* and are in my opinion very important for our understanding of today's Indian society. One of them is the fast growing, probably the largest in the world, educated and modern middle class (see, e.g., Fernandes 2006; Sen 2005, 2006).

NOTES

1. I appreciate the helpful comments by Duru Arun Kumar from Netaji Subhas Institute of Technology in New Delhi.
2. Contribution of Indian scholars, living in India, in Europe and in the US, to such very relevant disciplines like today's modern and postmodern social and cultural anthropology (see, e.g., Appadurai 1996, 2006), feminist studies or subaltern and post-colonial studies (see, e.g., Bhabha 1994; Loomba 1998) will not be directly addressed here (see also Connell 2007: 166–191), but will be touched upon.
3. The British Raj, or the British rule in the Indian subcontinent, lasted formally between 1858 and 1947. In 1947, the British Indian Empire was partitioned into two very large sovereign dominion states: the Union of India (since 1950—the Constitutional Republic of India) and the Dominion of Pakistan (as well as much smaller Burma). According to the 2011 census, India has a population of more than 1.2 billion people. Indian Constitution recognizes 212 tribal groups which together constitute about 7.5 per cent of the total population. Officially, the caste system was abolished. Hindi is the official language of the government, but English is extensively used in many public spheres as the 'subsidiary official language'. Hinduism, with more than 800 million believers, is the largest religion in India. The country is divided into 28 states and 7 union territories.

REFERENCES

Appadurai, Arjun. 1996. *Modernity at Large: Cultural Dimensions of Globalization*. Minneapolis: University of Minnesota Press.

——. 2006. *Fear of Small Nations: An Essay on the Geography of Anger*. Durham: Duke University Press.

Bhabha, Homi K. 1994. *The Location of Culture*. London: Routledge.

Burawoy, Michael, Mau-kuei Chang and Michelle Fei-yu Hsieh (eds). 2010. *Facing an Unequal World: Challenges for a Global Sociology*. Taipei: Academia Sinica and ISA Council of National Associations. Three volumes.

Connell, Raewyn. 2007. *Southern Theory: The Global Dynamics of Knowledge in Social Science*. Crows Nest: Allen and Unwin.

Fernandes, Leela. 2006. *India's New Middle Class: Democratic Politics in an Era of Economic Reform*. Minneapolis: University of Minnesota Press.

Indian Sociological Society. http://www.insoso.org/aboutus.htm (19 April 2012).

Kumar, Deepak. 2006. *Information Technology and Social Change: A Study of Digital Divide in India*. Jaipur: Rawat Publications.

Loomba, Ania. 1998. *Colonialism/Postcolonialism*. London: Routledge.

Modi, Ishwar. 2010. 'Indian Sociology Faces the World', in Michael Burawoy, Mau-kuei Chang and Michelle Fei-yu Hsieh (eds), *Facing an Unequal World: Challenges for a Global Sociology*. Taipei: Academia Sinica and ISA Council of National Associations. Three volumes, pp. 316-324.

Mukherjee, Ramkrishna. 1989. 'Indian Sociology or Sociology in India?', in Nikolai Genov (ed.), *National Traditions in Sociology*. Newbury Park and New Delhi: Sage, pp. 135–150.

Patel, Sujata. 2010. 'At Crossroads: Sociology in India', in Patel (ed.), *The ISA Handbook of Diverse Sociological Traditions*. Los Angeles: Sage, pp. 280–291.

Platt, Jennifer. 1998. *History of ISA 1948–1997*. Montreal: ISA.

Said, Edward W. 1978. *Orientalism*. London: Routledge and Kegan Paul.

Sen, Amartya. 2005. *The Argumentative Indian: Writings on Indian History*. London and New York: Allen Lane.

Singhal, Arvind and Everett M. Rogers. 2001. *Indian Communication Revolution: From Bullock Cart to Cyber Marts*. New Delhi and Thousand Oaks: Sage.

3

Modernization and Its Contradictions

Contemporary Social Changes in India

YOGENDRA SINGH

The modernization discourse in India emerged during the national movement for independence from the colonial rule. Its normative and structural ideals were: reconstruction of India to make it an economically developed, socially just and an egalitarian republic. These ideals were widely debated and were ultimately enshrined in the Constitution. Of course, we may recall that Gandhi and Nehru, the two architects of the modernization discourse and of modern India, had differences in their perception of what a future Indian model of modernization should be like, even though both were aware of the need for synergy and accommodation between their two world-views. The Indian Constitution reflects this effort, even though there would be many who may disagree with this interpretation. Nevertheless, the normative foundation and strategy of modernization was deeply influenced by India's historical encounter with the West and its trauma of having been colonized by a Western power. This issue was long debated in course of the national movement and reform movements launched during the colonial period. Also, most of the prominent leaders of the national movements had been educated in the British and European universities and were sensitive to the contributions that the republican and scientific-industrial revolution in Europe had made to their growth as global imperial powers. The significance of these factors in designing the Indian strategy of modernization, therefore, could not be minimized.

The colonial experience not only made Indian leadership conscious of the need to emulate the scientific and technological skills in which the West had gained leadership but also made them acutely self-conscious of the Indian identity, its tradition and culture which they universally acclaimed to be of enduring significance. Both Gandhi and Nehru not only reiterated this but made it an integral element in the strategy of modernization of India. Their visions envisaged the growth of a future modernized India in keeping with its traditions which had through centuries enjoyed a unity within enormous diversities. Both Gandhi and Nehru were proponents of preserving the local diverse traditions and cultural values, protecting the religion and culture of the minorities and other ethnic and regional communities. This, of course, had to be in keeping with the overarching values of a secular, welfare-oriented republican polity which ensured basic human rights, freedom and equality of opportunities to all its citizens in consonance with the normative framework laid down in the Indian Constitution. Nehru persevered with his espousal of a modernization model which promoted humanistic-spiritual values which could easily outcross the barriers of religion, caste or ethnicity within India and could build bridges of cultural and aesthetic linkages with the world community at large. Gandhi, a devotee and practitioner of the ideology of *ahimsa* or non-violence cherished a vision of modernity and processes of modernization which along with justice and empowerment to the people promoted a life world-view which promoted values of non-aquisitiveness, non-consumerism-hedonism and spiritually self-regulated way of life. These were contained in his principles of *ahimsa*. Both Gandhi and Nehru were champions of internationalism based on a global order founded upon the commitment to peace, equality and non-exploitation. Both rejected war and were emphatic about rejection of the uses of nuclear technology for warfare.

Sociology and Modernization Discourse

Sociology, including other social sciences in India, developed with the establishment of the university system by the British regime which had support of the Indian national leadership of the time.

But the shadow of colonial experience and the self-consciousness about the identity of India and its tradition among the intellectuals did deeply impact upon the discourse of modernization. Most of the 'pioneers' of sociology and social sciences questioned the western construction of the Indian society and its tradition as being partial or erroneous. For instance, Max Weber's emphasis on Hinduism as solely promoting 'other-worldly asceticism' in India which could not contribute to its industrialization and modernization or Karl Marx's use of the metaphor of 'sack of potatoes' to characterize the ancient Indian society (implying India as segmental society without interlinkages among the segments) were rejected because neither of these formulations were in consonance with the empirical realities as several studies conducted later established (Singh 1973, 1986). Yet, several studies of the Indian institutions by western sociologists and social anthropologists on religion, caste, family and kinship, etc., continued to postulate the viewpoint that supremacy of traditionalism came in the way of Indian modernization. Louis Dumont's thesis that the Indian social structure legitimized the principle of 'hierarchy' rather than 'equality' hence, by implication was a hurdle to modernization, was in tune with such formulations (Dumont 1970). Such formulations motivated a spate of studies of the Indian institutions, particularly religion, caste, family, village communities and tribal and ethnic minorities regarding their role in the acceptance of the programmes of development and modernization launched through the 1950s and 1960s by the Indian states and the Planning Commission.

The findings of most these studies do not support the thesis that the Indian tradition and traditional institutions were an obstacle to the promotion or acceptance of measures to modernization of the Indian economy, or hindered the entrepreneurial spirit for innovation and change. On the contrary, most of these institutions successfully adapted their traditional mode of thinking and institutional practices to bring them in tune with the demands of modernization. Studies of the entrepreneurial behaviour both among the Hindus and the Muslims in selected regions and towns revealed that continual flexible interpretation of religious ethics made it possible to override the stereotypical presumptions about these religions being an obstacle to entrepreneurial calling. Studies of entrepreneurship came up with similar findings and several of them invalidated the hypothesis of Max Weber that Hindu religion did not promote entrepreneurship. Family system was held to be another obstacle to innovation and enterprise, based as it was on the joint kinship obligations devoid of individual initiatives. But the study of the Marwaris in India, a very successful business community, in fact, revealed that the principle of jointness and cooperation in the families of Marwaris helped them to journey to far-off places to promote their trade and investment without anxiety about as to who will look after their wife and children in their absence. The continuation of the family mode of corporate ownership and management in many of the most capital intensive and modern business enterprises in contemporary India bear testimony to this reality (Timberg 1978). Similarly, about caste. Traditionally, caste defined occupation by birth for an individual. With revolutionary changes in the economy and social initiatives taken by the state to promote the processes of modernization, caste now could no longer be identified by one's occupation in most cases (Singh 1992). Yet, in some case, however, it also contributed to modernization. For instance, the peasant castes, with their traditional loyalty to farming led the acceptance of modern agricultural practices with innovations and new entrepreneurial business ethos. Similar is the case of the artisans and skilled castes. The 'green revolution' in agriculture during the 1970s which made India self-reliant in food production was led by the peasant castes in all parts of the country (see, Singh 1993).

In addition, the view that traditional value system inhibited the motivation for not only innovation but also consumption of material goods and commodities for expanded needs or for pleasure has been contested in a survey by the Anthropological Survey of India, which reports that among most communities in India (estimated 4,634 major communities) the lifestyle accepts meat eating, drinking and smoking. Not only men but a substantial majority of women in India smoke. In most regions, the communities have reported that having migrated from other regions there exists a degree of co-sharing of cultural traits across religions all over the country. This phenomena which was not unknown to the Indian intellectual community explains the resilience of India as it has met with the challenges and adapted innovatively to the institutional and behavioural demands of modernization (Singh 1992).

Modernization was often confused with westernization without taking into account its historicity, primarily the initial structural and cultural attributes of societies in their first encounter with this process. The significance of the historical factors, particularly in India with its own cultural and civilizational exposure of the centuries old history to other cultures with diversities enabling it to make adaptive accommodation with them was lost in such analyses. We have to take note that India in the past had evolved an economy with deeper roots in trade, manufacturing having linkages with other economies at the international scale. It had its own principles of division of labour, training of skilled manpower and accommodation of innovations. As I have attempted to argue in my *Modernization of the Indian Tradition* (1973), the weaknesses in this assumption were both logical and substantive. Assuming that 'new' modernization process, that was inaugurated in the west by its industrial and republican revolution, was driven by a world-view of science and technology, and it formed an essential element in any country's project of modernization is valid. However, the subtext in this assumption that assimilation of the scientific world-view would lead to the erosion of most traditional values and beliefs was only partly true, since this assumption primarily affected the instrumental cultural values and it traditional forms but could not make an impact on the 'fundamental values' that individuals and societies cherished. The validity of the instrumental values exists in the domains of making rational choices where means-end relationships are involved, such as the spheres of economic choices, adaptation to and innovations of new technology, health care, education and acquisition of skills, etc., where their validity or optimum results could be verified. As evidence suggests, most instrumental values which are modern have been not only widely accepted but also innovated upon in India. This has indeed shrunk the scope for many traditional values which axiomatically held sway over people's faith and behaviour in the past, but now encounter credible challenges from more rational and scientific alternatives. But also at the same time, the values emanating from the faith in the supernatural or divine forces, not only prevails but seems to have enlarged its hold on people's mind.

This peculiar co-existence of the instrumental and fundamental values in the process of modernization is not peculiar to India but tends to be a universal phenomenon. As a consequence of this mix we witness, on the one hand, commonalities of institutions and behaviour patterns across nations and cultures which are reflected in increased pace of globalization and homogenization, yet at the same time there is an increasing self-awareness and celebration of the sense of uniqueness and historicity among nations. As in the decades following the 1950s, the empirical evidence for this multiplicity in the forms of modernization in societies gained in substance, a rethinking on the nature of modernity and its grounding in diverse societies and cultures became inevitable. This coincided with theoretical concerns about positivistic foundations of earlier modernization theories, such as structural functionalism and historical materialism of the radical positivistic orientation, which fell under critical review or new forms of intermixing of paradigms.

Symptomatic of this development is the serious rethinking on forms of modernity and its historical roots in societies from 1970s onwards. In a symposium on modernity a decade ago the recognition of both the need to explore the nature of the early modernities, their historicity, variety and transition (Wittrock 1998; Subramanyam 1998), as well as the processes of continuities or linkages with its contemporary forms in various societies together with the phenomenon of 'multiple modernities' drew social scientists' attention to a major theme. S.N. Eisenstadt writes:

> The notion of 'multiple modernities' denotes a certain view of the contemporary world—indeed of the history and the characteristics of the modern era—that goes against the view long prevalent in scholarly and general discourse. It goes against the view of the 'classical' theories of modernization and of the convergence of the industrial societies prevalent in the 1950s and indeed against the classical sociological analyses of Marx, Durkheim, and (to a large extent) even of Weber, at least in one reading of his work. They all assumed, even if only implicitly, that the cultural programme of modernity as it developed in modern Europe and the basic institutional constellations that emerged there would ultimately take over in all modernizing societies; with the expansion of modernity, they would prevail throughout the world. The reality that emerged after the so-called beginnings of modernity, and especially after World War II, failed to bear out these assumptions. The actual developments in modernizing societies have refuted the homogenizing and hegemonic assumptions of this Western programme of modernity. (see, Eisenstadt 2000: 2)

Modernization and Structural Transformation

The Indian leadership had recognized early during the movement for freedom from colonial regime that imperatives of modernization of the Indian society involved a radical structural transformation of the Indian society and elimination of many of its cultural evils. Following independence, many radical measures of reform were introduced. The feudal system of zamindari, princely estates and various other forms of intermediary control on land and peasantry were abolished. This led to agrarian transition through which ownership rights over land were accorded to peasants. Consolidation of landholdings and land development and massive irrigation programmes were launched. The hereditary control on village panchayats was removed and replaced by a system of electoral participation of all citizens within a village community. This empowered most villagers who were traditionally deprived of freedom of choice in policy and programmes of management of village affairs.

At the macro level, the Constitution adopted in 1950 had already declared India a democratic republic with electoral civil rights to all its citizens irrespective of religion, ethnicity or caste distinctions within a framework of quasi federalism with distribution of powers between the central and the state government. These were radical measures with potential for basic structural transformation of the Indian society. These reforms were integrated with an industrial policy of mixed economy with state controlling the most of its crucial sectors (heavy industries) where intensive capital investment with long gestation periods was involved. A National Planning Commission was set up to guide and prioritize investment in social, infrastructural, economic and other related development policies. All this task necessitated availability of scientific data for policy intervention, and social scientists participated in this endeavour, including sociologists and social anthropologists. Social science research got substantial impetus from this initiative. Moreover, new institutional structures, such as the University Grants Commission (to invest and promote college and university education), councils to promote research and teaching in technical and scientific branches of knowledge, in school education, agriculture, medicine, technology and several other crucial sectors of knowledge received a very high priority as growth in these sectors and availability of skilled personnel was essential to realize the objectives of development.

It may be recalled that soon after independence following partition of the country, India was confronted with numerous geo-political and internal social tensions. Regional protests for new states within the Union were triggered by the claims and counter-claims before the States Reorganization Commission; quasi-separatist and left movements were active in southern states and agrarian problems including the dire food shortages were a perpetual problem. Structural changes, particularly in the agrarian economy and positive discrimination in favour of the traditionally marginalized, poor and exploited communities were an imperative. To attain this, provisions were made in the Constitution for reservation in jobs, educational opportunities and political participation, etc., for these communities labelled as the Scheduled Castes (SCs) and Scheduled Tribes (STs). Later, socially and educationally Backward Classes (BCs) were also incorporated in the scheme of positive discrimination. The policy interventions we have outlined above were intended to meet with these numerous challenges.

The first phase of modernization and social change that these measures ushered in India could be placed from 1950s to 1970s. During this period the state was a prime source of reform and investments to bring about development. Its results were first witnessed in the agricultural field which had invited substantial investment in education and research (establishment of research councils and agricultural universities), irrigation projects and innovations in agricultural technologies and inputs, such as new variety of seeds, new methods of credit, marketing and management, etc. This brought about, what is known in India, as a 'green revolution'; 'productivity in agriculture increased manyfold and soon the country became self-sufficient in matters of food grains. This change led to several long-term sociological consequences: a vigorous rural middle class comprising middle caste peasants (traditional cultivators) came into existence in all parts of India; since this caste/class base also had a substantial numerical presence (about 27% of population) it soon captured political power through electoral process in the states and realized a positive discrimination in its favour. They became the new 'Backward Classes' (BCs) of India. In a subtle manner 'green revolution' also changed the traditional pattern of authority and process of decision-making, particularly in matters concerning economic, political, techno-managerial, marketing and investment. It was passed down to the younger generation. However, in matters of gender relations and relations with the SCs/STs, the attitude the BCs remained authoritarian. Their views about women remained conservative with acute gender biases. Several studies of the consequences of 'green revolution' on women have found that women were displaced from a variety of occupational niches, consequently lowering their social status. Similarly, the social and cultural conservatism of the BCs also meant their overbearing or even hostile treatment of the SCs and STs in villages often triggering conflicts and violence. This particularly was reflected in the village level elections to Councils or Village Panchayats. The new structural changes had twofold implication: on the one hand, they augmented the modernization process in villages, on the other, they also seeded many sources of contradictions and conflicts in the rural communities.

This phase of social change (during the first two and a half decades since 1950) also introduced revolutionary changes in the political power structure that was not confined only to the villages but had regional and the national implications. The traditional monopoly on power held by the upper caste and landed gentry and the priestly castes was severely eroded. The change was more radical in South India where the upper caste comprised only a minority of about 3 per cent. But, in the North Indian states too, where they were in minority compared to the BCs, their monopoly on power came to an end. The republican electoral process thus changed the power landscape of India. The castes and communities which were traditionally marginalized, such as the SCs/STs and the Muslims gained tremendous electoral advantages as no single caste including the BCs could enjoy absolute majority on their own. On the other hand, as time passed, the reservation policy in favour of the marginalized castes began to show results, primarily and significantly it augmented the process of their social mobility and political influence. Taken together, these forces of social change also released tremendous entrepreneurial energy and upsurge of aspiration for more and more upward social and political mobility. Throughout this period, state remained a prime mover in matters of economic, social and developmental policies. It did succeed in creating a basic infrastructure and foundational resources for the first stage of modernization in India.

However, the limits of the state policies in many crucial areas also began to show by the end of the 1970s. Indian economy, throughout this period remained burdened with controls; the policy of import substitution and overemphasis on state control of capital investment, exports and imports and markets, etc. It succeeded in creating only a thin base of state favourite capitalism confined mainly to market standards. The Indian export market thus shrunk to only within the nation's boundary and to a few other socialist countries which had identical economic policies. The result was that other Asian countries such as South Korea and few others advanced at much faster rate leaving India far behind. China too introduced measures of liberal reforms in its economic policy by the middle of the 1970s. In India, all this did trigger a measure of rethinking. Committees to reform policies were set up. But no significant action followed. In addition, the positive outcome of the 'green revolution' and agrarian changes in villages also began to fade as it could only benefit a minority of the middle class farmers, but not the vast number of marginal peasants with land ownership of less than two acres. In many regions of India, due to lack of alternate avenues of employment the dependence on land led to partition and fragmentation of family landholdings as family size increased. The SCs/STs classes in villages too encountered distress and felt more alienated economically and socially from the fruits of growth and development. Not only the inequalities in rural social structure increased but also the awareness among the deprived sections about their relative deprivation contributed to a crisis of lag between aspirations and achievements.

The 1970s were also a period which witnessed several geo-political crises: Indo-Pakistan conflict and emergence of a new nation, Bangladesh which broke away from Pakistan, declaration of Emergency in India by the ruling Congress party, its electoral defeat and the end of its monopoly of decades since independence from political power, the mobilization of the BCs movement and emergence of coalition rule at the level of the Central government and subsequent political instability. For these reasons, with some exceptions in the sphere of social welfare and minor steps in economic reforms, no systematic policy interventions could be introduced. The policies pursued in the earlier decades had constricted the scope of export earnings for India and contributed to a crisis of foreign exchange and balance of payment.

The Congress party's return to power towards the end of 1990s occasioned a radical rethinking on economic policies. For the first time, effective economic reforms and opening up of the economy to enlarged participation from the Indian and foreign corporate groups were made possible. Liberalization policy increased the level of capital investment, import of new technologies of production and enlarged the market for the Indian goods within the country and abroad. This coincided with the revolutionary new developments in information technology and growth of the information economy. India's investment in higher technological and scientific education since independence gave it a natural advantage and more than in the manufacturing sector (where growth remained slow due to historical reasons), in the information sector it had an edge over others. India achieved phenomenal growth in the information sector of economy with a large measure of globalization of its services and manpower. As the capital investment of the private sector in various sectors of the economy increased in a large measure, it released the resources of the government for investment in the social and welfare sectors essential for balanced and sustainable economic and social growth.

The contemporary processes of modernization and social changes reflect these phenomena. Consistently during the past decade the rate of economic growth has been around 7 per cent making incremental growth in per capita and national income. This has given new energy to the local markets and there is phenomenal rate of growth in consumer industries linked with processes of globalization. The local consumer brands have withstood the penetration of global industries and a widespread process of 'glocalization' that is branding of the local products for global market is going on together with globalization. The quantum of investment of capital in various sectors of the Indian economy has sustained a high rate, and continues to generate employment for the educated man power. All this has added to the size of the Indian middle class, variously estimated from two hundred to over three hundred million now. Most of this mobility is in technological and information sectors of economy and has been possible because of long duration investment in higher technical and professional education. This is slowly changing the processes of urbanization and the growth is now no longer confined to the metropolitan or bigger urban centres. It is now percolating to the medium and smaller towns of India. Rapid urbanization is not without social problems such as growth of slums and migration not fully integrated with policies of rehabilitation. A remarkable growth is in evidence in the uses of information technologies, particularly use of cell phones now widespread both in villages and cities which has increased connectivity for communication by the people for social, commercial and other purposes. Internet use is slowly spreading not only to the towns but also in villages on the roadside which is used increasingly for governance, trade and utility conveniences on a large scale. Computers are replacing the traditional style of management of records in government offices all over India and process of governance and information retrieval, etc., now are almost largely computerized. All this adds to the processes of modernization and heralds significant social changes.

The traditional structures and functions of institutions such as caste, village community and occupational profiles have undergone basic changes not only in cities but also in villages across India. Most castes now no longer pursue the traditionally ascribed occupations for which they were known (Singh 1992). Caste has, with the exception of the rules of endogamy, lost most of its traditional attributes not only in cities but also in villages. Village communities have lost their traditional character of village centric integrative relationship of patronage and reciprocity but have become political communities with centrifugal interlinkages. New changes in the village panchayat (council) electoral processes (with 30% reservation of seats for women and reservation at the village level for SCs/STs and BCs) with constitutional obligations increasingly renders the traditional notions of caste and community in villages almost redundant. The politicalization of castes has, however, not minimized but increased the uses of castes as an electoral vote bank by political parties all over India. It forms the paradox of the Indian democracy which on the one hand celebrates civil principles and on other, gets increasingly embedded into institutions of primordiality, such as religion, ethnicity and caste (see, Singh 2009).

This forms one of the contradictions of the contemporary modernization of India. There are many other serious social structural contradictions from which the processes of modernization suffer. The growth so far has remained skewed in favour of the highly educated and professional categories of population. Those less educated or illiterate, who constitute more than 40 per cent of the population, have not benefited to the same degree. The poverty estimates now put the number of people below the poverty line to about 37 per cent which is abnormally high. The inequalities in access to the fruits of development have triggered violent movements in several regions of India, mainly those populated by the tribes, forest dwelling communities who find their social and economic conditions intolerable. Variously known as the Naxal or Maoist movements led by the radical left wing ideology, these violent movements are today putting a lot of pressure on institutions of governance and development. One added reason for the inequitable growth and modernization in India has been the states failures to remove illiteracy and not making schooling up to the secondary grade available to most of its rural, tribal and ecologically isolated communities. The state has, however, recently taken some strong steps to move forward in this domain by making right to education constitutionally mandatory and has launched a massive movement for 'education to all' which would take time to bear fruit. In the sectors of economy, the basic contradiction is now being faced by the crisis in agriculture as the shine of the 'green revolution' of the previous years has worn off and agriculture now faces scarcity of investment in technology, infrastructure, access to market and new practices of production and management. More than 55 per cent of the population is even today dependent mainly on agriculture. There is a need to provide alternative integrated avenues of employment to a majority of this population outside, mainly in the agro-industrial or other modern sectors of economy. Despite its realization the priorities of the states in the federation which are mainly charged with responsibilities in this sector remain fuzzy. To take India indeed towards an integrated direction of modernization, the resolution of these contradictions has to be resolved and prioritized.

Cultural Changes and Responses to Modernization

The significance of cultural modernization of India was realized by the Indian leadership as a part of the national movement. As we have mentioned, in the cultural encounter with the West, the need to accommodate many of the Western institutional and normative principle in the central domains of the Indian traditions and cultural values was recognized. Apart from Gandhi and Nehru, most other renaissance leaders were of the view that the best elements of the Indian culture (which were a plenty) had not only to be institutionalized and augmented for modernization but these had a valuable contribution to make in the integrative and sustainable response of India to emergent forces of change at the global level. A philosopher-saint and a great poet, Aurobindo Ghosh wrote 'the future civilization of India will be no more Asiatic modification of European Modernism like the present Japanese civilization but something truly Indian, and at the same time something of first-rate importance for the progress of humanity' (Aurobindo, in Sarma 1944). This vision for reconstruction of the global architecture of culture had a central place in both Gandhi and Nehru's projects of India's cultural modernization.

The national movement had generated several discourses on culture in India; not all of them were such as to promote harmonious cultural development. There was a Islamic discourse which led to partition of the country. As a counter point, a Hindutva discourse of cultural nationalism emerged; the Gandhian discourse of culture aimed at a harmonious cultural modernization with focus on those religious aspects of culture among all religions in India which manifested principles of unity and convergence rather than those highlighting differences. This perspective on reconciling the religious differences in India at the level of their commonality emerged as the vision of a 'composite culture' for India. This finds largely a reflection within the 'constitutional discourse' of culture as enshrined in the Indian Constitution (see, Singh 2010; Chandra and Mahajan 2007). Constitution not only gave religious freedom to minority religions but also ensured protection and promotion of their cultures and traditions. New major projects for institution building to preserve and promote the cultural heritage were undertaken. National academies and institutions were established to promote the classical and folk traditions of fine arts, dance, drama, music and literary forms by the federal and state governments; facilities for training, teaching and research were created. A national film institute was also established for training, research and archival responsibilities since the film industries already had a substantial cultural acceptance by people and were growing. The institutional and establishment aspect in all these measures of cultural support were intended to preserve tradition, but with nuances of modernization.

The institutional support to augmentation and protection of the literary and classical traditions of the Indian culture went hand in hand with efforts to strengthen regional cultures embedded in ethnicity and community. The real cultural resilience of India was provided by the continuity and adaptive capacities of the folk cultures and folk traditions. Sociologists made several studies of the significance of folk culture and its linkages with the classical literary cultural forms and traditions ever since the 1960s and 1970s; it formed an essential part of the numerous village studies that were conducted during this period. Much theorizing was also undertaken to use conceptual framework to capture the vitality of the folk traditions and its linkages with the classical (elite) traditions. Several studies of folk culture and communities revealed how elements from the classical traditions (also called the 'great traditions') were continually being borrowed and were integrated into the folk cultural traditions (also named as 'little traditions') of India, and similarly elements of the folk culture found a way to penetrate and get integrated with the cultural forms and styles of the classical elite traditions Marriott, an American anthropologist, termed it as the processes of 'parochialization' and 'universalization' (Unnithan et al. 1965). Comparative empirical studies of folk cultural traditions undertaken later also established that many styles and forms of cultural expression and celebrations, particularly of the family and caste rituals had similarities across regions and were not entirely 'parochial' in character. Both the folk and the elite or literary forms of cultural organizations had, therefore, a pan-Indian linkage and presence.

The studies of folk culture and its relationship with the classical traditions continued to engage the attention of sociologists and anthropologists through the following decades, and theoretical contributions continued to follow, based upon intensive empirical and ethnographic studies. Guy Poitevin provides us a new perspective on the relationship between the folk and the elite cultural forms in his numerous studies conducted recently. He posits this relationship as between traditions of 'orature' and of 'literature' which have survived in India through millennia right from the ancient period of history. The relationship between the two, the culture congealed in writing and that which found manifestation through the 'power of orality or vocality' existed in India in varying proportion throughout history and had not only an integrative but also contestational or even conflictual mutual relationship from time to time. He identifies this dialectical relationship that the 'power of vocality' had in India in fourfold dimensions: first, he posits that in ancient India orality had an overwhelming role; 'the modernist decoy of the superiority of writing over speech is an imported lure' he says; indeed, 'the excellence and prominence of the phonemes of utterances over the written signs was a distinctive and general feature of ancient India; second, there has traditionally existed 'an unbounded nexus of orality and writings which provided space for creativity for the folk culture in India'. Thirdly, oral tradition provided local communities a 'quiet resilience' which strengthened them and this manifests itself even today in India. The local communities through the power of their orality successfully contested many discriminatory elements in the 'sastric' or classical Brahamanical traditions. Finally, Poitevin opines that this opposition between the 'letter' and 'the voice' is poignantly explicated through the 'outspokenness of women' in the oral traditions. His own empirical studies adequately provide confirmation to these observations (see, Poitevin 2010: 33–41).

Implicit in this analysis is the latent class character that the power of the written text assumed as the new technologies of production, marketing and industrialization began to dominate the newly independent nations. The folk tradition as an alternate discourse of knowledge became largely redundant to most aspects of social change we characterize as modernization. Despite this shrinkage in the space for folk-culture and oral tradition of knowledge which is now largely in evidence in India, it retains its resilience in several areas of culture such as the graphic and plastic art forms, music, theatre and street plays, etc. There is evidence that such expressive aesthetic media have been effectively used in India to articulate protest, as well as to popularize new discourses in knowledge related to the areas of science, technology and health care and other concerns for social reforms and economic development. The irony of 'illiteracy' which continues in substantial measure in contemporary India is such that much of this has resulted from the essential demands of modernization (of economy, production systems and the tools of communication of knowledge, etc.) which render orality as irrelevant to its scripted discourses. It is noteworthy that illiteracy is predominant among the poor, the rural based and marginalized sections of society. These are also the sections where the folk cultural traditions remain active and articulate the power of vocality. The mismatch between folk culture and textual or literary forms of culture continues to persist in India despite its rapid leaps towards modernization and globalization.

The folk cultural traditions are also rooted in the sacred and secular domains of culture. This has, however, changed rather fast during the past few decades. A major factor, is the penetration of new technologies of production and communication all over India. In the spread of mass media of communication, the elements of the folk culture are increasingly and selectively being integrated in the programmes of television, telephone and internet discourses. Some vital aspects of this culture are also being lost, mainly those which were embedded in the order of nature, ecology and manual processes of production in agriculture. Women who constituted the strongest and popular media of these cultural expressions have been displaced from many aspects of their traditional modes of participation. The decline is also noticeable in several of the religious rituals which were a part of the folk culture. The penetration of market forces has brought a variety of products of folk art and culture into the national and global market which finds wider acceptance among the people. Similarly, impact of new medicines and health care techniques has made the role of the traditional healers and medicine men extremely marginalized.

Yet, most these changes do not as yet have meant total replacement of the past forms. The new technology, new middle classes and metropolitan-globalized cultural styles of life that are emerging as an influential factor do not imply that most people who have accepted it are totally detached from the traditional religious and ritual moorings of their culture. Not only is the emergent global culture in India linked with the local forms but it is also reshaping several of the traditional modes and forms of culture towards increasingly adaptive accommodation. Similarly, the power of the new media of communication, the internet, the computer and television not only extend towards the new goals of modernization but also celebrate and extend the reach of religious cultural forms and values with a new power of diffusion they have acquired. Thanks to progressive increase in migration, increasing strength of the Indian diaspora on the global scale and the increasing trends of multicultural and multinational nature of social and cultural contacts, and the globalization of market and work culture, noticeable changes in culture are imperatives and manifest. But these also demonstrate the resilience and adaptive qualities of traditional culture through accommodation of innovations and changes.

Identity, Culture and Modernization

An important contradiction that the cultural discourse on modernization today is confronted with, at the global scale, the new resurgence of religio-cultural self-awareness playing a central role in the formulation and definition of cultural identities. This exists in addition to the manifestation of cultural identities which have existed at the level of diversities of local and regional communities on the basis of differences of caste/tribe, ethnicity and region, etc. These latter expressions of self-awareness of cultural identities which have existed since centuries have no doubt sharpened with the coming into contact with new cultural attributes in modernization and globalization. But their encounter with modernization is embedded into a discourse which is far different from the religio-cultural manifestation of contradictions or even conflicts. These, unlike the identities based on the diversities of caste, ethnicity, etc., are loaded with ideological pronouncements of counter modernization discourses of different hues, with even pan-national linkages with formulations of multiple civilizational distinctions and differences. When we deal with the significance of cultural identities in the wake of forces of modernization and globalization it would be analytically conducive to deal with them separately, even though, as we would like to argue, the manner in which such identities conflict or conflate with modernization are determined largely by the historicity of each culture and its civilization.

India, with its enormous cultural diversities at the local level, did enjoy a unity of cultural ethos through times immemorial. At the local level, some recent studies have detailed the nature of these social and cultural diversities. It is reported that measured on the basis of cultural traits, India has six to seven distinct cultural zones; there are more than four thousand major communities with caste-like features, and none of its major minority religions—Islam, Christianity, Buddhism, Sikhism and Jainism—constitute a socially homogenous category as each of them is divided into hundreds of caste-like communities. It also reports that the shared cultural traits between several religious communities of the minorities with the mainstream religion, Hinduism is very strong. It reconfirms the concept of 'composite culture' being a significant feature of the cultural tradition of India, overriding the diversities (see, Singh 1992). Hence, among the contemporary global scene of the clashes based on religio-cultural formulations of differences which generates anxieties of 'clash of civilizations', India remains largely unaffected from conflicts emanating from such ideologies. This remains so, despite India having a very sizable proportion of minority religions such as Islam, Christianity and others.

This could probably be explained by the historicity of the traditional Indian social structure and its cultural tradition. Unlike in many other countries, India through centuries had provided for significant 'inter-structural autonomy' to its communities and people which also included the local and regional cultural domains. The significant structures were, first, the elements of social stratification such as caste and ethnic groups; second, the religious and ritual practices and their enforcement in society and finally, the political power and control over its administration and enforcement. India had a long history of several empires which had extensive political control over the entire nation. But the rulers, probably as a matter of policy, did not enforce control over the cultural practices of the local and regional social entities, castes, ethnic groups and regional communities. Castes enjoyed sufficient autonomy to carry on their cultural traditions, customs and ritual practices under the supervision of the caste councils (panchayats). Their network extended beyond a single village and they functioned as power centre of a sort with their collective mobilization of protest on issues which hurt their interest. The priestly class, similarly enjoyed full autonomy on religious matters in which the state and the rulers did not generally intervene. The power of the state, in the like manner, was exercised by and large without interference from the priestly classes. This arrangement continued until the end of the medieval period. Even the British colonial rulers, who were more inclined towards significant cultural and social reforms did more or less abide by this convention.

The process of modernization, however, began slowly to erode this autonomy as with major social reforms movements and policies of empowerment of the marginalized castes and communities, the tribes and minorities became a priority for the state after independence. Rapid strides were made towards expansion of higher education and research in most areas related to scientific and technological knowledge, crucial to successful modernization of economy and industry. Since the existence of major social and economic inequalities was recognized, measures were simultaneously taken for all-round social welfare and accelerated positive discrimination in favour of the poor, the minorities and the marginalized groups. Steps were taken to empower the women by a policy of reservation of seats for them in local councils, together with establishment of institutions for protection and enforcement of their human rights. Simultaneously, the rapid expansion of mass media, information technology, the television, telephony, computers and internet, etc., not only extended the exposure to communication for most people across rural and urban divides, but it also enlarged the scope of people's quality and intensity of participation in political and cultural activities. Most aspects of the information technology, particularly telephony has proved to be neutral to the divide between so-called literacy and illiteracy. Being skill based, mobile phones have empowered not only the educated middle classes but also the poor and illiterate citizens who have adopted it extensively for access to jobs, markets and economic activities, together with extension of private and public communicative relationships.

All this has contributed to enlargement of the scope of modernization in its generic normative and operational domain, but at the same time it has also sharpened the consciousness of cultural identities embedded into the diversity of Indian social categories, communities, castes, tribes, women and other local interest groups. Its impact on political culture has been such that on the one hand, it strengthens people's national awareness and sense of participation but on the other it reinforces the bonds of regional and sectional interests based on religion, caste, ethnicity and gender. The empirical studies of the televised programmes on multiple channels reveals the vigour with which a variety of them operate successfully with large audience appeal which reinforces their social, cultural and political identities even though in content, these programmes may range from kindling the values of modernization-globalization, nationalist viewpoint, religious traditions to sectional interests. The nature of these sectional identities does not, however, confront or challenge the normative principles and institutions of modernization or globalization. It is true that during the initial decade after 1991 when policies of economic liberalization opened the gates for rapid acceleration of the pace of modernization and globalization there was some initial resistance among the various communities and interest groups. The debate focused mainly on whether globalization would pose a serious threat to local cultures and local communities. As it turned out, the cultural resources of the local communities successfully met with most of the challenges that global exposure to other cultures brought in their wake. They synergized with processes of market exposure of several of their cultural resources and also realized that globalization simultaneously opened up opportunities for their cultural empowerment (see, Singh 2000). The traditional resilience of the Indian culture continues to persist with new adaptive responses to modernization even though it simultaneously reinforces people's cultural identities.

REFERENCES

Chandra, Bipan and S. Mahajan. 2007. *Composite Culture in a Pluralistic Society*. New Delhi: Pearson Longman.

Dumont, Louis. 1970. *Homo Hierarchichus*. London: Wiedenfeld and Nicolson.

Eisenstadt, S.N. 2000. 'Multiple Modernities', *Daedalus*, Vol. 129.

Poitevin, Guy. 2010. 'Folk Culture, the Oral and Traditional Forms of Communication', in Yogendra Singh (ed.), *Social Sciences: Communication, Anthropology and Sociology*. New Delhi: Pearson Longman.

Sarma, D.S. 1944. *Renaissance of Hinduism*. Benares: Benares Hindu University Press.

Singh, K.S. 1992. *People of India: An Introduction*. Calcutta: Anthropological Survey of India.

Singh, Yogendra. 1973. *Modernization of Indian Tradition*. New Delhi: Thompson Press.

——. 1986. 'Indian Sociology', *Current Sociology*, Vol. 34, No. 2.

——. 1993. *Social Change in India: Crisis and Resilience*. New Delhi: Har Anand Publishers.

——. 2000. *Culture Change in India: Identity and Globalization*. Jaipur: Rawat Publications.

——. 2009. 'Social Praxis, Conceptual Categories and Social Change: Report from a Village Study', *Sociological Bulletin*, Vol. 58, No. 2, May–August.

——. 2010. 'Cultural Discourse in India: Identity and Development', in Yogendra Singh (ed.), *Social Sciences: Communication, Anthropology and Sociology*. New Delhi: Pearson Longman.

Subramanayam, Sanjay. 1998. 'Hearing Voices: Vignettes of Early Modernity in South Asia, 1400–1750', *Daedalus*, Vol. 127, No. 3.

Timberg, Thomas A. 1978. *The Marwaris: From Traders to Industrialists*. New Delhi: Vikas Publishing House.

Unnithan, T.K.N. Deva Indra and Yogendra Singh (eds). 1965. *Towards a Sociology of Culture in India*. New Delhi: Prentice Hall of India.

Wittrock, Bjorn. 1998. 'Early Modernities: Varieties and Transitions', *Daedalus*, Journal of the American Academy of Arts and Sciences, Vol. 127, No. 3.

4

The Indian *Jāti*[1] and the European *Nation*

The Twins-Unlike Concepts of Mega-Tribal[2] Level

M. KRZYSZTOF BYRSKI

The oft and on quoted first line of Kipling's *Ballad of East and West*[3] has made many to think that the author of it was a herald of a sort of Euro-Asian apartheid which can never be bridged. But this is not so. It is enough to answer in affirmative a question whether what happens between Europe and Asia concerns already 'two strong men'? A meeting on equal terms is possible only of equally strong partners and obviously, not exclusively physical strength is meant here. There is no dearth of proofs that the era of absolute prevalence of the West over the East is passé. The first to contest the primacy of the West was Japan followed by the so-called 'Asian tigers'. Today, we witness vigorous development of China and last but not least, India is marking its presence among others in the software industry, Bangalore becoming fast the second largest 'Silicon Valley' of the world. If this be so, then—as Kipling wants—the two strong men already stand face to face, so there is neither East nor West any more. This to my mind is the unmistakable sign of globalization.

Nevertheless such meetings are heavily burdened with numerous misconceptions resulting from the fact that the West, following its victorious technological expansion, many a time imposed upon the East its language and consequently its own understanding or—more often than not—its misunderstanding of some basic ideas and concepts of the East, which—to start with—were wrongly defined and mistakenly named. Sometimes, the scale of consequences of such errors is immense and they do not only prevent mutual understanding but also make it difficult for the intellectual elite of the East to define properly its own identity. We shall try to tackle this problem which belongs to the domain of inter-cultural studies but trespasses also into the field of sociology. To begin with we shall take one of the basic notions of Indian civilization, which is the caste, i.e., *jāti.* Originally committed mistake in relation to Indian social reality, up to this day influences adversely not only the attitude of Westerners toward India and consequently toward their own civilization, but also the self-appreciation of the Indian civilization by the Indian intellectual elite itself, which to a large extent imbibed many a Western notion and concept. This flaw up to now impoverishes both our own and our Indian friends' perception of reality at large and to a certain degree hampers or at least does not facilitate ripening of pan-European self-awareness. For apparently it is nowadays mainly through dialogue between civilizations that such ripening may take place.

Thus, the immediate reason to tackle the problem of *jāti* and nation lies also outside India, in Europe. Nevertheless it should be of interest not only to Indians at large but also or even especially to Sanskrit scholars studying the traditional social doctrines of Indian antiquity which persist in having hold over social reality even down to this very day. The more so that it will be attempted to show how the study of the traditional social institutions of India may help in rationalizing processes through which willy nilly Europe will have to pass. The said reason is the vigorous process of European integration, which despite the current uneasy political and economical situation, will continue and—to be sure—should reach a positive result. The problems Europe—this north-western subcontinent of Eurasia—is currently facing are stupendous and while the process of unification within European Union will deepen, they are going to be even more challenging. This will be so because many nation-states find themselves under one political 'roof' or using the traditional Indian imagery under the 'shadow of one royal umbrella'. At the moment, most Europeans believe that it will be possible to coordinate policies of member states in such a way that they may preserve their full political sovereignty. But this is a fallacy. It becomes more and more evident while the European Union faces ever new and ever more demanding political exigencies close to its borders. The recent turmoil in the Arab world is the best example. But even earlier it became evident already in connection with the American war in Iraq and Afghanistan, that it is practically impossible to have one European foreign policy agreed upon by sovereign states. Even recently, with Lady Ashton supposedly coordinating EU's foreign policy some member states, including in this number Poland were not too ready to participate fully in the common policy towards Libya. At this moment an Indian reader of these words may ask a very natural question indeed: what role the experience of Indian civilization may play in helping to solve European political problems?

In order to answer this question we have first to mark that both India or better South Asia[4] and Europe are twins-unlike civilizations—the oxymoron intended! Territory-wise both are huge subcontinents of Eurasia of comparable size. But while India is a monolithic land mass, Europe is a sort of 'funny' peninsula, riddled with many 'Mediterranean' seas.[5] In both cases climatic variety between North and South is comparable, though both are very much unlike, taking into consideration the average annual temperature, which of course is much higher in India.[6] Although from the point of view of the population, India scores over Europe, yet the ethnic variety of both populations is very much alike,[7] as indeed the variety of spoken languages. In this case linguistic variety matches ethnic variety. In India it seems to be more pronounced than in Europe, for there we deal with at least four major language families, i.e., Indo-European (or Indo-Aryan), Dravidian, Tibeto-Burmese and Munda, while in Europe Indo-European definitely prevails. The number of speakers of the Finno-Ugric family is not many. To this we may add the large variety of scripts used in India and practically only the Roman script prevalent in most of Europe, with Cyrillic used by Russians, Ukrainians, Bulgarians and Serbs and the Greek alphabet prevalent in Greece and in the Greek part of Cyprus.

Similar variety concerns customs followed and confessions professed. But at the same time in both cases most obviously we have a common denominator of classical heritage connected with Sanskrit, Prakrit and Pali languages in India and Latin, Greek and Hebrew in Europe. It even goes much further back to that remote epoch when the hypothetical Indo-Europeans were one people speaking one language[8] and up till now we cannot liberate ourselves from the patterns of thought which were established then.[9] This may be going too far back, yet without undue emphasis we may suggest that in the global village it may carry some emotionally important meaning.

Passing on to the history of both civilizations we see that it is very comparably indeed ridden by wars and strife but at the same time marked by fabulous development of culture, science and technical skills and also by periods of unity and peace. In both cases also we have very distinct common value-systems and common aesthetic sensitivity though at the same time they are very different in character from each other.

We may thus safely conclude that both Europe and India may be considered twins who—not unlike those of the Bollywood films—were separated of yore[10] and nursed into adulthood by two different mothers: Mother Europe and Mother India.[11] Consequently, they have become very much unlike as 'personalities', at the same time being very much alike so far as their basic structure goes. It has been necessary to resort to the above argument in order to establish a viable premise for comparison, which is justified on the one hand by similarity, while on the other, differences make it exciting and edifying.

At this turn we have to explain reasons of our temerity to deal, without proper training in social sciences, with what appears to be largely a sociological problem. Yet, we trust that an outsider philologist may sometimes succeed in drawing attention to problems which Western science may tend to overlook. Here I mean the indigenous ancient Indian achievement in social sciences. The social structure of traditional Hindu society, well argued by indigenous scholarship[12] has been a domain of careful study also outside India for a very long time. It is enough to mention the classic *Homo Hierarchicus* by Louis Dumont, published in 1966 and listing already on twenty pages books and articles mainly dealing with this topic. Ever since this bibliography multiplied and today it will probably include close to one thousand books, not to count numberless articles in scientific journals. But we are not aware of any effort to treat indigenous Indian sociological concepts as valid points of reference in the evaluation of Western social reality. In such circumstances it is certainly very risky to venture into this field with a new concept of comparative nature at that. We decided to take this risk because in the given circumstances publication is the only way to verify the viability of the said concept.

The initial inspiration came from the field of linguistics. It was among others, Dumont who refers the Indo-European provenance of the word *jāti* which means 'birth' (*naissance*).[13] We may add that it is derivative of the verb *jan* meaning 'to generate, beget, produce, create, cause'.[14] Now, as the French word as well as its English counterpart 'nativity', which are cognate terms of the word 'nation' indicate, that this word being derivative of the Latin (*g*) *nascor, natus,* which means 'to be born' has to carry that meaning too, since the Latin word *natio* denotes 'tribe', 'generation', 'category of people'.[15] It appears therefore that the birth factor must have been crucial in coining these two terms in both civilizations. Could they then denote social categories somehow corresponding with each other? Our contention is that they play similar role in their respective civilizations bestowing upon their members comparable sense of belonging and comparable awareness of the group identity albeit appealing to different sensitivities (*sic!*). Thus, we feel that the question as to how come that Europe finds it so difficult to create one polity while India covering most of South Asia, on the whole finds one common polity quite congenial may be answered convincingly while invoking unusual correspondence of the notions of *jāti* and 'nation'. We may add that it is not easy for Europeans to define state in terms of civilization rather than in terms of nation, while for Indians the same is perfectly natural and legitimate. Here, of course, the political correctness would suggest the view that there is one Indian nation and therefore the Republic of India is the nation-state like any one in Europe. Yet, such an assumption cannot be accepted. It suffices to have a cursory look at the ways nation is thought about in Europe. Ernest Gellner offers two, what he calls, provisional definitions of nation, which he considers on the whole to be an elusive concept. The first one includes sharing the same culture, i.e., system of ideas, signs, associations, ways of behaving and communicating. To our mind this definition to a large extent applies to civilization as well. The second appears to have also a subjective tinge and consists of mutual recognition by members of one nation of their membership. Since these—he holds—are nations that make man. According to him,

> nations are the artifacts of men's convictions and loyalties and solidarities. A mere category of persons (say, occupants of a given territory, or speakers of a given language, for example) becomes a nation if and when the members of the category recognize certain mutual rights and duties to each other in virtue of their shared membership of it. It is their recognition of each other as fellows of this kind which turns them into a nation, and not the other shared attributes, whatever they might be, which separate that category from non-members.[16]

Further on Gellner draws our attention to cultural homogeneity that according to him is demanded by nationalism. He concludes 'that a homogeneity imposed by objective, inescapable imperative eventually appears on the surface in the form of nationalism'.[17] We would suggest that four underlined aspects of Gellner's opinion could be understood as the four main standard identifiers of a nation in Europe—more or less universally acknowledged, which in principle are: one language spoken throughout entire territory, native state executing sovereign rights over it and safeguarding mutual rights and duties, as well as the cultural and we would add ethnic homogeneity. About the last one Europeans are less explicit after the morbid experience of the World War II, but it still plays a considerable role in our perception of nation-state.

Now looking at India we notice that in spite of efforts to introduce one language, this identifying factor has been lacking up to this very day, nothing to say about ethnic homogeneity which is unthinkable for a population of more than one billion people. Yet this by no means makes the Indian state less viable because of considerable cultural or better 'civilizational' homogeneity, which the subcontinent owes to the Hindu society organized according to *varṇa-jāti* principle prevalent in the Indian heartland.[18] On the other hand one can hardly talk in the Indian context about Bengali, Gujarati, Marathi, Tamil or for that matter Uttar Pradeshi nations, although these entities are characterized by distinct common territory, language and even full-fledged though not sovereign but only autonomous state governments. Yet again ethnic homogeneity does not hold in all these cases. Still if the last criterion is not treated too rigorously, as indeed it is not any more in Europe, these Indian states on the surface seem to correspond perfectly to European nation-states. But while the citizens of the last are so attached to the idea of political sovereignty that they, up till recently, were ready to wage wars for its sake, the citizens of Indian states consider themselves just Indians and with some peripheral exceptions, which to my mind only confirm the rule, do not clamour for sovereignty, being satisfied with the sovereignty of the Federal Republic of India. Consequently, the question arises which factor is responsible for strong pan-Indian identity of the Indian people and which factor makes it so difficult for the people of Europe to transcend their narrower national identities in order to identify themselves, in addition, as Europeans.

Before we attempt to answer this question, let us try first to assess the social system of Europe, which we shall call national in contradistinction to the caste (rather strictly speaking: *varṇa-jāti*) social system of India. We shall try to look at it as if from the outside—a perspective which the author of this text acquired during fourteen years long stay in India. We shall also take into account the painful experience of the 20th century history of Europe.

The idea of a nation-state appeared there, only after the French Revolution in 19th century. According to Baszkiewicz, modern national awareness connecting nation and state was born during the time of Napoleon and mistakes committed by the French emperor contributed overwhelmingly towards its strengthening while development of industrial civilization additionally forged national bonds.[19] Tikekar also holds that

> development of modern nation state was linked to the industrial revolution, capitalism and a drive to create a common national culture and a common language. Along with capitalism the nation state has been a dominant Eurocentric paradigm for collective political organization and economic development as Europe experienced symbiotic development of state, nation and market.[20]

The comparative latecomers as nation-states to the political scene of Europe were Germany preceded by Italy. The so-called First World War being indeed a more or less domestic European war was the first massive evidence that a concept of nation-state is not a good proposal. Yet, this warning went unheeded by Europeans and they needed yet another bloody lesson of the so-called Second World War—this time the name being more justified since Europeans managed to get many more outsiders than before involved in their domestic slaughter. Further on the throes, through which the Balkans[21] has gone not so long ago, is the fresh case of the same illness which affects Europe. Other examples are not lacking.

The basic premise of the argument that follows is that the mega-tribal identity of the Europeans found its expression and fulfilment in the shape of a nation-state. Common language and by implication common culture, territory and state machinery have become indispensable 'identity factors' of such nation-state, to be supplemented with one more such identifier which we have already mentioned, i.e., ethnic homogeneity. Let it be repeated that nowadays after the morbid experience of the Holocaust during World War II, it is not any more politically correct to speak about nation in terms of its ethnic homogeneity and normally the term 'nation' is understood much more as tantamount to the Latin *civitas*, i.e., citizenship. We in Europe conveniently forget about the etymology of it although, what we may call 'womb factor', has invariably been very powerful in the self-perception of the nationhood.

In as much as officialdom tries to ignore it, in so much an average representative of each European nation treats it as a fairly important feature of national identity. If anyone would doubt this opinion, let him talk to the representatives of minorities in Europe—Roma, Jews, Arabs or Turks for that matter! Most certainly we have done a lot to make this discriminatory aspect of our social practice less obnoxious although it still is very much present. At the same time, a strong doubt persists not only regarding the question whether it can be totally eliminated but also whether it should be eliminated, since in a way it is only a broader aspect of family identity, the social *bona fide* of which no one even tries to question. For can we question the positive import of tribal identity which bestows upon us a sense of belonging and of loyalty due to blood relations? Hearing a familiar name we become positively alert to the fact that the bearer of this name belongs to our tribe. He might share our values and we may even find common relatives. What is then wrong with the European mega-tribes called nations that this aspect of their identity is shamefully excluded from modern socio-political discourse? What accounts for the fact that the etymology of the word 'nation' is consequently ignored?

Well, the reason lies in the nation-state concept, or to put it even more explicitly in the concept of one nation, one state and one leader (*Ein Folk, ein Reich und ein Führer*). This idea has been greatly discredited in the aftermath of the Second World War which was churned up with the slogans of the Nordic racial purity of Germanic peoples. It triggered a morbid process of putting into practice a maniacal theory that those of other races and especially those in Europe who tried to assert their homogenous nationhood even while they could neither claim their exclusive territory, common language nor their own state, have to be exterminated. No doubt, we think here about the Jews and the Gypsies whose fate left a shameful stigma on the European civilization, which cannot shun her responsibility for what happens now in the Middle East between Arabs and Jews who were practically evicted out of Europe. Even up till now similar problems have been haunting Europe in the Balkans, in Chechnya, Bask country and till recently the Northern Ireland. Europe finds it quite difficult to cope with these challenges. It smacks of a derision when we invoke Christian values of neighbourly love and universal unity in Christ but are unable to tolerate people ethnically and culturally different and even shorn of ambitions to create their separate state, when they wish only to share the same territory with us, although there is enough space for all of us. Let us repeat with emphasis that this incapacity of European civilization stems from the fact of a deeply ingrained fear that each and every mega-tribe called nation sooner or later will have to claim their separate territory neatly drawn on the map and carefully fenced out with barbed wire in real space; will wish to organize their own state administration and will introduce their own official language and finally purge such state of every alien ethnic element. May the Indian reader of these lines rest assured that this type of thinking is still fairly widespread in Europe and it is because of this that the Jews found it impossible to live as a distinct, though stateless nation in Europe, while in India they lived in peace for centuries as a separate caste (*jāti*)! Consequently they had to return after more than a millennium to their original homeland thus creating a new problem not only for the Middle East but for the entire world. The process of European unification may become an antidote to the illness diagnosed above but Europeans lack a proper perspective to apply suitable treatment. The social reality of India can provide such perspective.

The point of departure for the argument proposed is that the mega-tribal identity of Indians realized itself in the form of a *jāti*, i.e., a caste. Competence or occupation[22] has become the paramount identifier of it, closely followed by the notion of ritual purity which—we would insist—is an aftermath of the idea of competence considered as a primary criterion. Since we have to remember that originally the central point of reference so far as the competence of different members of the society went, was the sacrifice, i.e., *yajna*—an absolutely pivotal concept for the *varṇa* social system of which *jāti* is an integral component. It is the character of the involvement in sacrifice understood both as a liturgical act as well as the mechanism of entire existence, which determines particular competence of each and every participant and also determines the required degree of his ritualistic purity. This is the proper meaning of the *varṇa* passages of the Vedic hymn entitled '*Man (Purusha)*',[23] which by deriving *Brahmins* from the mouth of *Purusha, Kshatriyas*—from his arms, *Vaishyas*—from his thighs and *Shudras*—from his feet established the criteria of competence, which are valid universally. Since there can be little doubt that men occupy their given position in the society because of what they know, because of the power they wield, because of their economical means and last but certainly not least, because of what they can do using their physical strength and the skill of their hands. While the three following *varṇas* are self-explanatory, the first one requires certain elucidation. The name proper of the member of this *varṇa,* i.e., *Brahmin,* means 'the one who possesses *brahman*'.[24] In other words, the one who knows the *Veda,* which at that time was tantamount to knowledge as such. The term *vidvan* (knower) constitutes its equivalent. In the light of what has been said so far, it should be stressed that considering the *Purushasukta* a stratagem of cunning *Brahmins,* which was meant to ensure this *varṇa*'s paramount control over the rest of the society, is not correct. It simply testifies to the fact that subsequent malpractice of the system overshadowed its honest theoretical premises, one of which most obviously was the organic interdependence of all the four *varṇas,* exactly the way the four enumerated parts of the body of *Purusha* are interdependent. The *varṇa* society was conceived as an organic whole, a harmoniously cooperating social entity resembling modern societies, within which people are grouped according to their competence and of which trade unions are a modern expression, and governments by system of licences and diplomas ensure that only competent persons will be allowed to be active in professional walks of life. We may remember that the sacrificial fire of the ancient Aryans, a huge liturgical undertaking, required clear division of duties. There should be those who know the purpose for which it is lit and can elucidate it in words as well as know that fire is latent in dry pieces of wood, which require rubbing in order to generate it. There should also be those who would be responsible for organizing the work, for securing and preparing the ground for sacrifice and for protecting it from any external threat. Further on, there have to be those, who would supply commodities, which are to be cooked (offered as oblation!) and fuel. Finally, those also are unavoidable, who will do all the menial jobs involved and remove the remnants considered impure. If we translate this scheme into contemporary conditions, we may say that *Shudras* would be all those working nowadays in what broadly we know as services. *Vaishyas* would be all those running economy, finances and trade. *Kshatriyas* would be those responsible for administration, security and defence as well as government, so in their ranks active politicians will also be counted. Finally, *Brahmins* will be all those, who due to the knowledge they posses function in education, research and in the field of science serving the entire society with their advise also as philosophers and priests, and most naturally acting as its intellectual and spiritual leaders. This is precisely stated in the *Bhagavadgita* when Lord Krishna says: 'I have created the four *varṇas* according to the division of attributes and actions'.[25]

At this stage we have to bring up the notion of *varṇadharma*. Yet, first of all the term *dharma* alone has to be properly understood.[26] A common English equivalent of this term is religion. Those better informed would opt for virtue or law. None of these does real justice to the term. 'Dharma is the nature of thing' holds the Jaina treatise entitled the *Karttikeyanupreksha*.[27] It is this definition which makes this term all-embracing one. Everyone knows that any Sanskrit-English dictionary would offer at least two–three dozens of English equivalents of this term.[28] On closer scrutiny practically all of them may be reduced—or better—derived from this basic meaning, even the Buddhist *dharmas* or *dhamma*. Another important definition of the term comes probably from Shankaracarya[29] and it runs as follows: 'what upholds the worlds is dharma'.[30] Most obviously, 'the nature of things' upholds worlds. All whatever surrounds us is endowed with its proper nature. Liquidity is the nature of water, heat—the nature of fire and speech—the nature of men. And what is the nature of human society? What is its *dharma*? Yes, it is *varṇa* and *jāti*. It is hoped that after what has been said above such thesis will not appear presumptuous. The indisputable authority of the *Bhagavadgita* already referred to can be invoked in support of such contention. To this we may add the opinion of Mahatma Gandhi himself who wrote in the *Harijan* (September 28, 1934):

> The very first mention of *varṇa* in the Vedas likens the four *varṇa* to the four main parts of the body. Is the head superior to the arms, the belly and the feet, or the feet superior to the other three? What will happen to the body, if these members began a quarrel about the rank? The law of *varṇa* is one of absolute equality among all the creatures of God.[31]

Further on he wrote (25 March 1939) that 'varna does not connote superiority, it connotes different functions and different duties'.[32]

All this granted, one serious objection has to be raised. This objection is very strongly voiced indeed by the Western critics of the system. It assumes the form of an outright and most vehement criticism and opposition in India, especially on the part of those who are termed 'untouchables'. The objection concerns the fact that belonging to this or that *varṇa* is a birth right. In order to try to understand how it has come about we have to analyse another aspect of the traditional Indian social fabric, i.e., *jāti*—commonly known as caste.

Varṇas, i.e., very broad groups of society defined by competence, primarily based on the premises determined by the exigencies of the sacrificial ritual found solid grounding in the *jāti*, i.e., caste.[33] Philology is such a discipline of humanities that pays paramount attention to language and text. Words, their etymology and semantic significance are very important in this field. Thus, it is crucial to see what these two words really mean. *Jāti* as a derivative of the Sanskrit verb 'to be born' means 'birth', 'production' and also a particular group of people into which one is born. The easiest way to explain that is to refer to the body which is given to man at the moment of conception. The nature of our body is well known. We know well, what to do in order that it may serve us roughly speaking these hundred years, which are given to man as natural, maximal longevity of his life. Acting according to this knowledge is our *dharma*, our duty. Now, what would be the nature of human multitude, which we call society? What society has as it nature—its *svabhava?* What is it that should be sustained (*dhrita*) in order that it guarantees the optimal conditions for individuals, who create it?

Such system in ancient India, which we have already alluded to above, was called *varnadharma*. Among other meanings of the term *varṇa* 'property' also is included.[34] This is a category of competence par excellence. As we have already mentioned there are four *varṇas* of the traditional Indian society and for their existence the *Purushasukta* of the *Rigveda* is usually held to book, because it sanctifies this 'clever stratagem' aimed at the creation of hierarchic order and securing for *Brahmins* a dominant position. With the notable exception of Mahatma Gandhi, rarely indeed the organic interrelation of social functions is pointed to as the main idea of the hymn. Not so often, attention also has been given to the otherwise obvious fact that the four functions or if we continue to call them as above—the four competences enumerated have obvious universal import. It was a study of Polish scholar Stefan Kurowski titled, *The Theory of Kratoses* in which he, while trying to rationalize and explain the social processes that resulted in the Solidarity movement in Poland and consequently in the downfall of communism in our country, formulated the thesis that those processes resulted from natural tension between knowledge and work, which are more productive when diffused, i.e., when more and more people are participating and, power and wealth, which always tend to be centralized or to be concentrated. From this observation there was just one step to formulating an idea of four basic competences of *homo socialis*. These competences determine particular social roles of individuals such as work, power, wealth and knowledge. We can easily notice that they correspond perfectly with the vision of the *Purushasukta* and by the way, most probably it was not the source of inspiration for the author of this concept. The only difference is that knowledge is mentioned last on the list of the Polish scholar.[35]

In the light of what has been said above, the universal character of these criteria does not provoke objections. Modern societies are organized according to this principle as well and social roles are most obviously determined by what one knows (scholars, intellectuals, teachers, experts, engineers, free professions), by what one is able to achieve thanks to the power at one's disposal (politicians, administrators, military, police), by what means (financial mainly) one possesses (business people and manufacturers) and finally by what one can do offering his services in more or less physical sense (workers and servants of any kind). Practically the only objection that can be levelled against the *varṇa* system is connected with its hereditary character. Was it not because of that, the system could have been perfectly acceptable. Let us then try to see the logic behind the notion of heredity, which provokes so much criticism both in and outside India.

Now it is high time to have a closer look at the concept of *jāti*. As it is well known, this term in European languages has been replaced by the word 'caste'. The 'culprits' were for sure the Portuguese, who used this word at home with respect to their social divisions and found it a convenient appellation for the Indian *jāti*.[36] But the term 'caste' is also a cognate one of the Latin *'castus'*, which means 'pure'. One wonders whether cleanliness both in the purely hygienic sense as in the ritualistic one, which constitutes a very important aspect of the idea of caste and one of the two most important parameters of its identity, was not also at play in this case? Was it not this very aspect that impressed the first Portuguese who, when confronted with the Indian social system might have been struck by the sensitivity of Indians in this respect? Pure–impure, touchable–untouchable are the notions that to this very day determine behaviour of many people in India. So it is not surprising that several centuries back this could have struck so much that anonymous Portuguese, who decided then, that the word *'castus'* will be the most appropriate one to call the social group otherwise called by the Indians themselves a *jāti*. To repeat—this term—an obvious derivate of the verb *jan*—to be born, in contradistinction to the term 'caste', refers specifically to the genetic factor and most naturally implies also genetic purity of birth. Still, the most important aspect of its meaning is some sort of the genetic interrelation of all members of the group. Thus, such kind of community is implied here, which with regard to primitive societies is called a tribe. It seems therefore, that in the context of the Indian civilization the primitive idea of tribal community lay at the basis of the notion of caste. We shall call it a mega-tribal community, since most obviously it transcends such notions like that of a family or a clan as well as a tribe itself. It is precisely as in the case of the European idea of a nation. One of the important additional differences is the fact of lesser numeric strength and territorial spread of caste as compared to nation. It would be decidedly a mistake to treat caste as something imposed *per force* and to be rejected as soon as a possibility of rejection appears. The caste system does not owe its existence to violence or coercion directed against men free by nature. If we would treat caste in this way, we would have to treat nation in the same manner. In both cases we do not select our identity but it is given to us by the fact of being born from the womb of our mothers, who belong to particular social group be it nation or *jāti*. The acceptance of such identity is an aftermath of the fact that man is 'a slave of the womb'. Until now—thank God—there is only this unique way of entering society by every human being! So it can hardly be ignored.

One of the very important reasons for the persistence of the institution of caste has been the fact that the Indian civilization until modern times did not replace oral transmission of knowledge with the written (or printed) one. In such way it became an additional bond, which cemented the Indian *jāti*. For it has been within its framework that not only the DNA was being inherited but also it guaranteed the optimal mode of transmission of particular competence beginning with early childhood. The positive aspects of caste should not of course divert our attention from the negative ones, which can hardly be condoned. One of such aspects is that all those aboriginal tribes forced to assume competences treated by the caste society as impure and ignoble like sanitation, etc., are subjected to abysmal humiliation. Although they have right to exist still they are often treated like animals or even worse than animals. But even then they have hardly been threatened with total extermination. The so-called untouchables about whom we think here are a proof that the elites of the Vedic society could not properly discern the message of the *Purushasukta*. It does not provide sanction for eliminating any group of men from the scheme of the mystic body of *Purusha* and it forcefully establishes each and every man as *chaturvarnya,* i.e., possessing of four competencies—as long as he has capacity to speak and to ignite fire! The social division of competences is the result of projection of competences of individuals that make up society and of the need to have highest possible degree of specialization and efficiency.

These disabilities of the caste social system are well matched by the disabilities of the national social system of Europe. The mega-tribes of Europe, which because of some reason or other did not manage to acquire all three parameters of national identity, i.e., state, territory and language and wanted to function as castes (Jews and Gypsies, for instance) in the last count were threatened with total extermination, for which indeed not only the Nazis have been responsible but a sort of deification of the idea of nation-state, which is still pretty pandemic in Europe. If this is not enough we can add to the list two world wars and of course their numerous victims that were sacrificed on the altar of insatiable divinity of the (un) holy nation-state.

The carelessness of the Portuguese and other Europeans, applying the language of their own ideas to the description of other civilization, I hold responsible for convincing the Westernized Indian elites that the caste system is evil to the backbone and that it should be eliminated. In a similar way the English managed to convince many Indians that *dharma* is just religion and that—for that matter—we can separate it from politics, as if politics could have been deprived of its *dharma*, i.e., its proper nature. In order to understand the predicament of India, it suffices to imagine what sort of trauma Europeans would have to go through if someone would manage to convince our elites that nations are integrally bad and they have to be eliminated, if only because so much injustice has been committed in their name. Since in both cases it is totally impossible, we have to look for other solutions of the problems that our civilizations face. The integration of nation-states within the European Union is the way we in Europe try to cope with the problem of practical deification of nation-state that triggered innumerable conflicts including two world wars. In India on the other hand it is needed to change attitude towards the basic parameter of mega-tribal identity, i.e., mutual relationship of *varṇas* and *jātis*. Traditionally, four *varṇas* represent the criteria of competence according to which *jātis* are classified and grouped. Since nowadays the transfer of competence is no more taking place exclusively through oral communication, there is no need any more to effect such transfer within genetically interconnected group of people, i.e., caste, which previously guaranteed optimal achievement in this respect. But it does not need to invalidate *varṇas* as criteria of competence. Since, as we have already mentioned, each and every individual human being is endowed with these four competences so is each and every segment of society. Thus, any meaningful reform of traditional Hindu society should envisage a possibility of applying the criterion of *varṇa* within each *jāti*. This already happens as indeed it has been happening all along within nations[37] and it would be enough to show that this process does not contradict the traditional system but is only its adaptation to the new situation. First and foremost, it should be done and is being already *jāti* done through the process of educating intellectual elite (i.e., three upper *varṇas*) within those *jātis* that have traditionally been deprived of such elite. Self-respect of each *jāti* will depend on its ability to generate an internal *varṇa* system. In short, the remedy is proper interaction of the two principles—*varṇa* and *jāti*. We have to realize that the role of the *varṇa* principle does not exhaust itself while it is applied to any society taken as a whole. But it applies itself continually when any group of people tries to organize itself for the sake of participation in the doings of civil society. This, as a matter of fact, is now happening in India. Participation in the democratic procedures results in making the intellectual elites emerge in each and every caste and consequently a pride of belonging to it—no matter what its traditional position had been. Dalits, known earlier as untouchables, are the best extreme example, since originally they were refused the status of full-fledged human beings.[38] Yet, by no means is it the only one. It seems, therefore, that the reform of the so-called caste system is already taking place. What it requires is awareness that the Vedic *Purusha* while sacrificing himself and thus fashioning out of himself a human society, even more forcefully acknowledged the fact that each and every human being is by its very nature *chaturvarnya*. If so, then the feet of God out of which *shudras* were created do not deserve lesser respect than those created out of His head, arms or thighs.

Apart from Hindu social reform, there is one more problem that desperately awaits solution in India. This is the apparent divergence of interests of the two major communities of the Indian subcontinent: Hindu and Muslim. This problem in our view is also directly connected with the way both communities perceive their mega-tribal identity. Enough has been said above about the self-awareness of mega-tribal identity of the Hindus. We hold that in their case it is the caste that canalizes all requirements of belonging to a genetically interrelated group of people and thus permits them to enjoy what could be called 'the security of identity'. What then could guarantee such security to Muslims? We submit that Muslims see as the indispensable parameters of their mega-tribal identity and security, the Muslim state exercising sovereignty over particular territory and in somewhat special sense—the language (of the Holy Koran). It is rather obvious for us that this alongside the fear that becoming powerless minority in the democratic political system, which in their eyes is tantamount to the autocratic rule of majority, were two main reasons for the demand of separate state. Already in the 19th century, Sayyid Ahmed Khan (1817–1898) voiced such an opinion:

> Now suppose that all the English were to leave India. Then who would be the rulers of India? Is it possible that two qaums—the Muslim and Hindu—could sit on the same throne? Most certainly no! It is necessary that one of them will conquer the other and thrust it down.[39]

It was of course quite easy to answer the question, which one of the two would stand better chance to be thrust down. The problem was further complicated since because of their religion preaching equality of men, Muslims refused to accept the inequality of caste status. Especially since so far as their eating habits go, (they would not be prepared to give up eating beef), they practically could be considered only as outcastes by the orthodox Hindus. This situation seems to defy any remedy. Yet, in this respect, it is the political model in the form of a union fashioned on the pattern of EU, which to our mind could offer acceptable solution by harmonizing local sovereignty within continental political cooperation, thus giving Muslims assurance that their way of life regulated by *shariat* law will not be endangered.

Although in 1947, the Republic of India was divided in a way similar to Europe into several states based upon the linguistic principle and although each of these states got its clearly delimited territory as well as the self-government of considerable autonomy, still none of the states within the heartland of traditional caste system significantly clamoured for sovereignty. Such a demand was made only by Muslims, by Sikhs and by some frontier tribes, which do not owe any allegiance to the caste system. Would Marathas, Gujaratis, Bengalis or Tamilians have had entertained real national ambitions in the sense ascribed to such ambitions in Europe, India would not have survived as a democratic state. She would have either disintegrated into so many sovereign states or else would have turned into an autocratic totalitarian state long ago. As we tried to show, these ambitions are in traditional Indian society placed elsewhere, i.e., in the *jātis*. It is therefore, without any threat to the real unity of the Republic of India, that her parliament by its sovereign decision could bestow upon the present states the paraphernalia of sovereignty, remodelling the Federal Republic of today into the South Asian Union[40] of tomorrow. In such way the problem of Kashmir would be automatically solved. For such unilateral decision of the Indian Parliament could evoke similar response from the Pakistani Parliament to do the same with respect to the four constituent provinces of that country that nowadays enjoy only limited autonomy but by no means have been fully integrated into one monolithic nation. If the political thinking on both sides of the frontier and the Line of Control, quickened by the disastrous earthquake some time ago, could become capable of considering such solutions, the perennial problem of the subcontinent would be solved. For the postulated South Asian Union would in its capacity of a *rashtra (civitas)*[41] guarantee in equal measure, security for the Hindu and the Muslim mega-tribal identity.

In this context, there is yet one more very urgent and purely political challenge that India has to face. It is the so-called 'Chinese necklace' patiently and persistently built around India in Nepal, Myanmar, Bangladesh, Sri Lanka and Pakistan by Chinese Peoples Republic. If India wishes to score over China and win an upper hand in wooing her smaller neighbours, she has to prove her sincere belief in democracy and in fair treatment of smaller states in international relations. I am absolutely sure that India's smaller neighbours seeing Kashmir, Meghalaya, Mizoram, etc., enjoying sovereign rights within South Asian Union and observing the burgeoning, huge free market within that Union, would willingly opt for joining it rather than be dominated by autocratic China. Still one more reward will be in store for both India and Pakistan. Overnight they will gain so many votes in the United Nations. Then South Asian Union in concert with European Union could demand for the two Unions permanent seats in the Security Council, which may be occupied by rotation by the member states of both Unions!

Now, since we mentioned the north-western subcontinent of Eurasia called Europe, we are bound to notice that while the process of enlargement of the European Union continues and its inner cohesion grows, although not without occasional setbacks, the European civilization as a whole will have to become the main identity factor. In this light we have to reconsider the unquestioned prevalence in our thinking of locating our mega-tribal identity, which we call national in such ideas as sovereign state, sharply delimited territory and even our separate language. Especially that,

> nations as a natural, God-given way of classifying men, as an inherent though long-delayed political destiny, are a myth .... Nations are not inscribed into the nature of things, they do not constitute a political version of the doctrine of natural kind. Nor were national states the manifest ultimate destiny of ethnic or cultural groups.[42]

What then can be considered instead? It seems that the only identity factor, which would not threaten the European *civitas* with disruption, would be competence—something that stood the test of time in India although it did not emerge unscathed. The caste mentality is well satisfied with supra national (read: *para-jāti*) state. Caste does not require for itself a separate state. It requires a responsible one, which would guarantee to it its distinct identity and possibility to act within its proper competence. Such viewpoint seems to be endorsed by Gellner when commenting on educational system he writes that,

> the task with which that system is entrusted is to turn out worthy, loyal and competent members of the total society whose occupancy of posts within it will not be hampered by factional loyalties to sub-groups within the total community.[43]

The Swiss have a simple task. Their competence in banking, making cheese and watches as well as providing security guard to the Roman Pope is well known. Besides, they do not use one language. So even if they are deprived of fully sovereign state and their frontiers from international ones turn into administrative ones, their identity will not be threatened. The same maybe said about any European nation, provided it attaches more importance to its competences than to its frontiers. In a way it already began to happen in the domain of sports. Competence of our sportsmen feeds more and more our national pride and this trend spreads slowly to other domains of human activity.

So the time has come to reformulate and revalue determinants of our identity. Sovereign nation-states are blood drenched. Frontiers have been delimited with thousands of corpses of fallen soldiers. Let us hope that in the name of competence we shall not fight—we shall simply compete, while trying to avoid the pitfalls of the Indian caste system with its scorn for the lowly and with its inability to integrate those who define their identity differently—the sin equally stigmatizing the national system of Europe, which brought about the Holocaust. In spite of its obvious blemishes, the caste system proved its competence in safeguarding mega-tribal identity during last three thousand years. Let us then discard mental stereotypes and try to look at it impartially.

The European and Asian languages clutch themselves sometimes in a blind confrontation leading astray entire civilizations and making the true mutual understanding difficult. Providing proper form of inter-cultural communication among civilizations is a challenge of the 21st century. There have to be established proper equivalences between the European languages used in Asia and Asian languages, which could eliminate such misnomers as calling *jāti*—caste and not nation and *dharma*—religion and not nature of things or eventually even culture. We do not advocate any automatic transplantation of social institutions—by no means! It is not the Indian caste system that may be grafted upon European society but it is the way Hindus managed to safeguard during millennia their mega-tribal identities that should be of utmost interest to us Europeans.

Main hypotheses of the article:

(I) Byrski: Traditional Indic socio-cultural-political experience based on *varṇa/jāti* and dharma may have relevance in solving problems of group identity, citizenship, and nationalism in contemporary Europe.

Tilak: I am so glad that this article will force Indologists (both Indian and non-Indian) to reinterpret and revalue the enormous literature that has gathered around the founding concept of the traditional Indic social organization. We all will have to 'unlearn' almost everything that was drilled into our heads about the caste system and learn (or relearn) afresh about the *varṇa/jāti* complex.

(II) Byrski: (a) The category and the phenomenon of *varṇa/jāti* acts as a strong bond (*bandhu*) as well as an integrative force that promotes the pan-Indic identity which modern Europe lacks thereby preventing or undermining its cultural solidarity; (b) Such indigenous Indic cognitive, sociocultural, and political categories as *varṇa/jāti* and dharma may therefore be employed as valid points of reference in the evaluation of Western/European socio-cultural-political reality.

Tilak: It is true that birth in a given family/community automatically confirmed and conferred a specific social/ritual status on every individual in India. However, since very ancient times the *varṇa/jāti* dialectic was also used to integrate newly forming communities or communal groups by ranking them with reference to each group's competence, need, and desire to choose or opt for adopting and/or adapting to a specific trade and a corresponding lifestyle. Welfare, social status, and self-respect of each *jāti* (and its members) therefore have been a function of each *jāti*'s ability to generate an internal i.e., self-endorsed and self-validated system of governance and competence based on the scale of *varṇa* as outlined in the *Purushasukta* of the Ṛgveda. The *jātis* or nations (modern European equivalent of *jāti*) were expected to compete with each other (rather than fight each other) for recognition (or de-recognition) of a higher (or lower) socio-cultural status. This assured a 'secular' mode (to use an equivalent modern term) of state polity (*dharma sāpeksha rāstra*) in which citizenship (*civitas*) of each founder group was recognized, protected, and preserved. Lapses in observing the ascribed and prescribed norms of dharma (based on the individual's *varṇa/vaya/liṅga*) resulted in the downward or upward movement of the individual (and eventually the community) on the scale of *varṇa*.

(II) Byrski: Why and how this natal/mobile and cohesive sense of being born from the same womb disappeared from modern Europe? The principal reason is (1) the Portuguese use of the term 'casta' for *jāti* and its description as an evil system; it is not clear whether the use was a genuine misunderstanding or a deliberate distortion; (2) more recently, ideology as reflected in the slogan 'One land, one language, and one leader' and popularized by the Nazis may have been the cause of this disappearance.

Tilak: The failure or difficulty encountered by Westerners (and Indic academics and intellectuals who uncritically follow them) in understanding the integrative scope and application of *jāti* may be traced to the fact that in the Western political theory and polity it is the state and the political processes (such as democracy) and ideologies (secularism for instance) that are principally implicated in the business of holding a nation together and keep the societal system going. In India, on the other hand, it is *jāti* and dharma that are pressed into service to cultivate a sense of belonging and to cope with and manage diversity and keep society functioning. Socio-culturally speaking, besides *jāti* (dharma), other integrators of cohesion like *bhakti* (devotion to one's chosen deity) and *rīti* (dharma) (local custom) have been found useful. All are united by a common celebration of wholeness and 'competence' as you put perceptively.

Samavāya: integrative force of jāti

As opposed to its current, colonially dictated meaning of 'caste' *jāti* denotes the logic of classes, of genera and species (Ramanujan 1990: 53) and by extension a federation of cultural communities as in the concept of *jana jāti*.

jāti-based integration typically involves incorporation into a larger unit; i.e., (re)alignment into a larger whole the scattered entities. From the Indic perspective this kind of unity is rooted in the relationship called *samavāya*, which is different from synthetic unity (conjunction = *samyoga*) that typically brings together two are more entities that may essentially be different. *Samavāya*, on the other hand, is a unity based on the permanent or eternal relation between two or more entities one (or more) of which *inheres* in the other. It is to be remembered that the 'many' emerge (or are born) out of 'one'. Thus, the *Vaiśeṣika classical texts describe samavāya* as a connection (*sambandha*) that is sui generis (that is, inherent or natal) connecting *relata* in a relationship of 'container' and 'contained' or of dependence and support (*ādhāryādhārabhāva*) (see Halbfass 1992: 147).

To put it differently, the universal resides in the individual and particularity via some enduring substance. Thus, we may say that the cloth as a whole (*jāti*) is in the threads (individual members and families that make up a given *jāti*).

(III) Byrski: In modern Bengali *jāti* is used in the sense of nation an important factor is the fact of sharing a common womb or birth (FN # 14). To that extent *jāti* is akin to Latin *natus* or *nasci* i.e., being born (p. 171; fn # 15); formation of a nation (*jāti*) through a shared birth process that assures organic interdependence is already formulated in the *Purushasukta* of the Ṛgveda.

Tilak: This is well put. Even today, when used as an adjective, the word *jātiya* carries the sense of 'national' as in the 'Bangladesh Jatiya Party', which is a political party in Bangladesh, a splinter-group of the original Jatiya Party that was founded by the former president of Bangladesh, Hossain Mohammad Ershad.

(IV) Byrski: The successful and meaningful integration of Jews into the Indic sociocultural world is an example that may be repeated in Europe especially in light of the discriminatory treatment meted out to the gypsies (Roma) in Europe.

Tilak: The inclusive character of the Indic tradition fosters acceptance and affirmation of cultural, ethnic, religious, and social diversity or plurality which was reaffirmed and strengthened through such concepts as *varṇa, jāti,* and dharma. Different *jāti* and *varṇa* groups received their *raison-d-être* as autonomous communities that always sought the middle ground. The middle ground, however, did not imply a *common* ground, since it may be contested. All that is shared is agreement on the purpose that organizes the content. If conflicts arise, they arise not on the existence of the absolute (say, *brahman, nirvāṇa* or dharma, but on its identity, its manifestations, and the relative value of the ways of attaining it. It is not the absolute that is at issue, but the relativities.

The concept of *jāti* assures that an individual or a group is free to establish a separate corner and a spatial/temporal context for itself. One of the characteristics of Indic thought is precisely that it does not normally aim at a synthesis because it allows the holding of even contradictory beliefs together (though they can be kept separate through an integrative relation of *samavāya*). This tendency is comparable to people speaking many languages readily recognize and acknowledge that the sun or the moon could be male in one language and female in another. Just as multilingual speakers do not fuse different languages into a synthesis, so Indians do not aim at synthesis of their various beliefs or dharmas in a synthetic whole (see Ferro-Luzzi 1997: 297–298).

Needless to say, von Stietencron was moved to observe that Hinduism created a culture of accepted and recognized multiformity generating tolerance between religions and ideologies to a degree, which civilizations based on Judaism, Christianity and Islam, were never able to achieve (1997: 48).

(V) Byrski: Replace the present federal constitutional republic by a South Asian Union.

Tilak: Indian Ocean Community as suggested by Dr Kalyanraman in his recent book entitled *Indian Ocean Community: Uniting nations on path of progress* would be a preferable alternative. Kalyanraman sees *Rashtram* (his name for the Indian Ocean Community) as a counterpoise to the European Union or Community that would be capable of providing new developmental opportunities for over a third of humanity. In the long run it can contribute to setting up of a more equitable and just global order in which Europe and India together can offer a viable stabilizing sheet anchor.

NOTES

1. It is the only Indian term in writing of which we use diacritical mark for long ā, just in case a reader would wish to look up this word in Sanskrit dictionary. Otherwise the anglicised transcription has been adopted.
2. The term 'mega-tribal' is being introduced here in order to embrace both the idea of nation as well as that of caste.
3. 'Oh, East is East, and West is West, and never the twain shall meet, Till Earth and Sky stand presently at God's great Judgement Seat; But there is neither East nor West, Border, nor Breed, nor Birth, When two strong men stand face to face, tho' they come from the ends of the earth!' (Kipling 1950, pp. 137–144).
4. South Asia is a subregion of Asia comprising the modern states of Afghanistan, Bangladesh, Bhutan, India, Maldives, Nepal, Pakistan and Sri Lanka, members of South Asian Association for Regional Cooperation (SAARC). It covers about 51,435 thousand square kilometres (*Uniwersalna Encyklopedia* 2006, pp. 96–97).

5. Jelonek 1996 mentions 27 such inland seas.
6. In the Indian subcontinent the maximal one is +26.8EC and minimal is +18.10EC. In case of the European subcontinent it is +17.11EC and –8.08EC (*Geograficzny atlas świata* 1997).
7. The population of the Indian subcontinent (SAARC countries) as in 2005 is 1462,671 thousand (*Uniwersalna Encyklopedia* 2006, pp. 96–97). It is three times as large as that of Europe (513,000,000 [1994] without the European part of the erstwhile USSR [*Geograficzny atlas świata* 1997]).
8. 'Without placing too much reliance on the actual absolute figures produced by glottochronology, we may note that the lexicostatistician, Norman Bird, has reported a strong co-occurrence of Indic with Iranian words: 85 per cent of Iranian words from his list have Indic equivalences ... 77 per cent of Hittite words in the list have co-occurrences with Indic roots too' (Renfrew 1987, p. 193).
9. Mallory 1989, p. 272.
10. East Anatolia may be considered part 'of the early "homeland" of people speaking a very early form of Indo-European, around 7000 BC' (Renfrew 1987, p. 174, 266, 269, 272).
11. According to Popko, the forefathers of Aryas left Anatolia and sometime during second millennium BC reached India. This might have happened after the last glacial period and that it is difficult to determine the motive that made them leave more hospitable region for less hospitable one. Thus, the hypothesis that deluge might have been responsible for the dispersion of Indo-Europeans acquires considerable probability (Popko 2003, pp. 145–148).
12. We keep in mind here the ancient sphere of scientific enquiry called *dharmaśāstra* and the classic treatise entitled *Mānavadharmaśāstra*.
13. Dumont 1966, p. 55 and 161.
14. Monier-Williams 1899, p. 410. It may be added that in modern Bengali language *jāti* means also 'nation'.
15. Nation c. 1300, from O.Fr. nacion, from L. nationem (nom. natio) 'nation, stock, race', lit. 'that which has been born', from natus, pp. of nasci 'be born' (Old L. gnasci; see genus). Political sense has gradually taken over from racial meaning 'large group of people with common ancestry'. Older sense preserved in application to N.Amer. Indian peoples (1640s). Nation-building first attested 1907 (implied in nation-builder). [http://www.etymonline.com/index.php?term=nation] (29.04.2011).

16. Gellner 1983, p. 7.
17. Ibid., p. 39.
18. It is true that in India, cultural homogeneity sometimes cuts across linguistic diversity: Hindus 'speak the same language' even when they do not speak the same language (Gellner 1983, p. 109; Kedourie 1971, p. 20).
19. Jan Baszkiewicz in his excellent essay in the Polish language entitled 'State and Nation in Europe at the Turn of XVIII and XIX Centuries' gives also a brief account of how the idea fared in Europe and in the United States of America. He mentions two schools of thought concerning the idea of nation; one of Johann Gotfried Herder holding that nation is formed by phenomena independent of human will and often not even realized consciously, like common destiny, culture, customs and mother tongue. The other is the French school, which holds that nation is inherited from the past and forms itself as a result of conscious processes expressing human will and political will as well (Baszkiewicz 2005, p. 237).
20. Tikekar 2008, p. 51.
21. The Balkan wars were a series of conflicts that led to the disintegration of the former Republic of Yugoslavia. Occurring over a decade-long period between 1991 and 2001, these conflicts ultimately affected all six former Yugoslav republics—allegiances were largely split along republic borders. All of the conflicts had underlying ethnic, political and religious origins [http://www.squidoo.com/Bosnia] (29.05.2011).
22. Dirks 2001, p. 49.
23. For *Purushasukta* (RV. X.90. 11–12), see Panikkar 1977, pp. 72–77.
24. The meaning implied here is 'the sacred word', 'the Veda', 'a sacred text'.
25. Edgerton 1965, p. 24 (IV.13). This translation is rather cryptic if not mistaken for it interprets *chaturvarnyam* as *'the fours caste-system'*. This is wrong for *varṇa* is not caste but it is a fourfold categorization of castes according to competence and ritualistic purity. Caste is called *jāti* in Sanskrit.
26. Byrski 2006–7, pp. 63–70.
27. This Jaina treatise formulates this definition as follows: *dharmah vastusvabhāvah*. Svāmi-Kumāra 1997, p. 364 (XII.478).
28. See Monier-Williams 1899, p. 510.
29. The famous Indian philosopher (788–820 CE).

30. Sanskrit: *dhārayati lokān iti dharmah*.
31. *The Encyclopaedia of Gandhian Thoughts* 1985, p. 360.
32. Ibid.
33. Singh 2003, *passim*.
34. Joanna Jurewicz drew my attention yet to one more meaning of this word, i.e., a letter, sound, vowel, syllable and word, which may have been substantial in the context discussed. Categorization of human competences of course requires suitable terminology. As *varṇas* denote order of sounds, so applied to human beings they signify social order. Writes she in a paper to be published soon in 'Oriental Studies: Past and Present', proceeding of the International Conference of Oriental Studies, Warsaw, 2010, *Rocznik Orientalistyczny*, vol. 65, no. 1, 2012. '... the use of the word *varṇa* to denote social classes could be motivated not only by the anthropological features of the people but also by thinking about language as the social phenomenon. The social states are the *varṇas*, sounds of the God's language ...'.
35. Kurowski 1983, *passim*. The Greek term *kratos* means 'strength, power, rule'. See also Byrski 1980–81, pp. 654–661.
36. Rothermund 2008, p. 199.
37. Our Indian friends should know that the role, which the Nazis ascribed to Poles, was that of menials exclusively and that they did their level best during World War II to eliminate the three upper *varṇas* of our society physically in order to turn us into slaves. In the Indian context, in the past this used to be achieved by forbidding lowest castes even to listen to the Vedas being recited—Vedas, which were tantamount to knowledge.
38. Bhimrao Ramji Ambedkar (1891–1956) responsible for drafting the Constitution of India and Kocheril Raman Narayanan (1921–2005) the tenth President of the Republic of India, both were dalits (untouchables) highly respected.
39. Gandhi 1990, p. 36.
40. This idea in somewhat different terms has been considered by Ranjit Kumar 2005, *passim*. The author suggests that the South Asian Association of Regional Cooperation may be remade into South Asian Union. But the difference in size and power between India and all other member states of SAARC, including Pakistan precludes the success of this project.
41. Very much welcome support in such an understanding of this term comes from Professor G.U. Thite, who holds that *'there is no word for*

"nation" in Sanskrit. The word "rāstra" means state and not nation'. This information I found on the jacket of *Kātyāyan-Śrautasūtra,* New Bharatiya Book Corporation, Delhi, 2006. Yet, I would insist that the proper word for 'nation' in Sanskrit is *jāti,* although it does not mean that its understanding in India and in Europe is identical, but both cater to the same need of mega-tribal social security.

42. Gellner 1983, pp. 48–49.

43. Ibid., p. 64.

REFERENCES

Baszkiewicz, Jan. 2005. 'Państwo i naród w Europie na przełomie XVIII i XIX wieku' (State and Nation in Europe at the Turn of XVIII and XIX Centuries), in *Cywilizacja Europejska* (The European Civilisation), edited by M. Koźmiński, Warszawa: IPH & Collegium Civitas.

Byrski, Maria Krzysztof. 2006–7. 'Dharmaśāstra: A Natural Science', in *Sanskrit Studies,* edited by Wagish Shukla, New Delhi: Special Centre for Sanskrit Studies, JNU.

——. 1980–81. 'Is Manu's Varnadharma an Obsolete Sociological Concept?', *The Adyar Library Bulletin,* XLIV–XLV: 654–661.

Dirks, Nicolas B. 2001. *Castes of Mind: Colonialism and the Making of Modern India.* Princeton: Princeton University Press.

Ferro-Luzzi, G. Eichinger. 1997. 'The Polythetic-Prototype Approach to Hinduism', in *Hinduism Reconsidered,* edited by Gunther D. Sontheimer and Hermann Kulke, Delhi: Manohar, 294–304.

Gandhi, Rajmohan. 1990. *Understanding the Muslim Mind.* New Delhi: Penguin Books.

Gellner, Ernest. 1983. *Nations and Nationalism: New Perspectives on the Past.* Ithaca, New York: Cornell University Press.

Halbfass, Wilhelm. 1992. *On Being and What There Is: Classical Vaiśeṣika and the History of Indian Ontology.* Albany: State University of New York Press.

Jelonek, Adam. 1996. *Encyklopedia Geograficzna Świata—Europa* (Geographic Encyclopaedia of the World—Europe). Kraków: Opress.

Jurewicz, Joanna. 2012. 'Oriental Studies: Past and Present', *Rocznik Orientalistyczny,* 65, 1.

Kedourie, Elie (ed.). 1971. *Nationalism in Asia and Africa.* London: Weidenfeld and Nicolson.

Kipling, Rudyard. 1950. *Barrack Room Ballads* and *Departmental Ditties*. New York: Arcadia House.

Kumar, Ranjit. 2005. *South Asian Union*. New Delhi: Manas Publications.

Kurowski, Stefan. 1983. *Teoria Kratosów* (The Theory of Kratoses). Warszawa: Liberta.

Mallory, James P. 1989. *In Search of the Indo-Europeans: Language, Archeology and Myth*. London: Thames and Hudson.

Popko, Maciej. 2003. 'Archeologia, genetyka i praojczyzna Indoeuropejczyków' (Archeology, Genetics and Homeland of Indo-Europeans), *Archeologia*, LIII.

Ramanujan, A.K. 1990. 'Is There an Indian Way of Thinking?', in *India through Hindu Categories*, edited by McKim Marriott, New Delhi: Sage Publications, 41–58.

Renfrew, Colin. 1987. *Archeology and Language: The Puzzle of Indo-European Origins*. London: Pimlico.

Rothermund, Dietmar. 2008. *India: The Rise of an Asian Giant*. New Haven: Yale University Press.

Singh, Kumar Suresh. 2003. *People of India—Introduction*, II Revised Edition. New Delhi: Oxford University Press.

Svāmi-Kumāra. 1997. Kārttikeyānuprekṣa, Śrī Parama-Śruta Prabhāvaka Mandal, Agās.

Tikekar, Maneesha. 2008. 'Nation, State and Identity Conflicts in South Asia', in *South Asia and Central Asia: Building Political and Economic Linkages*. Islamabad: Institute of Regional Studies.

von Stietencron, Heinrich. 1997. 'Hinduism: On the Proper Use of a Deceptive Term', in *Hinduism Reconsidered*, edited by Gunther-Dietz Sontheimer and Hermann Kulke, Delhi: Manohar, 32–53.

ENCYCLOPAEDIAS AND DICTIONARIES

Geograficzny atlas świata (World Geographic Atlas). 1997. Warszawa–Wrocław: PPWK.

The Encyclopaedia of Gandhian Thoughts. 1985. A.T. Hingoorani and G.A. Hingoorani (eds). New Delhi: All India Congress Committee (I).

Uniwersalna Encyklopedia (Universal Encyclopaedia). 2006. Warszawa: Wydawnictwo Naukowe PWN SA.

Monier-Williams, M. 1899. *Sanskrit–English Dictionary*. Oxford: The Clarendon Press.

5

Decolonization and the Entangled Histories of Science and Philosophy in India*

DHRUV RAINA

This paper seeks to investigate the nature of entanglement between the academic concerns of historians of science and the discipline of Indian philosophy since the commencement of the decade of decolonization. The exploration is prefaced by a lengthy discussion about the modern scientific community in India. The problem to be discussed is the encounter, and possibly its nature, between the modernity of science and the engagement with philosophical reasoning in the 'Indian' traditions. The sociologist Niklas Luhmann perceptively pointed out that science unfurled as a frame of thinking and acting that had never to establish its modernity, unlike other fields of human culture and experience or, more so, even 'modern society' (Luhmann 2002: 61). But stretching the Luhmannian point a little further it could be argued that the disciplinary differentiation and speciation that characterizes the changing frontiers of knowledge in the West, has cast a cordon sanitaire that demarcates the discussion between the philosophical conceptions of knowledge and that of science (Rosenberg 1998).

---

* The second part of this paper draws upon my article 'Knowledge', in Akira Iriye and Pierre-Yves Saunier (eds), *The Palgrave Dictionary of Transnational History*, Basingstoke: Palgrave Books, 2009, pp. 620–626.

Consequently, one of the outcomes of this rear guard action of philosophy that is traced back to the nineteenth and early twentieth centuries is the institutionalization of a discipline referred to as the philosophy of science, as the final realization of the Cartesian project. Thus, while philosophy of science is enveloped within the disciplinary folds of philosophy, it distinguished itself from other subdisciplines of philosophy, inasmuch as it approached its subject-matter or object domain in terms of a dichotomous separation of fact and value, and the other Cartesian dichotomies. However, since the 1970s the emergence of the sociology of knowledge has since made deep inroads in contesting this dichotomy, but the heated battle continues, as attempts are made towards reconciliation between what appear just now as irreconcilable positions (Ziman 2000; Longino 2002).

The institutionalization of science in modern India in the twentieth century is apparently marked by a paucity of philosophical reflection on the nature of the foundations of science within the scientific community, some notable exceptions within the scientific community notwithstanding.[1] This is not an accusation nor does it suggest that there is no awareness of the philosophical foundations of the science being practised (Raina 2003). By and large, within the Indian scientific community, over the last century or so, the conception of science as a cultural universal has prevailed, that in the first two decades of the twentieth century found expression in a triumphalist scientism. In fact, it is rather surprising that leading physicists like Meghnad N. Saha and Satyendra N. Bose who were closely networked with the quantum theory/quantum mechanics generation of scientists-philosophers, moulded in the German ideal of the kulturträger, did not participate or take an explicit view on the foundations of quantum mechanics. Was this on account of a lack of philosophical engagement or that they entertained a different notion/interpretation of quantum theory or theory itself?

In any case, the disenchantment that characterized the last three decades of the twentieth century, and the consequent epistemic deprivileging of science produced a number of debates on the question of scientific method, appropriate technology, ecological movements, big dams, forestry, not to mention a version of the 'culture wars'. In each of these debates, the character of the nature of science was discussed, polemicized and the public image of science somewhat eroded, without in any way denting state support for science. By and large, in these last decades, scientists were on the defensive, where old images of science were recycled in order to revive old and perhaps some new dreams. These dreams did not reflect the changing epistemology of science, or the changing character of the relationship between science and state, science and society. The idea of science as cultural universal incarnated itself in a pattern of speaking about science in the ever present tense.

Nevertheless, there were some very important exceptions that included A.K.N. Reddy, Satish Dhawan and Madhav Gadgil. Their philosophies of science differed from each other but were not radical enough to overthrow the apple cart of science as cultural universal. They were certainly concerned with the question of science in society and the interests science in India served, as well as the social values and considerations scientific and technological regimes encoded. If they still operated within the terms set by the use-abuse model of science, what was more important was that the model did not offer an excuse or mode of exculpating themselves of moral or political responsibility—in fact, they pressed for scientists' involvement in issues of societal concern.

But the possibility of evading moral responsibility gave cause for concerted critique from the social sciences from the 1970s onwards. In the first instance, this criticism came from neo-Gandhians who had mounted a civilizational-national critique of the West, science and modernity (Nandy 1988; Visvanathan 1997). I shall not delve into this criticism because it has been discussed elsewhere in great detail. Irrespective of whether this neo-Gandhian critique was anti-science or not, it projected a new topos of alternatives. In other words, it challenged the path-independent stadial models of historical and social evolution (Visvanathan 1997). This it substituted with the idea of there being other possible and equally likely worlds that had been condemned to the underground of both India as well as the modern West (Uberoi 2002). This was an important milestone in engaging with the present of the sciences and most certainly de-privileged the epistemic authority of science, even if this did not alter the trajectory of scientific or technological evolution.

Strategically, the projection of alternatives into the public imaginary triggered a number of initiatives within civil society, that could well be considered new social movements across the political spectrum and civil society initiatives. The inventiveness of these social movements played a small role in democratizing the upper-caste, patriarchal culture that characterized the world of institutionalized scientific research and higher education. It also brought different ways of knowing, into a more substantial engagement with that of modern science. More substantial in this new sense, or more likely new order, would mean a greater degree of reflexive engagement with other ways of knowing and possibly suspending, if only temporarily, progressivist and received ways of thinking. If these developments resonated with trends in postmodern thought, they could also be seen as an exemplification of another global trend, namely the transition from an earlier phase of the scientization of society, to a more self-conscious one of the socialization of science (Nowotny et al. 2001).

Philosophically, the issue manifests itself in a different form. Modern Indian philosophers have, in the twentieth century, constantly engaged with the status of classical Indian philosophy. The relationship between the two has been a difficult one and could be seen as a distorted by-product of late colonialism. It appears as if the very prerequisite for the contemporary Indian philosopher's metier is to define his or her relationship with the enormous corpus of classical Indian philosophy. The problem was addressed in a paper by Peter Schreiner titled, 'The Indianness of Modern Indian Philosophy as a Historical and Philosophical Problem' (Schreiner 1978). The salient concern of the paper, both historical and philosophical, is the relevance of the notion of Indianness to academic disciplines currently practised in the universities. It is suggested that the notion of Indian as an attribute of Indian philosophy 'was probably introduced by Western and non-Indian authors' based on an ideal of India prevalent among British and German Orientalists. The resolution of the problem of Indianness requires confronting the construction of Orientalist images of India, characterized as philosophical, spiritual and mystical, and their subsequent distortion or modification at the hands of Indian philosophers (ibid.: 35–36).

The dilemma further manifests itself as an outcome of the translation of meaning, goals, methods and questions of the classical Indian philosophical project into the idiom of contemporary Western/modern philosophy. In this task of cultural translation of the traditional into the modern, the Indian philosopher is often burdened with the task of establishing the relevance of classical Indian philosophy to contemporary philosophy; and for some reason that has been the destiny of classical Indian philosophy in its relationship to the Western philosophy in the twentieth century. This has been no different from the case of rendering the history of science in India as linking up with the trajectory of modern science.

In the case of philosophy, till the second half of the last century, Western philosophers largely believed that there was no such thing as the Indian philosophical tradition in the sense that Western philosophy existed. Once we discount both the patent Eurocentrism behind the claim and the construction of the Indian philosophical tradition as either purely metaphysical or mystical we come to the question whether we should see the philosophical enterprise as a cultural universal or we proceed to reduce the underlying similarities and differences across cultures. Typically, two dichotomies that characterize debates in Western philosophy, the fact-value dichotomy and the theory-practice dichotomy, are absent in the Indian tradition. But Western categories percolate into thinking about Indian philosophical theories. The philosopher, Jitendra N. Mohanty suggests that to overcome these dichotomies one needs to think from within a global perspective, employing western categories and inspired by eastern examples (Mohanty 2009: 147).

By and large, modern Indian philosophers have centred the focus of Indian philosophy along three orthogonal axes. Each of these proposals has attempted to locate the central problematic of Indian philosophy. The first of these reconstructions whose vintage and public reception is rather extensive argues that the concerns of Indian philosophy are primarily spiritual or metaphysical and this is what sets out an identity for Indian philosophy that distinguishes it from other philosophical traditions. One way of understanding this reconstruction of such a diverse and complex philosophical system is to locate the reconstruction as a pathological response to the colonial project, which produced a protectionist response in terms of an external material world governed by the laws of science and an internal spiritual realm that was grasped by Indian thinkers (Chatterjee 1993; Raina and Habib 1996). The table below summarizes this response:

West	*India*
Mastery of the external world	Mastery over the internal world
Seeking to control the material realm	Seeking to control the spiritual realm
Inventors of modern science	Pioneers of the science of spirituality

In this sense, the agenda of Indian philosophy in the foreground is merely a spiritual response to European constructions of India during the late colonial period. Furthermore, it has been argued that the integration of Indian philosophy into the idiom of modern Western philosophy was undertaken by leading Indian philosophers such as Radhakrishnan, who possessed a deep and close knowledge of the corpus of classical Indian philosophy in Sanskrit. The idea then that spiritualism is the essential component of Indian thought was elaborated further by many other philosophers such as R.D. Ranade, Karl Potter, T.M.P. Mahadevan, Ramachandra Gandhi.[2] In a way then, as Raghuramaraju suggests, while this view of Indian philosophy arose as a reaction to one construction of Indian philosophy, it thrived upon the differences between India and the West (Raghuramaraju 2006: 13). On the other hand, the Indologist David Zilberman turned to Indian philosophy; for he felt that traditionally in Indian civilization, philosophy enjoyed the status of a 'system of culture'. Thereby, he shifted the standard essentialization of Indian philosophy, as other-worldly, in the opposite direction where it occupies the centre of culture:

> ... philosophical activity of thinking was organized as a specific form of the material production of meaning, and the cultural significance produced by that kind of thinking turned out to be of central importance for the reproduction of the whole system of Hinduism (Zilberman 1988: 3).

The difficulty with this approach is that Indian civilization is conflated with Hinduism at whose core are the Hindu systems of philosophy, to the exclusion of other equally significant systems such as Buddhism, Jainism, Islam, and the other heterodox systems. This conflation characterized the work of a number of other philosophers such as Radhakrishnan and Mallik (Schreiner 1978). In pointing out the difficulty with Zilberman's characterization, I run the risk of clubbing him with nineteenth century Indologists whose influence on the construction of Indianness of Indian philosophy has been substantial. But like Radhakrishnan and others argued, so does Zilberman that these philosophical systems, as different from the others, are not religious philosophies, since philosophical concerns were never coupled with the personal devotion or the lack of it of the philosophers (Zilberman 1988: 4). Thus, reckoning with the differences between literary production of Western and Indian philosophical texts, the latter being more technically oriented than discursively reflective, the essential difference resided in that Indian philosophical systems '... can be understood as a constituent of objective reality, rather than as an abstract mental reflection upon it' (ibid.: 3).

While the very idea that the systems of thought in antiquity were expressions of a nation's thought and culture, would certainly raise a number of contemporary eyebrows, for underlying the thesis is a philosophical ideal and approach that enfolds the unity of India as a political idea (Schreiner 1978: 34). Nevertheless, once this connection is decoupled it should be possible to look at the schools of philosophy functioning within an extended geographical cosmopolis.

The diametrically opposed view, a marginal one though, has been proposed by Debiprasad Chattopadhyaya, arguing that it is materialism that constituted the hard core of Indian philosophy, and its epistemic and socially radical possibilities were in part responsible for its being swallowed up in the maelstrom of idealism that subsequently swept across classical Indian philosophy (Chattopadhyaya 1959). While on the surface of it, one could have problems with this kind of an explanation there are two parts that centre the discussion on Indian materialism that warrants some elaboration. First, the idea that there was a materialist tradition in Indian philosophy that constituted the diversity of classical Indian philosophy, and that this school, however problematic its sources may have been, posed difficult philosophical questions for rival schools is an important insight worthy of consideration. Second, Chattopadhyaya very carefully in his subsequent work divulged the importance of the relationship between the schools of logic such as the Nyaya and the schools of traditional Indian medicine such as the Ayurveda (Chattopadhyaya 1979). Chattopadhyaya's inspiration could have been an early twentieth century history of science authored by B.N. Seal, *The Positive Sciences of the Hindus* (Seal 1915) and he went on to argue that of all the knowledge systems of ancient India, it was only medicine that qualified to be a science in the modern/Western sense of the term. A very arguable and contested thesis.

This was a new twist to the debate, for herein resided the suggestion that in the logical traditions there was much that was germane to the practice of science. I do not wish to suggest that Chattopadhyaya was the inaugurator of a discourse that several philosophers working on classical Indian philosophy would deepen or thicken. But certainly, there was an argument that several thinkers would take up independently to bring classical Indian philosophy into engagement with contemporary Western philosophy and more particularly modern science. Interestingly enough, as Western philosophy was dislodged from its pedestal as adjudicator of knowledge with the rise of the sciences, one of the ways of retaining its relevance for the practice of science was to reserve for itself the meta-theoretical enterprise of philosophy of science and the social sciences.

The third reconstruction of the classical Indian philosophy highlights the point that it is rationalism that constitutes the core of Indian philosophy. And it is along these axes we encounter a number of Indian philosophers such as Matilal, Dayakrishna and Mohanty who are in dialogue between contemporary Western philosophy and classical Indian philosophy from a number of perspectives, logical or phenomenological or meta-theoretical (Raghuramaraju 2006). Consequently, this approach alongside the materialist reading, important differences notwithstanding, strives to imbue classical Indian philosophy with contemporary relevance unlike the case with the other sciences of India, where the past of science is condemned to some musee imaginaire without any contemporary relevance. This is true despite the essential difference wherein classical Indian philosophy confronts contemporary Western philosophy. Does this mean that contemporary Indian philosophy cannot articulate itself but through the spectrum of classical Indian philosophy and not directly confront contemporary Western philosophy.

However, most explorations of the cross-cultural dialogue between philosophical traditions have been set within the frame of the Western philosophical tradition, which provides a vocabulary and a grammar within which to apprehend or translate the Indian philosophical tradition. In addition to the existing Western scholarship on Indian philosophy, there exists a large body of scholarship on Indian philosophy produced by Indians writing in English. This raises another set of meta-theoretic questions dealing with the different modalities of dialogue between distinct philosophical traditions. In other words, what is and how does the comparative method function. Naturally, in posing these questions, we cannot find answers to them purely within the philosophical realm and one approach that could be pursued could be labelled a sort of social epistemology.[3]

The weight of traditions, disciplines and theories, gives meaning to this central concern with what the Indian traditions consider knowledge to be. And this entails clarifying how modern scholars comprehend these traditions and how their ancient, medieval and early modern commentators have understood them. Other than the deep hermeneutic problem that plagues any such project in translation or commentary, there are conceptual barriers that separate Indian philosophy from Western philosophy. But these barriers were erected by formulations that became philosophically institutionalized and portrayed, not just Western philosophy but Western thought as intellectual, discursive, abstract, theoretical, axiomatic-deductive and Indian philosophy and Indian thought as intuitive, experiential, pragmatic and computational. In these binaries of the history of ideas, the Indian philosophical tradition was constructed as guided by practical goals and that of transforming human existence (Mohanty 2001: 83).

Two contemporary Indian philosophers Matilal and Mohanty had dedicated themselves to the task of demolishing these barriers and the latter suggests that the goals of Western and Indian philosophy frequently cross each other, in the sense that Western philosophy has a practical side to it as well, just as Indian philosophy has theoretical components (ibid.: 84). To our generation this may seem, to employ a usage common among mathematicians, 'intuitively obvious', but the weight of intellectual and cultural institutions had prevented earlier generations from seeing through this point. Further, an issue that needs to be addressed is that Indian philosophy itself is internally quite diverse and these large constructions of systems, such as Indian philosophy collapse the internal distinctions between the different schools that comprise the Indian philosophical tradition. And, the Indian philosophical tradition often collapses onto what Western philosophy has classified as Hindu, Buddhist or Jaina philosophies. In Western accounts of Eastern philosophy, the term itself comes to connote either Indian or Chinese or Japanese philosophy—the one to the exclusion of the others (Mohanty 2001: 84).

The question of how colonialism and Indology shaped the ideal of Indian philosophy is central. There is a rich literature on the subject that seeks to locate knowledge and power in British India and that draws insights from the work of Foucault and Said. There are several perspectives in understanding of how colonialism transformed the coordinates of understanding Indian knowledge systems. Despite the differences, Orientalism appears as a shorthand for the 'imperial sociology of knowledge' (Pinch 1999: 390–393). These differences arise from differences in the understanding of the establishment of colonial rule in India. Thus, Chris Bayly (2000) addresses the importance of the knowledge received in the making of empire; and how a new information order that is created subsequently structures commerce and politics (Pinch 1999: 395). Whereas Cohn, Inden (1999) and others elaborate how the creation of knowledge about India contributed to the furtherance of the imperial project. Colonialism as post-colonial scholarship has detailed for us, produced 'complicated' forms of knowledge that Indians had constructed but were codified and transmitted by Europeans' (Cohn 1997: 16).

A number of factors shaped the encounter of seventeenth century Europeans with Indians; of these three were of prime importance. Firstly, the Europeans lived in a world of 'signs and correspondences', whilst the Hindus and Muslims 'operated within a substantive theory of objects and persons' (ibid.: 18). The spectacles through which the English viewed the divinely created world was apprehended through the senses and comprehended empirically. In invading India, Cohn contends, Europeans had unwittingly encroached upon the native epistemological space which they believed could be grasped through translation by establishing correspondences (ibid.: 53). This in turn shaped their encounter with the languages of treaties and philosophical systems of India and subsequently their reception and translation. In the eighteenth and early nineteenth century, the British desire to learn Sanskrit was fuelled by a scholarly curiosity in India as it was by a desire for the more efficient governance of Bengal (ibid.: 26). But the early translations of Sanskrit texts were undertaken from intermediary translations of these texts first into Persian and then into English (Cohn 1997: 27). This was to change with the foundation of the Asiatic Society of Bengal towards the last decades of the eighteenth century.

The comparative method developed out of several strains of European thought that included technologies for the textual construction of a history of Europe, these were now extrapolated to the study of India. The European preoccupation with the 'origin of things' was reflected in the questions and technologies of comparative history that included the collection and classification of texts and languages in the hope of establishing original versions of texts, pure languages and of establishing a chronology (ibid.: 54). In this manner the comparative method through its power of classification facilitated the control of 'variety and difference' (ibid.: 55). The linearity of the comparative narrative was oriented either forward as was done in the case of European history or as a hurtling down from a pristine authentic past as was done by some Europeans and Indian scholars—the discovery of the pure versions, it was contended, would reverse this degeneration (ibid.). Thus, the colonial project that resulted in the production of dictionaries resulted in the creation and alteration of the languages of the region and thus altered radically the access of both future generations of Europeans and Indians to the past (ibid.: 55).

This brings us to the point whether we post-colonialists will ever be able to access the past as 'undistorted' by the experience of colonialism or the encounter with the West. This historiographic perspective is an outcome of paradigmatic changes in recent history writing that disregards the articulation of 'timeless structures and mentalities' and focuses instead on questions of agency (Minkowski 2001). In fact, post-colonial scholarship has ignored the social history of knowledge on the eve of colonialism which in a way reinforces the perspective that colonialism certainly marked the end of the Sanskrit episteme and thereby changed the rules for the generation of knowledge on the subcontinent (Pollock 2000). I think there are two simple presuppositions at stake. Outside the cultural encounter between East and West, one could as well ask in the European context what the writings of the ancient Greeks would have meant without the works of the Arab commentators on those texts (Montgomery 2000). Further, we can then ask whether even a Western philosopher can access ancient Western philosophy in terms that are unmediated by two millennia of history. The

Indian philosopher, Matilal rejected the objection that twentieth century attempts to articulate the ideas of the ancients were futile. On the contrary while the motivations of philosophers from different periods and cultures might differ, there were important philosophical questions and puzzles that continued to be of contemporary relevance, these included 'the problem of knowledge and its criteria, the problem of perception and the status of the external world' (Matilal 1986: 2–3).

In which case, how do we transit from the discussion of 'knowledge' in one system to another, when there are differences in some essential conceptions? What needs to be reckoned with is that the epistemological vocabularies in the two traditions is comprised of terms considered synonymous, but actually denote different concepts. Thus, we are in addition to the preceding discussion led to ask of the utility of the comparative method. A comparative historian of science, Joseph Needham for one felt that the comparative study of the science and civilization of China would enable him to rethink the presuppositions of Western civilization and social science theory.

The comparative method is then an unavoidable activity for cultural amphibians (Said 1985) and for those philosophers attempting to render one tradition comprehensible in the language and vocabulary of another. The task for the philosopher is to ascertain the nature of the philosophical enterprise, and the relevance of the comparison of ideas and theories to the philosophical goal of studying 'things-in-themselves'. One of the arguments cited by Mohanty is that comparative philosophy is an unavoidable enterprise for cultural amphibians, forever rendering one tradition in terms of another or translating from one language into another.[4] But then, one must ask what philosophy is—is it about things in themselves or about the comparison of ideas, concepts and theories? According to Mohanty, comparative philosophy is a second order discipline as a result of which it falls short of genuine philosophy. It nevertheless serves the important role of liberating philosophers of dogmatically inhabiting their own traditions and thereby, free philosophy itself (Mohanty 2001: 85). If that be the case, then comparative philosophy inasmuch as it leads to the clarification of our philosophical ideas and theories could as well be as crucial as mainstream philosophical activity, even though its nature is that of a metaphilosophy.

The discussion on the comparative approaches of Mohanty and Matilal seeks to point out that the discourse on the character of knowledge in the Indian tradition is really a social-epistemological one, and may throw some light not merely on the philosophical enterprise but play up similarities between the conception of knowledge in the Indian tradition and the insights emerging from the sociology of scientific knowledge. Zilberman's investigations commenced with a comparative elaboration of the notion of epistemology in Indian theories of knowledge and the Western tradition (s). This examination was prompted by his understanding that analogy was a central problem in modern philosophy of science, language and phenomenon, and that Indian philosophy provided some very interesting insights (Zilberman 1988: xx). This intellectual journey is similar in spirit to that of Matilal and Mohanty, though Zilberman himself comes in from a different cultural or philosophical tradition.[5]

Zilberman was particularly disposed to the perspective of the social dimensions of knowledge though he approached the problematic differently. In his work titled, *The Birth of Meaning in Hindu Thought*, his focus was on the sociological presuppositions of Indian epistemology and formal logic (ibid.: xix). In attempting to explicate the sense in which Hindu systems of thought constitute epistemic disciplines, Zilberman was aspiring to reform the whole idea of philosophy, as the object for a new science he calls, 'science of philosophies' (ibid.: 1). Put it differently, Indian philosophy offered a categorical framework for meta-philosophy. The several systems of Indian philosophy were not to be viewed as different philosophical systems but part of the categorical apparatus that would be required in the making of philosophy as an object of the science of philosophy.

An interesting feature is that the three projects of Matilal, Mohanty and Zilberman coruscate at a particular conjuncture of philosophical thought, namely in the 1980s. A conjuncture produced by the linguistic turn in philosophy and the social turn in the philosophy of science. Zilberman sees his own project as an entirely novel one, the historical necessity of which was announced by the times (ibid.). This conjuncture marks the end of a philosophical project through its century long attempt to become more scientific (Suppe 1977). Secondly, in the domain of the sciences, the recognition of the normative constitution of science rendered it into an object of investigation of a second order discipline such as the science of culture. Consequently, in the circumstance that philosophy is drawn towards science in itself becomes the object for a second order science (Zilberman 1988: 2). In this sense, particular disciplinary moments in the philosophy of science and the sociology of knowledge occasion the sorts of projects that are being discussed.[6]

However, Zilberman went on to argue that Indian philosophy could never produce a science. Surely when taken literally, ample historical evidence would disqualify Zilberman's claim. Nevertheless, when read meta-theoretically, it could be taken to mean that a good meta-theory does not always generate a good science. And here too, the recent history of logical positivism would stand out as testimony to the point being made. Debiprasad Chattopadhyaya for one, arrived at the opinion quite contrary to Zilberman that the only discipline in the ancient Indian world that could be counted as a science was medicine, which benefited from the methodological interventions of the philosophical schools such as that of the Nyāya (Chattopadhyaya 1979). The fruitful possibilities within the tradition were nipped in the bud by the gradual hegemony of the idealist thought and the obstacles posed by the caste hierarchy of Indian society. Zilberman's radical thesis then is not so distant from Chattopadhyaya's thesis, but the former attempts to limit the sociological reduction of philosophical activity to the caste organization of Indian society. As pointed out earlier in the essay, Zilberman on the other hand sees Indian philosophy to be a unique system generating factor of Indian civilization. If that be the case, then the structure of Indian philosophical thought contributed to the growth and development of social organization rather than the base generating the superstructure (Zilberman 1988: 5).

While recognizing that any dialogue between Western and Eastern philosophy will take place in a Western language, Western philosophical categories take precedence in the dialogue and define the terrain of the dialogue. But having said that, the two central concerns of Indian philosophy according to a modern Indian interlocutor, discussed here, is the reconstruction of classical views and critically examining modern perspectives. One such modern perspective is that of social epistemology that addresses the social dimensions of knowledge or rational belief. And this raises the first point of intersection between Western epistemology and its Indian counterpart. Social epistemology or social theory reflexively examines the conditions under which it theorizes about what counts as knowledge; it potentially is meta-theoretically oriented as well. These two dimensions, it could be summarily argued, are of significance in Indian theories of knowledge and attempts have been underway to orient Indian epistemology along such meta-theoretic lines within the rubric of not merely comparative philosophy but philosophy proper.

However, the question of the identity of Indian philosophy in its relation to the practice of contemporary philosophy has continued to be an issue more than half a century after India became independent of colonial rule. This naturally has led many philosophers and sociologists to ask as to what constitutes the spirit or nature of Indian philosophy. The scholar, Attipate K. Ramanujan in a much discussed paper titled 'Is there an Indian way of Thinking' set out an East-West distinction in terms of approaches that were 'context sensitive' and those that were 'context free' respectively (Ramanujan 1989). If that indeed be the case, we are forced to ask ourselves the question as to the 'sense in which Indian philosophy exists'. At least as far as the discussion in the sociology of scientific knowledge is concerned, there appears to be some consensus that contextualism concerning scientific knowledge does not necessarily entail lapsing into some version of relativism. Some of the major debates on the social constructivism have centred around the issue. In which case, the dichotomy in terms of context sensitivity and context neutrality breaks down.

In the same vein, Ganeri circumvents the entire issue of the identity of the Indian philosophy by rejecting the East-West dichotomy of the norms of reason, arguing that paradigms of reason that include among others instrumentalism and the epistemic conception of reason are to be found across both cultures (Ganeri 2001a: 3). But then how does one address the problematic of concepts in translation? Are we not reading the extension of epistemic concepts from the Western tradition into the Indian philosophical tradition? Ganeri denies combing the Indian philosophical tradition with a Western concept of rationality, for if this were indeed the case, then inter-systemic understanding would be impossible because the same could be said of concepts such as 'perception, thought, language or morality'. But, it is pointed out, that any of these concepts are not internal to a philosophical theory but are concepts about which there can be many theories (Ganeri 2001a: 4). The central problematic for Ganeri arises from the diametrically opposed goals of the history of philosophy and philosophy proper. Ostensibly, the history of philosophy has for its goal the recontextualization of ideas, and situating an author in an intellectual milieu. On the other hand, the avowed goal of philosophy is to decontextualize ideas, separating it from the contingent conditions of its formulation. As result, the philosopher engaging with Indian philosophical theories is justified in working with 'the modern philosophical idiom as a generally shared and convenient vehicle in which to frame his discussion' (ibid.). One could wonder then how epistemological contextualism operates within philosophical discourse, or is this contextualism only limited to the history of philosophy.

I wish to conclude this reflection, having argued that the history of sciences in India commenced in historical narratives premised on science as a cultural universal. In the 1950s, the first decade of decolonization, though these concerns prefigured half a century earlier, the instrumentalization of the historiography of science promoted a 'me-too' variety of history, seeking to counter a Eurocentric history of science by establishing precedents or genealogies of contemporary theories of science and in the past of science in India. This research orientation attempted to accomplish two things. On the one hand, it represented the struggle for cognitive justice, a precious and central concern of the newly independent nation. On the other, it legitimated the state's investment in science, both as a new knowledge form, but more importantly in the programme of nation-building.

In the domain of Indian philosophy too, there have been several attempts to engage with its diversity and variegated nature, in an attempt to emphasize its continued relevance. Philosophers have over the past century emphasized different aspects as part of its central concerns. If in the early half of the twentieth century greater emphasis was placed on its spiritual preoccupations, with the passage of time attention has shifted to linguistics, logic and in the more recent past its relevance to the philosophy of sciences. As a result, it could well be conjectured as the presence of modern science became more visible within Indian society, and science moved if not to the centre, then to one of the epicentres of contemporary culture in India, the turn to Indian philosophy's resources of rational thinking and meta-theoretic deliberations became more pronounced. This conjuncture constituted the locus of concerns around which the two discourses revolved over the last three decades.

The important feature to be noted in this discussion is that homologous concerns arise both in the sciences and philosophy. These concerns are prompted from the problematic assertion that modern science and reason were the prerogatives of the Western intellect. In the entangled narratives we have been discussing the effective keywords are 'science' and 'reason', which have been construed as the two epicentres of the discourse of the modernity of the Indian nation. The history of science drew upon the philosophical idea of reason to foreground the antiquity of a version of science in India. Philosophy would emphasize the central place of reason and rationality in the Indian tradition, and the modern incarnations of these epistemic faculties were manifest in logic, mathematics and the sciences of ancient India.[7] The rise and decline of the sciences was consequentially a sign of the eclipse of reason, and the ascent or descent of reason was concurrent with the rise or eclipse of the sciences. In the twentieth century where science had risen to the position of the grand legitimator (Pels 2003), the decontextualization of reason and science could be seen as a move to go beyond the dichotomies we have inherited. On the other hand, the attempt to contextualize reason and science could be seen as the flip side of efforts to integrate different knowledge forms within mainstream discourse on science and philosophy.

NOTES

1. Amongst this group of scientists who bothered to question the nature of science and interrogate the relationship of science with Indian society from the post-colonial era one must count Satish Dhawan, Madhav Gadgil, Roddam Narasimha, A.K.N. Reddy, B.M. Udgaonkar, and E.C.G. Sudarshan.
2. According to Ganeri, Radhakrishnan was in a way responsible for portraying India's intellectual past as 'essentially spiritual' and that it was stimulated by the problems of religion, and was 'subjective, speculative and synthetic' (Ganeri 2001: 2).

3. In the introductory chapter of her book *The Fate of Knowledge*, Longino points out that Charles Sanders Peirce, John Stuart Mill in the nineteenth and Karl Popper in the twentieth centuries discussed the social dimensions of knowledge and suggests that Popper is considered to have originated social epistemology (Longino 2002: 3–7).
4. Despite his commitment to a global philosophical perspective Mohanty has also argued that the pursuit of Indian and Western philosophy should be independent projects employing their own idioms, language and metaphors (Mohanty 2002).
5. I make this remark rather tentatively, for it becomes increasingly difficult to pin down a philosopher's identity especially when discussing the work of amphibians such as Mohanty who was an authority on Western phenomenology and an important contributor to Constitutive phenomenology (Mohanty et al. 1991). Matilal dedicated his work on perception in Indian theories of knowledge to Michael Dummett and Peter Strawson, and David Zilberman tries to redefine the Western philosophical enterprise in terms of Indian philosophy himself came in from Russian Philology and Russian Indology.
6. One modality of the East-West encounter was to explicate the rationality of the knowledge systems of the East in terms of the rationality of Western thought by searching out cognitive homologies between the two and then locating the former within the conceptual architecture of the latter (Raina 2003). This modality, a colleague and I have referred to as the methodological imperative (Raina and Habib 1993). Zilberman does not attempt to bring either Indian or Western philosophy closer to the epistemic organization of science (Zilberman 1988: 2). In that sense his project is not orientated by the methodological imperative.
7. This could also be seen as a response to what Serres has called 'science's bid to take over the totality of reason', that was historically schematized as 'reason later, unreason before' (Serres with Latour 1995: 51).

REFERENCES

Bayly, Christopher A. 2000. *Empire and Information: Intelligence Gathering and Social Communication in India, 1780–1870*. Cambridge: Cambridge University Press.

Chatterjee, Partha. 1993. *Nationalist Thought and the Colonial World: A Derivative Discourse*. Minneapolis: University of Minnesota Press.

Chattopadhyaya, Debiprasad. 1959. *Lokayata: A Study in Ancient Indian Materialism*. New Delhi: PPH.

——. 1979. *Science and Society in Ancient India*. Calcutta: Research India Publications.

Cohn, Bernard S. 1997. *Colonialism and its Forms of Knowledge: The British in India*. Oxford: Oxford University Press.

Ganeri, Jonardan. 2001. 'Introduction: Indian Logic and the Colonization of Reason', in Ganeri (ed.), *Indian Logic: A Reader*. Surrey: Curzon Press, pp. 1–25.

——. 2001a. *Philosophy in Classical India*. London and New York: Routledge.

Inden, Ronald. 1999. *Imagining India*. Oxford: Basil Blackwell.

Longino, Helen. 2002. *The Fate of Knowledge*. Princeton: Princeton University Press.

Luhmann, Niklas. 2002. *Theories of Distinction: Redescribing the Distinctions of Modernity*. Stanford: Stanford University Press.

Matilal, Bimal Krishna. 1986. *Perception: An Essay on Classical Indian Theories of Knowledge*. Oxford: Oxford University Press.

Minkowski, Christopher Z. 2001. 'The Pandit as Public Intellectual: The Controversy over Virodha or Inconsistency in the Astronomical Sciences', in A. Michaels (ed.), *The Pandit: Traditional Sanskrit Scholarship in India*. New Delhi: Manohar Publications.

Mohanty, Jitendra N., Dagfinn Follesdal and Thomas Seebohm (eds). 1991. *Phenomenology and the Formal Sciences*. Dordrecht and Boston: Kluwer.

Mohanty, Jitendra N. 2001. *Explorations in Philosophy: Essays by J.N. Mohanty*. Edited by Bina Gupta. Oxford: Oxford University Press.

——. 2002. *Between Two Worlds: East and West*. Oxford: Oxford University Press.

——. 2009. 'Science and Poetry, Fact and Value', in *Lectures on Consciousness and Interpretation*. Oxford: Oxford University Press, pp. 146–153.

Montgomery, Scott L. 2000. *Science in Translation: Movements of Knowledge through Culture and Time*. Chicago: University of Chicago Press.

Nandy, Ashis (ed.). 1988. *Science, Hegemony and Violence: A Requiem for Modernity*. Oxford and New Delhi: Oxford University Press.

Nowotny, Helga, Peter Scott and Michael Gibbons. 2001. *Re-Thinking Science: Knowledge and the Public in an Age of Uncertainty*. Oxford: Polity.

Pels, Dick. 2003. *Unhastening Science: Autonomy and Reflexivity in the Social Theory of Knowledge*. Liverpool: Liverpool University Press.

Perrett, Roy P. 1999. 'History, Time and Knowledge in Ancient India', *History and Theory*, 38, 3: 307–321.

Pinch, William R. 1999. 'Same Difference in India and Europe', *History and Theory*, 38, 3: 389–407.

Pollock, Sheldon. 2000. 'New Intellectuals in Seventeenth Century India', *The Indian Economic and Social History Review*, 38, 1: 3–29.

Raina, Dhruv. 2003. *Images and Contexts: The Historiography of Science and Modernity in India*. Oxford: Oxford University Press.

Raina, Dhruv and S. Irfan Habib. 1993. 'The Unfolding of an Engagement: The Dawn on Science, Technical Education and Industrialisation', *Studies in History*, 9, 1: 87–117.

——. 1996. 'The Moral Legitimation of Modern Science: Bhadralok Reflections on Theories of Evolution', *Social Studies of Science*, 1: 9–42.

Raghuramaraju, A. 2006. *Debates in Indian Philosophy: Classical, Colonial and Contemporary*. New Delhi: Oxford University Press.

Raju, Poolla T. 1985. *Structural Depths of Indian Thought*. New Delhi: South Asian Publishers.

Ramanujan, Attipate K. 1989. 'Is there an Indian Way of Thinking', *Contributions to Indian Sociology*, 23: 41–58.

Rosenberg, Alexander. 1998. 'The Rise of Logical Positivism', in Robert Klee (ed.), *Scientific Inquiry: Readings in the Philosophy of Science*. Oxford: Oxford University Press, pp. 10–15.

Said, Edward. 1985. 'Orientalism Reconsidered', *Race and Class*, 2: 1–15.

Seal, Brajendranath N. (1915) 1985. *The Positive Sciences of the Ancient Hindus*. Delhi: Motilal Banarsidass.

Schreiner, Peter. 1978. 'The Indianness of Modern Indian Philosophy as a Historical and Philosophical Problem', *Philosophy East and West*, 1: 21–37.

Serres, Michel with Bruno Latour. 1995. *Conversations on Science, Culture and Time*, translated by Roxanne Lapidus. Ann Arbor: University of Michigan Press.

Singh, Navjyoti. 1999. 'Phenomenology and Indian Philosophy', *Journal of the Indian Council of Philosophical Research*, 3: 109–132.

Suppe, Frederick. 1977. *The Structure of Scientific Theories*. Urbana: University of Illinois Press.

Uberoi, J.P.S. 2002. *The European Modernity: Science, Truth and Method*. New Delhi: Oxford University Press.

Visvanathan, Shiv. 1997. *A Carnival for Science: Essays on Science, Technology and Development*. Oxford: Oxford University Press.

Zilberman, David B. 1988. *The Birth of Meaning in Hindu Thought*. Dordrecht: Reidel Publishing Company.

Ziman, John. 2000. *Real Science: What it is and What it Means*. Cambridge: Cambridge University Press.

6

State and Democracy in India

PRATAP BHANU MEHTA

This paper proceeds in the following order. In the introduction I make some remarks about the study of Indian democracy and try to give a formulation to what exactly one is looking at in considering democracy versus authoritarianism in India. In the next section, I argue that the real challenge for Indian democracy is, what I call, the gap between democracy and legitimacy. This is a specific theoretical notion that does not question the legitimacy of democracy. But it asks two questions: Does democracy necessarily produce outcomes that all citizens can accept? I discuss some theoretical issues in relation to democracy and legitimacy and argue that the relationship between these two concepts is contingent. In order to produce accountable institutions, the gap between legitimacy and accountability needs to be bridged. But this gap can be bridged only by taking into account the regulative ideal of politics that citizens operate with. What are the set of expectations that citizens bring to politics, and how do these expectations shape what democracy produces. Despite many imperfections, democracy is a form of government that aspires to honour the standing of citizens as free and equal persons. While there is considerable debate over the degree to which democracy promotes or impedes growth, there is less doubt that the democratic aspiration is itself a vital component of development. Recognizing the status of individuals as citizens rather than mere subjects, expanding their rights and their freedoms to define their own lives, protecting them from the exercise of arbitrary power and making government accountable through greater participation of the governed, are central components of the development aspiration itself. Representative constitutional democracies are a mode of organizing government through which these aspirations are recognized. Yet in practice, the actual functioning of democracies often honours the promise of accountability only in its breach. This paper is an attempt to examine the obstacles to producing accountable government even in well-established democracies. In particular, it pursues two lines of inquiry. First, it examines the degree to which inherited forms of social inequality cast a long shadow on democracies and distort its functioning. In some ways, this is a familiar argument: inequalities in wealth for instance, often determine access to power. But this paper's argument is that social inequality may distort the functioning of democracy, by redefining the very meaning of politics in such societies in such a way that a politics of common citizenship becomes difficult to achieve.

The second line of inquiry this paper pursues is this. In democracies the actual organization of government, the authority structures that assign particular responsibilities to particular parts of government and define the pathways through which government power flows, are exceedingly complex. To some extent, this complexity is inevitable in modern societies. But this paper examines, briefly, the degree to which the mode of organizing authority in a democracy can also impede the creation of accountable government. Section two looks at features of the regulative of ideal of politics in India that have enhanced the gap between democracy and legitimacy. The final section looks at different institutional aspects of accountability and treats, in turn, questions of institutional design and the impediments to making electoral accountability more effective. The paper treats all of the questions simultaneously, because its central argument is that these different aspects of the accountability problem are related and attacking one in isolation does not help.

Introduction

India has, in many ways, been something of a curiosity in discussions of democracy and authoritarianism. India remained an outlier by the lights of most theories of democracy that look at structural variables to predict the prospects of a country instituting it and remaining a democracy such as class structure, extent of ethnic diversity, level of income and education (Moore 1966; Lijphart 1999; Przeworski et al. 2000). The sense of intellectual surprise at Indian democracy was captured in a recent conference when one of the participants, paraphrasing Groucho Marx, said about Indian democracy, 'It looks a like a democracy. It talks like a democracy. But don't be fooled by that. It really is a democracy'. It is something of a measure of the success of Indian democracy that whatever other anxieties might be expressed about its future—its capacity to deliver material well-being to large number of its citizens, its capacity to create a sense of national identity itself without conflict, its capacity to manage social tensions arising out of the process of development—a slide into an authoritarian system of governance is not high on the list. India does well on other measures of success in a democracy: voter turn outs, turnover of incumbents, the empowering of new groups, the maintaining of a core set of liberal freedoms, civilian control over armed forces, political contestation. Democracy in India is as much of an established fact as its success is a matter of surprise to political scientists.

How does one think about the Indian democratic experience? This question has both an explanatory and a normative dimension. I do not want to go deep into the explanatory dimension. But I want to make one methodological general remark about how one goes about explaining such 'success' as the Indian democratic experience has had. I think one big change in the studies of democracy is that the focus had shifted from a *theory* explaining Indian democracy to concrete *mechanisms* by which this democracy has been sustained (Khilnani 1997; Mehta 2003; Guha 2007; Kapur 2000). These narratives of Indian democracy, rather than emphasizing one or two variables—a propitious class structure, or cultural norms or such things—emphasize the extent to which a whole host of factors, from the colonial legacy to the character of India's inherited institutions, from the beliefs of its leaders to the character of social divisions, interact with each other to sustain democratic institutions. But the important point that emerges out of these narratives is this. Indian democracy is an ongoing exercise in *political improvisation*: its trajectory has not been determined by structural conditions, but has, at each step, been shaped by a number of contingent political choices. It is often said that modern India is creation of politics; arguably the same is true of Indian democracy. An explanation of its success and limitations, does not lie outside of the space of politics. The weakness of a lot of the earlier literature on Indian democracy was that it was united in its impulse to explain Indian democracy in terms outside of the space of politics, rather than through politics itself and the concrete and contingent choices made by the myriad actors who make up Indian democracy. Obviously, there is some sense in which background structural conditions matter, but much of the literature does not acknowledge the extent to which choices have shaped outcomes.

In some respects it is an astounding fact that there was near unanimity in the nationalist movement as early as the 1920s that India should have universal suffrage, when no precedent would have warranted reposing confidence in a largely unlettered and unpropertied population being given the vote. It is a remarkable fact that, with some limitations, India's principal political party in the nationalist movement, the Congress chose to organize itself along democratic lines, at least providing mechanisms for incorporating new groups as they emerged. It is a remarkable fact that the mainstream of its anti-colonial movement distanced itself from a politics of violence, which had a fundamental impact on the character of political organizations that occupied mainstream space in India. It is a remarkable fact that the Indian Constituent Assembly managed to come up with a remarkable constitution, that still potently defines so many of the normative aspirations of democratic India. The choice of a first past the post electoral system, the introduction of mechanisms like reservations for marginalized groups, the moderation that allows twenty party coalitions to get into relatively stable governments, or even Indira Gandhi's decision to lift emergency rule in 1977, are not easily explained in terms of background structural conditions. It is astonishing that India's political class is reluctant to undermine the legitimacy of an independent commission such as the Election Commission that oversees the independence of elections in India. These are just some of the remarkable choices made by political actors, choices that are not easily explained by in non-political terms. Indian democracy has been imaginatively constituted rather than structurally determined.

Before I get to the heart of the paper, a few more preliminary points. The first is about the relationship between democracy, authoritarianism and nationalism. Nationalism is often said to be the crucible of modern democracy (Greenfeld 1992). In some sense India is no different. Colonial rule in India rested, amongst other things, on two propositions: that India was not a nation with any sense of corporate identity; it was not capable of self-government because it was not a *people*. Second, that it was not ready for democracy. Under such conditions any critique of colonialism must assume that the colonized society can be a self-governing nation. But Indians could demand self-determination only by appealing to the authority of a new presence in the social imaginary of something called the Indian people. But this would require privileging their status as members of this people—as citizens of nation being born over more restrictive older identifications such as caste or region. But the remarkable thing about this process is that the Indian nation emerged through a *political* negotiation with these identities, rather than erasing them. But more importantly, it was almost impossible to conceive this people coming into being without granting them a modicum of participatory access. In short, anti-colonial nationalism in India tended to carry democratic ideas along its logical train. Here paradoxically, an act of political imagination turned the colonial argument on its head. The colonial argument went: India cannot be self-governing because it is not a people. The nationalist argument went: the idea of an Indian people can be constituted only through shared institutions of participatory access. It does not have an identity outside of this process and mechanisms of political negotiation and participation. This point is of some importance because there is a sense in which many Indians believe, rightly, that India can be a nation only so long as it is a democracy; there is no nation building project outside the democratic framework. If India had sustained periods of authoritarian rule, the idea of India itself would be in jeopardy; it is a nation conceived and sustained through political negotiation.

But this point is also an important way of characterizing the specificity of the Indian anxiety about authoritarianism. First, it is a remarkable fact that wherever the Indian state has tried democratic incorporation of its diversity, it has largely succeeded. State subverting secessionist movements are more likely to emerge when the Indian state acts in an authoritarian rather than democratic mode. Second, the spectre of authoritarianism towards particular groups arises often when there is an attempt to benchmark Indian identity outside of the space of politics, to see it not as a product of an ongoing democratic negotiation, but to locate it in a particular 'ethnic' characteristic like religion or race. The spectre of authoritarianism in India is not associated with the suspension of the electoral process or military takeovers, but with the possibility that certain political movements will define a conception of India that will be exclusionary, and therefore, authoritarian in relation to certain groups. While this tendency has a presence in Indian politics, it has not garnered sufficient power to dislodge India's democratic credentials. But the sense that 'no democracy, no Indian nation' has, to a certain extent helped sustain democracy.

A second preliminary point is that the attraction of democracy for Indian elites has been precisely that it is ameliorative rather than revolutionary. Nothing illustrates this better than the case of land reform. Contrary to most eighteenth century fears of democracy, it has turned out to be, as Tocqueville prophesied, a relatively conservative force. There are very few instances of radical land reform measures being voted in through democratic means; most radical land reforms have involved a degree of violence and coercion. While the ideological commitment to democracy amongst Indian elites was undoubtedly very strong, their sense that democracy could be used to create their power anew in a new form was equally sharp. In some senses the slowness of democracy in delivering social and economic change, its capacity to blunt radical edges, turned out to be an advantage from the point of view of democracy. To minimize the impact democracy has had on the transformation of social relations in India, or to deny its ability to open these up for contestation would be to falsify the record. But equally, to deny that most democracies are not radical when it comes to redistributive politics, would also be to miss out on one of the sources of its attractiveness to elites.

Just as a heuristic contrast I want to pose the following question. Does representative government automatically imply responsive government? Here is general consideration I have in mind. Suppose there was a government that claimed legitimacy in terms of certain process that authorized it, namely elections. Suppose you asked this particular government: Why should you be considered the legitimate government of X? The answer involves some appeal to a process by which the government came to be constituted? Legitimacy in this sense is legitimacy on the input side. Such a government would, ex hypothesis, do all it can to ensure that it masters the process that gives it the right to be the legitimate government, particularly win elections. Its bedrock claim would be that it is a representative government, in some sense of the term. It is not representative simply because it says so, but that there is *some process* that makes it representative.

Now suppose there was a government that could not appeal to such a regularly instituted process to claim legitimacy. It might appeal to other things to claim legitimacy: pragmatic considerations, historical claims, ideology. But this regime's claims will simply be *its* claims, there is no independent process through which the extent to which these claims are shared by the population at large can be validated. In short, there is no independent legitimacy on the input side. Such legitimacy as this government claims will be on the output side, trying to convince more people that this government is indeed the best for them.

Which government would be more 'responsive' to the people? You could cut the argument both ways. At one level you could say that a government whose legitimacy has to be constituted through the electoral process has to be responsive; government whose legitimacy is not so constituted needn't be. On the other hand, think of the reverse possibility. A government that is constituted through the electoral process is responsive to the extent that it needs to stitch together some kind of electoral support. But it is possible that under some circumstances stitching together this support has little to do with being responsive. We know that elections can be very blunt instruments of accountability in terms of the way they aggregate preferences. The degree to which it is blunt instrument will depend upon a lot of factors: the party system, the system of voting the nature of preference formation and so on. But it is in principle possible that mastering the art of winning elections may not have as much to do with responding to the public at large as we would like to think. But this regime will still not be illegitimate; in a curious way, the process will act as a palliative against discontent.

On the other hand, a 'non-representative system' could, under certain conditions produce a great degree of responsiveness. This regime might say: 'For our legitimacy we cannot appeal to a process. We have to keep delivering outcomes that ensure levels of dissatisfaction do not cross a certain threshold. Such a regime could, under certain circumstances, depending on its ability to process information, etc., be more responsive. It might have to work harder to secure its legitimacy, precisely because it does not have the support of a 'process' behind it. Of course, such a regime is unlikely to do justice to the intrinsic normative value of democracy; but it could along certain dimensions of well-being, be very responsive.

This stylized contrast has two points. The first is to suggest that the degree to which particular regimes are responsive, and the dimensions along which they are responsive is an interesting empirical question. One fruitful agenda for India-China comparisons is to ask just this kind of question. In the nineteenth century Hegel said something to the effect that China was all state, no civil society; India was all civil society, no state, a contrast that still has some heuristic value. Perhaps the twenty-first century analogue would be the following: India is a representative system, but there are question marks about the degree to which it is responsive. China claims to be a responsive system, but there are interesting issues about the extent to which it can do so without being 'representative'.

The rest of this paper, rather than looking at Indian democracy in self-congratulatory mode, tries to look at the gap between representation and responsiveness in the Indian system, which is perhaps a more germane version of the authoritarianism versus democracy contrast. In the next section I give this gap a more theoretical formulation and then explore some institutional mechanisms which need to be addressed if this gap is to be closed.

Responsiveness, Legitimacy and Democracy

Any discussion of responsiveness, especially in democratic societies, misses a good deal if, it does not begin with some account of the relationship between two key concepts—democracy and legitimacy. In many discussions the relationship between these two concepts remains obscure and often leads to a fundamental confusion over the requirements of good governance. Indeed, it is my contention that the fundamental challenge of creating accountable institutions is to bridge the gap between democracy and legitimacy. But bridging that gap requires two things: first, properly designed institutions and second, an appropriate conception of politics, that is an account of the norms and expectations that citizens bring to their political conduct. In the first part of the paper, I briefly elaborate on this point.

What do I mean by the gap between democracy and legitimacy? The association of the two concepts is largely contingent. The concept of legitimacy concerns the reasons persons who stand in particular political and social relations have for accepting those relations. Legitimacy involves an answer to the question: are political relations in which citizens stand in relation to each other, or to those who exercise power over them, acceptable to them? Put in utopian terms, the modern understanding of legitimacy is this: legitimacy obtains when the terms of the political relations, and the reasons given for the exercise of political power, are mutually acceptable and freely chosen.

Democracy, on the other hand, is a way of constituting political power such that its exercise receives popular authorization. In order for this authorization to be meaningful, we stipulate certain baseline conditions. This popular authorization must take place against the backdrop of political equality and basic freedom. A proper theory of democratic governance will have to connect two things: a political practice, namely, popular authorization with a standard of justification, and the idea of mutual acceptability. Popular authorization alone cannot bear the burden of legitimizing the exercise of governing power. It is possible that citizens may experience a certain kind of alienation even from a political process where practices of popular authorization are well established, if these practices do not produce outcomes that are mutually acceptable.

There are many ways of explaining the gap between democracy and legitimacy. Most explanations focus on the ways in which the workings of popular authorization are distorted by the operations of power in any given society. Actual democracies work in the context of a good for social and economic inequality and manipulation that, in turn, bears upon democracy itself. Other explanations focus on the ways in which the institutional organization of power within democracies can impede the production of mutually acceptable agreements. There is much truth in these cautionary tales as empirical studies of functioning democracies reveal. But these accounts miss out on one important dimension that I would like to stress here. For democracy to realize in political practice the requirements of legitimacy, it is necessary that those participating in democratic politics share common beliefs about the aspiration of democracy: reaching mutually acceptable agreements. These shared beliefs about the aims of democracy must shape political conduct. It is important to emphasize that there is nothing intrinsic about the practice of democracy to suggest that citizens will, in fact, share the ambition of reaching mutually acceptable agreements.

The political theory of democratic legitimacy relies on a resource that democracy itself cannot produce or secure: the practical and regulative aim of those engaged in democracy to reach mutually acceptable agreements. Democracies, such as India's, can be stable for a variety of reasons: for instance, the contingent balance and fragmentation of power among different groups may enable practices of popular authorization to take place. But, the fact that a democracy is institutionalized does not entail that citizens share some regulative ideals about democracy. However, this poses a challenge for any conception of accountability. For accountability to be possible the practices of citizenship, the ensemble of values by which citizens orient their conduct toward each other, must include the desire to find mutually acceptable agreements. Otherwise, the core question of accountability—accountability to whom and at what terms—cannot be answered. In short, if citizens do not aspire to live in a world governed by terms that all can freely accept, then it is difficult to give theoretical and practical content to accountability.

If the aim of accountability is to produce policies and relations we could, as citizens, freely accept, then citizens have to be governed by the desire to find mutually acceptable agreements. They must share the regulative aim of reaching agreement by coming together to reason publicly as free and equal persons. Too often in technical debates over accountability, we lose sight of the overall normative underpinnings of accountability. These depend on the practices of citizenship, the expectations and demands citizens place on each other.

Accountability, Legitimacy and Politics: The Indian Case

Indian democracy, deeply entrenched and competitive as it is, is not governed by a shared ideal of finding mutually acceptable agreements. Instead of this ideal, politics is marked by a conception of competition in which to hold the state accountable is to gain access to its power and the goods it provides. It is not to produce a politics of accountability to all those affected by the state's decisions. I argue that competitive ideal of politics is a product of two things: first, historical legacies of inequality and second, a particular conception of the state. These inflect some of the parameters by which the state is held accountable. But taken together, they impede the creation of a society where people are governed by relations they find acceptable.

Democratic aspirations are in some senses tied to the idea of equality. The idea of equality is complex and immediately invites the question, 'Equality of What?' Income? Wealth? Political Equality? Opportunity? But understanding the political trajectory of Indian democracy does not require beginning with an answer to this question. In any society, especially democratic ones, the meaning and scope of equality will be fiercely contested and will be the basis for ideological divisions. Rather, it is the psychological impulses that lie behind the demand for equality; the existential burdens that any demand for equality seeks to address that leave their imprint on politics. The varieties of structures, caste, class and patriarchy, which maintain and reproduce inequality, are all too familiar, and Indian society exemplifies many of these to an unconscionable degree. But inequality is not simply a structural condition in which people find themselves; a condition measured by such objective indicators as Gini coefficients or development indices. Inequality is resented, and becomes salient for politics, because it is experienced as an existential burden that inflicts complex psychic costs by diminishing a sense of self. Not all forms of inequality are unjust. And, the ways in which the experience of inequality shapes the self is a complex subject. But fundamentally inequality imposes the profoundest existential burdens when it is seen as denying individuals the minimum regard due to them, or when it constantly puts them in situations that are experienced as humiliating.

It is now a commonplace observation, thanks largely to Rousseau who most vividly wrote about the psychic burdens of inequality, that most human beings, unless they have been dehumanized to an unimaginable degree, place some value upon themselves (Rousseau [1756] 1997). This does not mean that they are selfish; it is rather that they place some value upon themselves and wish that this value be somewhere affirmed. The institutions and practices of most inegalitarian societies deny individuals this basic form of recognition, the recognition that they are valuable in some sense, that they have some moral standing. In most societies this quest for having one's worth affirmed will take debased forms. The only way in which you can secure acknowledgement by others is either by seeking to dominate them, or by putting a convincing show of attributes and accomplishments that are capable of winning the acknowledgment of others. Inegalitarian societies, where there is no public acknowledgment of individual self worth, will be characterized by both a fierce competition to dominate, and paradoxically, an exaggerated sense of servility. These are the two strategies of securing acknowledgement. Both desire to dominate and a kind of self abasement, Rousseau suggested, would lead us to lead inauthentic lives: lives that were not governed by values and concerns that were properly our own. Such societies would also frequently give individuals reasons to consider their self-respect injured: inegalitarian societies will routinely humiliate its members.

The aspiration to democracy is in part an aspiration to have one's moral worth acknowledged. The charge that an arrangement or a set of procedures is 'undemocratic' carries moral resonance, not simply because it describes a faulty procedure, but because it is accompanied by the sentiment that, in being undemocratic, someone's moral standing has been slighted. Acknowledgment by others of your moral worth is at least partly constitutive of an individual's sense of self-respect.

What institutions and objectives can satisfy the minimal requirements of acknowledging people's moral worth is a debatable one? But at the very least, freedom from abject necessity, removal of invidious and humiliating forms of discrimination, some equality of opportunity and access to a set of goods that are minimal requirements for being a capable agent in the modern world. The great liberal hope, embodied in the Indian Constitution, was that ameliorating serious material deprivation, and an effective equal standing in the eyes of the law would go some way toward mitigating the desire to have one's worth affirmed, either by dominating others, or by having one's own sense of self-fashioned by what we think might get others attention.

The paradox is that the more unequal the background institutions and practices of society, the more likely it is that politics will be a struggle to displace the holders of power, rather than an ambition to bring about social transformation. The struggle to move ahead will not be a common struggle for justice—for little commonality exists—but a competitive quest for power. A society that is adept at humiliating its members is, as Rousseau convincingly argued, more likely to make them adept at humiliating others than it is to teach them about justice. This perhaps explains one of the paradoxes at the heart of Indian politics. There are few other democracies where the universal language of injustice, rights, even constitutionalism is so profusely used and has become part of so many political mobilizations. But it is a stratagem for particular individuals or groups to gain access to power, not an acknowledgment of the due claims of all. Discourses of law, constitutionalism, rights, justice, obligations, do not signify that a particular set of values are being taken as authoritative and these set genuine moral constraints for individuals. Rather, they are the languages in which particular grievances are expressed or interests advanced without the least acknowledgment of reciprocal or parallel interests and grievances of others. A sense of justice toward someone presupposes a sense of reciprocity; it presupposes that you acknowledge others. The more the social distance, the less likely that such reciprocity obtains. It is quite possible for a democracy to experience great clamour for recognition by particular individuals and groups without these resulting in diffusion of norms of justice. This follows the general pattern of the ways in which Indian society has been democratized. Democracy in India has advanced through the competitive negotiations between groups, each competing for their interests, rather than the diffusion of democratic norms. It is, in that sense, a contingent outcome of social conflicts, not necessarily a deep-seated norm. The purpose of political mobilization has not been to make the state more accountable, but to get access to or share in its power[1] (Mehta 2003).

This conception of politics was most dramatically manifest in the way in which citizens often thought of the state. Given the commanding presence of the state, underwritten by an ideology of state-led development, access to state power became, for good or for bad, the principal means of improving the life chances of individuals. Politics, through access to state power, has become the swiftest route toward social mobility. In a strange kind of way, compared with the market, or educational institutions, politics of all kinds, from the most ambitious aspiration for power to the interest in gaining smallest benefits, came to be seen as a surer route to social mobility. Access to the state gave jobs and a likely class status that was better than anything available outside the state; the discretionary power the state conferred on all its officials was experienced by many as empowerment, or at least an escape from the subordination that resulted from being at the receiving end of that power. Access to state power was about the only way of ensuring that one counted for somebody.

But the consequence of the growth of the state and its undoubted success in producing a kind of social mobility is attended by a paradox, namely, that once the state is seen as a means for social mobility, it is not, for the most part, seen as the provider of public goods. The state is adjudged to be successful, the more opportunities for large numbers of private individuals it can create through its own spending: if the number of government jobs expands for instance, even when not required, this is adjudged to be a political success, regardless of the opportunity cost this form of job creation imposes on others. The state exists primarily to satisfy the private interests of collusive interest groups. The raison d'etre of politics, the aims of public representation are no longer to respond to fundamental issues impinging upon common life but to organize the state's power in such a way that its resources can be channeled in the direction of particular groups or individuals to protect their exclusive interests. This form of competitive politics can produce an equilibrium that sustains democracy. But it is quite compatible with a wide gap between democracy and accountable institutions. And this gap can be bridged only if citizens change their understanding of what politics is about.

Accountability: The Institutional Story

To begin with, we operate with a basic and simple concept of accountability: for a person or institution X to be accountable to an agent Y is for X to act on behalf of Y, and for Y to be empowered by some formal or informal mechanism to reward or sanction X for their activities.

While the basic concept is simple, the institutional expression that makes accountability effective is far from simple. First, the range of principles and the agents to whom they are accountable is vast. Second, the mechanisms for eliciting accountability are often very complex. But there is a conceptual problem. There is a series of tensions internal to the concept of accountability. The various ingredients we associate with accountability: transparency, responsiveness, representativeness and so forth, may not harmonize with each other. Transparency is sometimes in tension with responsiveness and representation in tension with both. The crucial point is that harmonizing the different components of accountability cannot be done by conceptual fiat. It is an empirical matter addressed by institutional design and the concrete work of politics. The question is not: what is the concept of accountability? It is rather, how different states make tradeoffs between different components of accountability.

The Importance of Institutional Design

The Indian state secures legitimacy and is held accountable through a diverse range of institutions: executives, legislatures, courts, police, regulatory authorities, bureaucracies, commissions of inquiry, independent statutory bodies, development agencies, and so on. Sometimes, a broad-based ideological vision may impart to this myriad of interlocking institutions, laws and agencies a degree of coherence and semblance. But even under the most homogeneous of ideological constellations these institutions often compete with each other, set bounds on what other institutions can do, interpret directives in their own peculiar way and provide the structures of accountability. Numerous studies of political and economic development in India have long recognized the important role the state plays as an autonomous actor—that is, its capacities to often act free from societal constraints and manipulate them and its capacities to set the agenda for society. Nonetheless, with the exception of the literature on central banks and more recently on the judiciary, there is little systematic analytical work on India that examines the myriad of institutions, both formal and informal, the commitments to procedures, the formal and informal incentives within state institutions, through which the state is both constituted and enabled to act on the one hand, and constrained in its powers and capacities on the other.

Much of this neglect of the diversity of the institutions within the Indian state, the mechanisms by which they are held accountable, and the problems that arise from adverse incentives within institutions, has stemmed from certain methodological proclivities. In Marxist or structuralist inspired paradigms which dominated the political economy of the Indian state, the state was simply considered epiphenomenal to social forces. As such its own internal constitution, rules, incentives and procedures had at best marginal bearing on outcomes. Economic approaches to the state have paid more attention to the broad incentive structures that result from overextended and excessively dirigiste states, but for the most part its focus has been to demonstrate how the state has been captured by interest groups. The constitutive institutions of the state, particularly in poorer countries, remain, for the most part, a 'black box'. Relatively little attention has been paid to the relationship between institutional design and accountability.

For example, take the case of agents that enforce legal accountability. These include not only agencies of law enforcement such as the police, or the judiciary such as the courts, but also the investigative arms internal to bureaucracies and governments.

There is a general consensus in India that these institutions of accountability have underperformed. The Indian judiciary is a case in point. On the one hand, the judiciary has been extraordinarily active in calling the executive branch to account. The explosion of public interest litigation has meant that the judiciary is a conduit through which citizens make the executive accountable on a whole range of issues, such as health, sanitation, environment and social justice. But the overall effectiveness of the judiciary is very much open to question. For one thing, as the limitations of public interest litigation has demonstrated, the judiciary can at most provide immediate redress in a specific set of cases, but its power to generate enduring legislation that is widely enforced is extremely limited. But the main weakness of the judiciary has been its own institutional shortcomings, rather than its ability to sanction the executive branch. As the Malimath Committee noted, using data from India's courts, there were a staggering 28 million cases pending in 1996 (Mehta 2004). But most of the weaknesses are internal to the working of courts and a product of adverse incentive structures. There is wide variation in the management of case loads among different Chief Justices. Other factors influence the disposal rates of cases considerably: the extraordinary laxity in code of conduct of lawyers, the length of workday, norms of classification and allocation of cases among judges, the reliance on long oral arguments and procedures for taking witness depositions, provisions for appeals, the schedule of court fees, the structure of payments to lawyers can all have a vast impact on the performance of courts. All these measures, that were ostensibly designed to render the courts more transparent, have, by their cumulative effects, rendered them less responsive.

The effects of judicial delays are momentous. Delays mean that the use of 'extrajudicial methods' to alter the stakes in a judicial dispute become more attractive, especially since these methods themselves are unlikely to be punished swiftly. The more extrajudicial institutions such as system of patronage are resorted to as a means of resolving disputes, the more fairness, transparency and certainty are likely to be sacrificed. By and large, the judicial system has, because of its own internal micro-dynamics, been unable to hold politicians accountable in an effective way. And politicians used to a system that protects them from punishment are more likely to weaken the judicial system. Indeed, it is arguable that judicial reform will be the lynchpin of any effective accountability. The example here is meant to illustrate a simple point: the micro-dynamics of individual institutions can have wide system effects on accountability.

Elections and Accountability

India is a robust and contentious parliamentary democracy. Elections are one of the principal mechanisms of sanctioning the conduct of politicians in a parliamentary democracy such as India and holding them accountable. But elections can often be a blunt instrument of accountability.

In order to hold governments accountable, voters must be able to assign clear responsibility for government performance. But the ability to assign clear responsibility can be limited in several ways. In the first instance, voters need information about how their representatives voted in parliament on a full range of issues. It is arguable that in India voters do not have or do not seek much of this information about representatives. The press and the public debate almost never carry detailed information about how members of parliament voted on particular bills or what legislation they introduced as private bills. In some respect, this lack of information is not as serious as might first appear, because in a parliamentary system each individual legislator's record is less important than the positions taken by the party. But even party manifestoes avoid cataloguing legislative accomplishment in any significant detail.

One particular aspect of the lack of information is particularly important in the Indian case. This has to do with the time horizons of the electorate by which they judge government performance. Ideally voters ought to be concerned about their welfare not only during the present term of the government but also the impact government decisions have on prospects of their future welfare. This requires that they make inferences about the impact, policy is going to have on their future welfare. These inferences are notoriously difficult to make and theories of voting behaviour have tried to wrestle with it.

In the case of India, a few things are very clear. First, the impact of policies on well-being is judged less by aggregate future expectations of the impact of policies. Notoriously, aggregate measures such as growth have seldom been political issues in India. Governments have routinely lost elections with high growth rates. Because of the dominance of the agrarian sector, aggregate measures of employment have not played a part. The one measure of well-being to which the Indian electorate is extremely sensitive is inflation, especially of essential commodities. This measure affects a large number of people, in a direct and transparent way, but it also indicates a preoccupation with present welfare rather than inter-temporal gains.

This has a profound effect on the incentives this sets up for politicians. The time horizons under which politicians operate crucially determine policy outcomes. Politicians have less of an incentive to enact policies whose benefits are distant and uncertain. Most Indian politicians operate with short time horizons; this makes them risk averse in that they are not willing to sacrifice present constituencies for possible future gains, unless those accrue within the time horizon of the next election.

Second, for reasons that Hamilton pointed out in *Federalist* 70, accountability is very difficult to assign in cabinet executives. In circumstances where the lines of decision making are obscured, the questions of who is to be held accountable becomes notoriously difficult. The problem of assigning responsibility plagues the civil service as well. A large class of decisions is 'collective' decisions within the civil service, in the sense that there are more than one signatories before a file can be approved. Often, decisions are made by 'committee' which makes accountability difficult. Ostensibly committees serve to prevent individual officers from acting arbitrarily. In practice, the large numbers of committees make civil servants dependent upon each other, in that they know they will require the cooperation of their colleagues on some future occasion. This leads them to sign on to decisions which they might not individually agree. In doing so, the decision is granted collective legitimacy which makes accountability difficult. The institutional mechanism by which the line between one civil servant and another is blurred makes accountability difficult (Das 2001). The management procedures and the incentive structures of the Indian Civil Service are such that individual responsibility is very difficult to establish. Indeed, as a general rule, Indian institutions do not have clear lines of authority, hence the lack of accountability.

Third, in principle, voters must be able to vote out of office parties responsible for bad government. But the nature of the electoral system makes the connection between voter preference and government formation more indirect. For one thing, in a first past the post system, the number of seats that a party gets in parliament is not in direct proportion to the number of votes they receive; second, which parties form government is not a function of aggregate voter preference but of the way in which votes are distributed geographically; third, under conditions where no party is in the majority, the making and unmaking of governments is even less a direct consequence of voter choice. This has become more true of India in an era of coalition governments. In many instances, voters do not know what coalition a party is going to be part of once elected. Coalition governments blur the lines of responsibility even further. In instances where small parties are held responsible for arbitrarily breaking governments, their conduct is cashiered. But whether praise or blame can be assigned for policies is less clear.

Fourth, elections as a mechanism require that the opposition both closely monitor the government and inform the citizens. In principle, the opposition has incentives to monitor government and to inform voters about the performance of incumbents. Yet the existence of an opposition that can effectively articulate a critique of government cannot be taken for granted. In some instances smaller opposition parties can collude with government; in others, the opposition may be too deeply divided and preoccupied with internal fights to monitor incumbents. Such is now arguably the case with India's parliament. There is compelling evidence that both the quantity and quality of deliberation in India's parliament has declined substantially in the last decade or so. As one commentator pointed out, opposition parties monitor only a very small range of issues and bills closely; legislation related to most departments passes virtually without debate or notice. One telling statistic about India's upper house of parliament, the Rajya Sabha, is revealing in this respect. In 1985 this chamber of parliament spent a total of 791 hours discussing government bills; in 1996–97 this number was down to a mere seven hours (Kapur and Mehta 1998). There is virtual unanimity that parliament has become ineffective in its monitoring functions.

Opposition parties face another dilemma. They cannot always oppose the government for they may be blamed for obstructing business; nor can they let the government get away with credit for enacting legislation. Opposition is effective when it neither colludes with nor obstructs the government. Arguably, this dilemma is keenly pronounced in recent Indian parliaments. There are numerous examples of legislation that are held up in parliament because: (a) either some small party that is part of the coalition government is exercising veto power; or (b) many parties do not want legislation passed not because they disagree with the contents of the legislation but because they do not want the government to be able to garner credit for passing it. Given the fragmented character of parliamentary composition in India, the pace of legislation is extremely slow, even when there is substantive agreement among the parties. For instance, a bill to liberalize insurance markets in India was first introduced in 1993 and took full six years to pass (for details, see Kapur 2000).

Beyond these large structural constraints, effective accountability depends upon how access to power is organized. While a complex topic, here I will gesture only at two blockages that prevent citizen access to decision making. The first is the lack of effective intra-party democracy. The key mechanism for organizing power in democracies is political parties and their structures can often mould the ways in which citizens express their aspirations. In India, political parties generally mediate citizen access in ways that impede accountability in a number of ways.

First, political parties in general are not transparent and deliberative forums. They do not educate their members in the issues and do not act as conduits of information for political activists. Whatever their other disadvantages, intra-party primaries have a profound educative function on the rank and file of voters. Election campaigns in India are relatively short and the lack of intra-party democracy implies that groundwork preparation is not done. Second, parties do not allow for the genuine preferences of voters to manifest themselves clearly. The criteria for candidate selection is non-transparent and uninstitutionlized. This often prevents key information about voter preferences from flowing up party conduits and prevents them from selecting candidates that are the most appropriate for particular locations. The net result is that parties can impede rather than enhance representation. Given the high cost of entry, parties have the power to restrict voter choices rather than expand them. Rather than being 'institutions that knit the state and society together' (Kohli 1987), the lack of inter-party democracy can help keep them apart. More subtle forms of accountability therefore require a pluralization of the sites of accountability and a greater expansion of the forums for deliberation. The great disjuncture in Indian democracy is that the rules of political advancement within political parties are arbitrary and can circumvent accountability. Genuine intra-party democracy is an essential component of restoring accountability to this process.

Politics and the Unresolved Question of Accountability

The second great blockage remains the relationship between finance and politics. A reform of the ways in which elections are financed remains the single most difficult challenge for Indian democracy. The need to raise money for elections, combined with unrealistic, unworkable and unenforceable existing laws on campaign finance, produce profound distortions in the working of Indian democracy. At least some of the roots of corruption lie in the imperatives to raise finance in a context where the cost of elections is high, the legitimate rewards of office low, the chances of re-election uncertain, and the organizational effort required to mobilize voters is massive. The repercussions of the existing ways of collecting campaign finance are felt across all areas of public life.

Most democracies attempt to regulate election finance in four ways: they can limit political expenditures of parties; place limits on private donations and contributions; offer public funds for contesting elections; or they can introduce measures that bring about transparency in the process of generating funds. The idea behind the last measure is not so much to restrict fund-raising activities, as it is to provide information to the voters on who is raising money from whom.

But the challenge for the Indian state is that the widespread opaqueness of its financial system makes it difficult to monitor such financial flows. Arguably, realistic campaign finance reform cannot be achieved unless whole sectors of its economy, such as real estate markets that generate 'black money' and the system of taxation that more effectively scrutinizes the flow of money that makes elections possible, are reformed. But it is a vicious circle where India will not get reform of the state in part because of the need to generate rents to finance elections, and an unreformed state will continue to be ineffective in regulating election money.

State financing of elections has not been much tried in India. In almost all democracies, except the United States and United Kingdom, the proportion of public financing of elections has been consistently rising in relation to private funding. There are challenges to public funding however. It appears from comparative experience that public funding, ironically, works better in systems that are already effective and transparent to some degree. For public funding formulas to be effective, certain conditions have to be met. First, public funding must encourage rather than supplant private funding, because if seen as a substitute for private funding it becomes prohibitively expensive. Second, public funding should be fair and transparent. It should not be a means for already existing party oligarchies, which usually derive their power from their ability to raise funds, to strengthen their hold on parties. In short, public funding presumes that political parties are transparent, well run and considerably democratic in their internal workings. Most Indian political parties have no effective intra-party democracy, and in the absence of serious reform in party structures, public funding is unlikely to yield good results. Third, one should not overestimate the degree to which public funding can be a panacea. Every single European country with public funding of elections, from Germany to Italy and Belgium, has continued to experience financial scandals relating to politics.

The fourth prong of regulation, transparency, has been very weak in India as well. Although party accounts are supposed to be audited regularly, these have proved to be an ineffectual check on party finances. Much of the recent effort by bodies such as the Supreme Court and the Election Commission has been to try and strengthen the disclosure requirements for political parties and candidates. Declaration of a candidate's assets, regular scrutiny of part accounts that require the disclosure of all donors who contribute more than 10 thousand rupees, and the filing of party tax returns are all steps in the right direction. A tax return is hardly the most reliable register of the true well-being of most Indians. Inducing transparency in election finance is parasitic upon the state being able to better regulate other non-electoral institutions that impinge upon election finance.

Any sensible strategy for regulating campaign finance will have to work on all four of these dimensions simultaneously and bring them together in sustainable, realistic and imaginative ways. But unless election finance is made into a serious issue, access to power and accountability will both be impeded. It is perhaps no accident that, as a recent study found, the average net worth of those who run for parliamentary elections in India is at least over ₹ 10 million (over $ 2 million); a testament to the fact that the political system remains inaccessible to the poor. Unless a genuine solution is found, money will continue to usurp politics, or in

Gibbon's words, 'corruption will remain the one infallible sign of our liberty'.

Economic Policy, Public Action and Accountability

Probably the single most important puzzle at the heart of any study of accountability in India is why has India's record at poverty alleviation not been better? Why is there less pressure on the government to deliver a whole range of crucial services such as health and education? These two questions are analytically distinct: the first can more readily be explained by poor policy choice; the second demands closer scrutiny. These puzzles are compounded by the fact that an historic explanation for India's lack of failure in this respect does not hold. It suggested that either the poor do not vote, or some form of coercive or clientelist relationship prevents them from voting on their true preferences. In the case of India, where there is now reasonably disaggregated data available on voter turnouts, the picture is exactly the opposite of what this explanation hypothesizes. First, the incidence of coercion exercised by local elites in voting matters has decreased significantly and social relations have been politicized to the extent that old fashioned clientelist relations are difficult to sustain. Second, the poor in India have tended to vote more than the middle classes and the rich, rural turnouts are better than urban turnouts and, in recent years, lower and backward castes have voted more than upper castes (Yadav 1999). Yet they have not been able to extend concerted public pressure in areas of health and education. One measure of this is captured in government spending statistics on health and education. In education, the central and state governments spent 4 per cent of GDP for all levels of education in 1996–97 or 13.4 per cent of total government expenditures, which is below the developing country average of 17.5 per cent for all developing countries. India's public spending on health is very low: 1.2 per cent of GDP, which places it among the lowest quintile of countries. There is wide variation among Indian states on these matters. State expenditures on education, for example, range from 3–7 per cent of GSDP and from 16 to 29 per cent as a share of total state expenditure. The reach of public criticism has been much less effective in Indian democracy when the deprivations people face fall short of the extreme hardships that, say, famines signify. The state's failures in these areas are well known. What is less well understood is the demand side of the equation. Why is political mobilization on *these* issues less effective? Can one just assume that this is simply a product of the *state's* failure or is there something about the structure and ideologies in civil society that impedes the formation of *effective demand* for health and education?

There are complex reasons for this phenomenon that will bear serious scrutiny. First, as with any claim with respect to India, there is wide regional variation in the mobilization for collective action on these issues. We would submit that, empirically, this is the least understood area in Indian politics, and our understanding of the ways in which governments can be held more effectively accountable, hinges on an answer to this question. The range of factors that influence the extent of collective action for the provision of public goods is complex. It has been shown, for instance, that the Indian states whose land distribution arrangements have historically displayed the greatest inequality also have low collective action for public goods (Kohli 1988). Two large North Indian states of UP and Bihar both have the most inegalitarian land distributions and the greatest political apathy compared with the southern states of Kerala, Karnataka, Tamil Nadu, and so forth. The latter states historically had more egalitarian land tenure systems and were also the beneficiaries of more effective land distribution after independence. It appears that some degree of redistribution of assets is necessary before demands for public provision become more effective. The second key factor facilitating collective action for public goods seems to be the existence of a cadre-based party of the left that can facilitate mobilization on class lines, as Kerala and West Bengal have had. These parties have been instrumental in both producing land reform and increasing public provision (Dreze and Sen 1995; Dreze and Gazdar 1996; Kohli 1988). Third, Indian states with a longer history of social mobilization, such as resistance to caste discrimination, are also more successful in collective action for the provision of public goods. Again, South India, which has had a much longer history of anti-upper caste movements compared with the North, provides good evidence for this point. It seems that anti-upper caste movements in the South were a precursor to more effective mobilization for tenancy rights, land reform and education (Menon 1992). It has been very clearly demonstrated that India's poor record in the provision of education and the abolition of child labour owes something to the ritual stratification that caste produced (Weiner 1990), and a history of anti-caste movements seems to lead to better public provision in general. North India has only recently begun to experience such anti-caste movements and their outcomes are still indeterminate.

Perhaps, this is an appropriate point to raise a question that needs further study in the Indian context. There is some evidence in the literature that, in terms of the relationship between class and ethnicity, the best results are obtained for the poor when mobilization along class and ethnicity coincide rather than clash. The former, termed 'ranked ethnic systems' (Horowitz 1985), seem in democratic settings to produce the most effective forms of collective action for the poor. The distinction between ethnicity and class does not mark the politics of all societies but, in India, these have been seen as rival locus of mobilization. Ethnicity, in general, has been seen to be an easier locus of collective mobilization. Mobilization along class lines alone has on the whole been much less effective than instances where class and ethnicity have co-mingled. The Communist Party of Kerala was more successful because it was both an anti-upper caste movement and could draw upon a repertoire of caste symbols, as well as a class movement (Varshney 2005).

It is not the case that the exercise of franchise has not had a significant impact on economic policy and poverty alleviation programmes. But the nature of this sort of accountability has to be studied more carefully. There are three ways in which that impact is visible. First, as Sen has very effectively argued, India's ability to avoid significant famines in post-independence era has largely been a function of democratic pressures being brought to bear upon government. Second, in comparative terms, India's aversion to inflation has been attributed to the workings of electoral politics. Inflation has been the simplest measure of people's current well-being; its impact direct and widespread. Third, politicians have preferred what are known as 'direct' methods of poverty alleviation. It has been shown that in the case of food and agricultural subsidies there is a very direct link between increases in subsidies and electoral cycles (Chibber 1999). Of course, direct methods of poverty alleviation are preferred for many other reasons. Direct monetary transfers are administratively easier to enact than long-term structural changes; they can be more easily targeted at the discretion of politicians. But, cumulatively, the kinds of pressures that have been brought to bear through the franchise suggest that immediate benefits are electorally more salient than long-time horizon changes.

Accountability and the Politics of Reform

What about dominant interest groups' ability to impede accountability? A traditional explanation of India's poor economic performance was precisely this: a tripartite collusion of rich farmers, public sector professionals and industrial capitalists exercised an effective lock over government policy. None of these classes was powerful enough to singly dominate the state, while their combined fears about the consequences of altering state policy meant that change was structurally inhibited (Bardhan 1985).

This powerful and influential explanation accounted for much stagnation in Indian economic policy. But this explanation has been less useful in thinking about the process through which India has, during the last decade, undertaken a serious economic liberalization programme. Bardhan's explanation suffered from two weaknesses. First, it was too deterministic and underestimated the political room for manoeuvre possessed by political elites. Second, Bardhan failed to follow through on the implications of his own argument. Bardhan posed the following question: 'why the dominant classes, who have so much to gain from long-term economic growth, do not pull together in their long-run collective interests and cooperate in dredging the stilted channels of surplus mobilization and investment which were in danger of being overrun by patronage and subsidies?' His answer was that it was difficult to mount collective action in large and heterogeneous coalitions and hence elites took action to change the system in a way that would lead to their long-term interests. But the logic of this argument can also be turned on its head. This argument would also suggest that, when government does take action, it would be difficult to mount collective resistance against its policies. In other words, the very phenomenon that explained stagnation might also explain how government could, with artful manoeuvre, initiate change. Governments can initiate change and it is often difficult to mount resistance against it. They can exploit divisions between interests and take advantage of the ambiguities that surround the effects of policy to seize the initiative (Jenkins 2000).

But these changes can be taken only under certain conditions that underlie the character of policy making in India. First, the reform programme has succeeded to the extent it has, largely because it has been gradual and has noticeably involved a major public debate. Observers of parliamentary debates over reforms have noticed that most governments have not acknowledged that they were undertaking radical action. A broad vision that underlies the reforms has seldom been argumentatively justified or explained to the public. In fact, the rhetoric of continuity is more pronounced than the acknowledgment of disjuncture. On the one hand, this makes the government's intentions less transparent to the public and, in that sense, renders it less directly accountable. On the other hand, by avoiding debates on ideological fundamentals, the government also avoids a potentially damaging polarization. This allows it, oddly enough, to be more *responsive*. Second, gradualism has allowed governments to avoid shocks. The one sense in which economic reforms can become an issue in mass politics is if they lead to a major shock to the economy. Indian politicians and policy makers have, by and large, been risk averse, in part because electoral compulsions force them to avoid policies that might potentially be experienced as a shock. It would be fair to conclude that, in India's case, electoral accountability renders policy makers risk averse.

Third, policy makers are risk averse in another sense. Politicians are concerned less with the aggregate consequences of economic policy and more with the impact these have on their distributional coalitions. They like, in other words, to manage the distributional consequences of their policies. This does not mean they are averse to change. What it implies is that politicians will use policy to solidify new constituencies and raise resources from new sources before they go against the interests of old ones.

Therefore, the decisive determinant of reform in the Indian context is not whether the state is granted autonomy from social forces or whether key parts of the bureaucracy can be insulated from public pressure. The key question is whether policy makers can use policies to generate new groups that can sustain reform and devise creative compensatory schemes that can allow for divide and rule tactics to flourish. Neither structural constraints, nor open accountability, nor electoral pressures, but political creativity determines the nature of policy reforms in India (Sachs et al. 1999).

In Lieu of a Conclusion

This paper has highlighted different facets that go into making of a politics that is more accountable and responsive. In particular, it has emphasized that the norms and expectations citizens hold each other to, the design of institutions and the manner in which power is organized, all matter for accountability. But the paper is also a cautionary note against any quick fixes. Indeed, any purely administrative solutions that bypass the messy process of politics, are not likely to succeed or be enduring. The only alternative is creativity and improvization that uses the small openings and incentives that entrenched structures provide and transforms them into virtuous cycles of hope. Just a cursory glance over institutional reforms in India will throw up many moments where such reforms are possible. For instance, all the distortions in the representative process and the decline in legitimacy of institutions such as the parliament, provided an opportunity for non-elected institutions, such as the judiciary and India's independent election commission, to produce a measure of accountability. Most recently, the promulgation of a Right to Information Act has empowered citizens by giving them access to one crucial component of accountable government: information. In terms of economic reform, the Indian story is best described as one that involves creative disequilibrium. For instance, the state, for its own political economy reasons, facilitated the growth of a number of industrial groups, which in turn grew in ways that they could demand more reform of the regulatory system. Decentralization is taking place in slow and halting steps. Together, greater access to information, the devolution of power, and the rise of new regulatory systems have brought about incremental change. But fundamentally, the debate over decentralization and such reforms returns us to the question I started with: what conception of politics do we operate with? It seems to me that the fundamental issue in the decentralization debate is not technical institutional design but 'trust'. All the arguments used against decentralizing power—lack of capacity, local elite capture—are arguments that could equally be levelled against Indian democracy, and are essentially paternalistic. Imagine if our founding fathers had heeded the advice of European Social Theory against introducing universal suffrage based on these grounds. What we need is a similar 'leap of faith'. Decentralization will not be the panacea for all ills, but it has the potential for transforming the structure of politics, from a politics of identity to a politics of public goods. On some understandings, China is more decentralized because decentralization is a way of the centre shoring up its own legitimacy. But the conditions under which political systems devolve power downwards is an interesting question.

The list of incremental measures that have cumulatively had an impact is long. No equilibrium in a political system is so stable that reforms cannot take place. But the central point is that these come about because political and social entrepreneurs seize the moment, as it were; not because there is a predetermined policy template. This may make the reforms sound arduous, but then politics is nothing but 'the slow boring of hard boards'—to use Weber's resonant phrase. While this chapter has dealt largely with the challenges of institutionalizing accountability, there are many experiments underway to empower citizens more effectively. For instance, the right to information, while not a panacea, will certainly help citizens monitor the delivery of social services better. But, in the final analysis, accountability is only possible when the romance of a particular kind of politics is restored, a politics that recognizes that the good of citizenship is impossible without reciprocity. As India and China move forward, they will face many common challenges. But some think these common challenges are more economic than political. After all the question of what shape China's political system will take in the future remains uncertain. And India and China will have vastly different political systems. But, perhaps if we take the representation, responsiveness framework some common *political* challenges also emerge.

As the Chinese thinker Qin Hui put it in a striking formulation:

> What is excessive now is not liberalism or social democracy, but oligarchy and populism. It is therefore essential to critique both oligarchy from a liberal standpoint and populism from a social democratic standpoint.

When I read these words I wonder whether there can be any better formulation of the challenges for Indian democracy.

NOTE

1. To some extent, this is a feature of all existing democracies. No democracy approximates the idea of mutual reciprocity outlined here. But, in each of these instances, it is background historical inequalities that act as lasting impediments to achieving reciprocity. So this argument is valid not only for India, though the degree and nature of inherited inequalities may vary considerably.

REFERENCES

Bardhan, Pranap. 1985. *The Political Economy of Development in India*. Oxford: Blackwell.

Chibber, Pradeep. 1999. *Democracy Without Associations*. Ann Arbor: University of Michigan Press.

Das, S.K. 2001. *Public Office and Private Interest*. Delhi: Oxford University Press.

Dreze, Jean and Amartya Sen. 1995. *India: Economic Development and Social Opportunity*. Delhi: Oxford University Press.

Dreze, Jean and Haris Gazdar. 1996. 'Uttar Pradesh: The Burden of Inertia', in J. Dreze and A. Sen (eds), *Indian Development: Selected Regional Perspective*. Delhi: Oxford University Press.

Greenfeld, Liah. 1992. *Nationalism: Five Roads to Modernity*. Cambridge, MA: Harvard University Press.

Guha, Ramachandra. 2007. *India After Gandhi*. New York: Ecco Press.

Horowitz, Donald. 1985. *Ethnic Groups in Conflict*. Berkeley: University of California Press.

Jenkins, Rob. 2000. *Democratic Politics and Economic Reform in India*. Cambridge: Cambridge University Press.

Kapur, Devesh. 2000. 'India: 1999', *Asian Survey*, January.

Kapur, Devesh and Pratap B. Mehta. 1998. 'Parliament as an Institution of Accountability', Working Paper, UNRISD, Geneva.

Khilnani, Sunil. 1997. *The Idea of India*. New York: Farrar, Straus, Giroux.

——. (Ed.). 2005. *India's Public Institutions*. Delhi: Oxford University Press.

Kohli, Atul. 1987. *The State and Poverty in India*. Cambridge: Cambridge University Press.

——. (Ed.). 1988. *India's Democracy*. Princeton: Princeton University Press.

Lijphart, Arend. 1999. *Patterns of Democracy*. New Haven and London: Yale University Press.

Mehta, Pratap B. 2003. *The Burden of Democracy*. Delhi: Penguin.

——. 2004. 'The Constraints on Electoral Mobilization', *Economic and Political Weekly*, Vol. XXXIX, No. 51: 5399–5403.

Menon, Dilip. 1992. *Caste, Nationalism and Communism in South India*. Cambridge: Cambridge University Press.

Moore, Barrington Jr. 1966. *Social Origins of Dictatorship and Democracy: Lord and Peasant in the Making of the Modern World*. Boston: Beacon Press.

Przeworski, Adam, Michael E. Alvarez, Jose Antonio Cheibub and Fernando Limongi (Eds). 2000. *Democracy and Development: Political Institutions and Well-Being in the World, 1950–1990*. New York: Cambridge University Press.

Rousseau, Jean J. [1756] 1997. *The Social Contract and Other Political Writings*, Victor Gourevitch (ed.), Cambridge: Cambridge University Press.

Sachs, Jeffrey, Ashutosh Varshney and Nirupam Bajpai (Eds). 1999. *India in the Era of Economic Reforms*. Delhi: Oxford University Press.

Varshney, Ashutosh. 2005. 'Democracy and Poverty', in Deepa Narayan (ed.), *Measuring Empowerment*. Washington, DC: The World Bank.

Weiner, Myron. 1990. *The Child and State in India*. Princeton: Princeton University Press.

Yadav, Y. 1999. 'Politics', in M. Bouton and P. Oldenburg (eds), *India Briefing*. New York: M.E. Sharpe.

7

Rethinking Civil Society and the Public Spheres[1]

Pathways of Indian Modernities in Global Conversations

ANANTA KUMAR GIRI

It is Jurgen Habermas (1981) himself who quite some time ago had challenged us that now we need a new philosophy of science which is not scientistic. It is worth asking Habermas and all of us sociologists, for whom sociological engagement is nothing more than an elaboration of the agenda of modernity, whether we need an understanding of and relationship with modernity which is not modernistic. This inquiry is at the core of understanding paths of civil society and experiments with modernities not only in India but also in Europe, East Asia, Africa, Latin America and around the world. Both conceptions of civil society and modernity suffer from a profound modernistic bias and is part of the post-traditional telos of modernistic sociological theorizing[2] and here, though the recent discourse of multiple modernities initiated by Shmuel N. Eisenstadt (cf. Sachsenmaier et al. 2002) has suggested some new possibilities, the approach of multiple modernities as that of universalistic modernity of Habermas suffers from a modernistic bias when it comes to understanding tradition.[3] Prefiguring my argument, I wish to submit that appreciating the significance of Indian modernities from Buddha to Gandhi challenges us to understand the relationship between modernity and tradition, state and society, religion and secularism in a new way through a multivalued logic of autonomy and interpenetration rather than through the dualistic logic of modernity. Such a dualistic logic has impoverished our understanding of civil society and modernity in the West itself, what to speak of illuminating our historical paths and tryst with modernities in India.

The subject of Indian modernities is quite vast and here I just wish to state that Indian modernities have emerged out of processes of criticism, creativity and struggles through history as in the revolt of Buddha, the rise of Upanishadic spirituality, Bhakti movements in medieval India, movement for a new renaissance in 19th century, and the multidimensional anti-colonial and post-colonial struggles for freedom.[4] Tryst with modernities in India have involved a transformative dialogue between reason and tradition, tradition and modernity, and rationality and spirituality which has shaped their paths, contents and visions. These modernities have generated their own public spaces of coming together, dialogues and public deliberations which bear parallels to what we speak of civil society in the modern West. Civil society is not only an epistemic project, it is also an ontological project; in fact it is a project of ontological epistemology of participation going beyond the modernistic privileging of epistemology and dualism between ontology and epistemology. Taking inspiration from Bhakti movements, Kabir, Nanak, Mira Bai, Sri Aurobindo and Gandhi, we can realize that the significance of Indian modernities lies in bringing to the fore strivings for multidimensional self-development where self-transformation contributes to world transformation and where an aesthetics and ethics of servanthood is an important mark of being modern rather than the will to power.

But such an open-ended approach to civil society and paths of Indian modernities seems to be missing from certain dominant sociological theorizing in India. For scholars such as Andre Beteille (2001) and Dipankar Gupta (1997), civil society is a modernist category of thought and practice guaranteed by state. Beteille writes: '[...] I will not try to give a definition of civil society but instead sketch out the context in which it may be meaningfully described. While doing so, I would like to repeat that civil society is a feature of the modern world, and it will serve little purpose to look for alternative forms of it in the medieval or ancient world'

(2001: 294). For Dipankar Gupta, '[...] if tradition is allowed to gain the upper hand then it is not civil society and with it the concomitant growth of freedom that develops' (1997: 141). In discussing the potential for formation of civil society that the social mobilization of Bharatiya Kisan Union of Mahendra Singh Tikait of Uttar Pradesh, Gupta says:

> When it comes to the laudable objective of curbing liquor and drug addiction, here too methods are traditional and repressive. Even if some one gives some one the legitimate contract to vend liquor, the outlet should be forcibly closed (ibid.: 145).

But Gupta does not look into the repressive apparatus of the state itself in flooding villages with liquor. While talking about Mahendra Singh Tikait, Gupta writes the following, among others: '[...] many of his followers have told me that on several occasions the BKU chief leaves a meeting and goes to his prayer room where he is not to be disturbed' (1997: 60). But Gupta does not ask what significance prayer has in this movement leader's personal life as well as in his conduct in the public sphere. Such a derisive attitude is an instance of a modernistic bias and disdainful attitude towards tradition. Understanding civil society and paths of modernities in India challenges us to overcome this.

Towards a Multidimensional and Multivalued Understanding of Civil Society

We need a multidimensional understanding and realization of the sphere of civil society and its multiple activities, but for this, we need to overcome the dualism between tradition and modernity, right and good (cf. Habermas 1990), civil society and good society (cf. Beteille 2001) and institutionalization and mobilization. I suggest that the field of civil society consists of an autonomous space but interpenetrated by overlapping and interpenetrative circles of society, religion, state, market, social movements/voluntary organizations and self. Civil society is not only a space of 'mediating institutions' (cf. ibid.) but also of mobilization where mobilization refers not only to socio-political mobilizations but also socio-spiritual mobilizations including reflective mobilization of self (cf. Giri 2004).[5] In the same vein, state and civil society are not to be conflated with each other.

Society and civil society are not co-terminous—civil society refers to that conscious and mobilized aspect of society which strives to create a space of critical self-reflections and public deliberations. Despite contentions and struggles, state and civil society are related again in a logic of autonomy and interpenetration and here social movements, different mediating institutions, and voluntary organizations play an important role. Civil society is also nourished by the support from market. Contributions from actors from market such as corporate leaders and other market leaders contribute to the resource base of civil society. In so far as the relationship between religion and civil society is concerned, one great challenge here is to overcome the dualism of religion and secularism. While for Beteille (2001), civil society is mainly a secular space, for Uberoi (1996) and Oommen (2001a) civil society is a space where religious associations and critical spiritual movements are also at work.[6] Finally, civil society is also a space of work of self, in fact self is an actor in all the intersecting and interpenetrating dimensions of civil society—society, state, market and religion. The quality of work of self and its mobilization in civil society and its above interesecting dimensions determine the quality of civil society.

Critical spiritual movements such as Bhakti movements in Indian history have been important actors in articulating paths of Indian modernities and generating a space of autonomy, self-realization, social transformation and world transformation. Bhakti movements created a new social space of caste and to some extent gender equality and they embodied inter-religious dialogue. For Chittaranjan Das (1997), the Sant tradition is a product of creative and transformative dialogue and encounter between Hinduism and Islam.[7] The participants of Sant tradition and Bhakti movements challenged people to go beyond accepted boundaries and generate a new space of togetherness.[8] The leaders of Bhakti movements wrote in people's language, not in Sanskrit. Their literature has been one of love, protest and affirmation, and for understanding paths of modernities in India we need to understand the public sphere of creativity in language, religion and society that the Bhakti movement created. This is not possible as long as we are bounded to a priori dualistic logic of modernity and civil society which puts religion and civil society in two separate boxes.

Such an approach to civil society has a wider global significance, for example, understanding the relationship between Islam and civil society. As Nakamura Mitsuo writes urging us to take Gellner's views on the impossibility of civil society and Islam only with a pinch of salt: '[...] for centuries Islamic civilizations have developed their own versions of civility and civil society which are different from the West. These have included the independence of Muslim communities (*ummah*) from the state under the spiritual leadership of the *ulama* (Islamic scholars), rule of law to protect personal life and property, religious and ethnic pluralism, consultative and consensus methods of decision-making. In short, there has been civility and public sphere in Islamic world in its own ways including mechanism to control the arbitrariness of state power and to guarantee the autonomy of diversified associational life' (2001: 5). According to Madjid, '[...] the notion of civil society or civilized society coined in the constitution of Medina by Prophet Muhammed makes a genuine part of the common heritage of mankind' (quoted in Mitsuo 2001: 5). Giving the examples of voluntary organizations and political movements such as Nahdaltul Ulama and Muhamadiya, Mitsuo urges us to understand the religious resources for Muslim voluntarism in Indonesia. In his work on civil Islam in Indonesia, Robert Hefner (1998) also urges us to understand its role in democratization of politics and society in Indonesia. But Hefner makes a larger point that calls for consideration from those of us who are bonded to a 'post-traditional telos':

> Viewed from the ground of everyday practice rather than the dizzying height of official canons, the normative diversity of traditional societies is far greater than most sociological models imply. As in China, Romania, and Islamic Indonesia, there are always 'underdeveloped possibilities'—values and practices that hover closer to the social ground and carry unamplified possibilities. These low-lying precedents may not appear in high-flying discourse. Nevertheless, they are in some sense 'available' for engagement and reflection, even if they have long been overlooked in public formulations. Under conditions of cultural globalization or cross-regional transfer, some legal actors may seize on exogamous idioms to legitimate and elevate principles of social action (such as equality, participation, etc.) already present in social life, if in an underdeveloped, subordinated, or politically bracketed manner. (ibid.: 20)

Here Hefner may have to consider that there are underdeveloped possibilities not only in so-called traditional societies but also in so-called modern societies. As there is underdeveloped possibility for participatory politics in the so-called traditional societies there are underdeveloped possibilities for reflective mobilization of self in contemporary modern and postmodern societies as well.

While civil society and reflective mobilizations of self have manifested themselves in varieties of societies some of the unique features of their manifestation must not be lost sight of. This calls for a non-judgmental global comparative engagement with various manifestations of civil society, reflective mobilizations of self and spiritual movements in societies and histories. In India socio-religious and socio-spiritual movements such as Bhakti movements generated new spaces of self and societal realization but it did not offer a direct political confrontation of governing regimes. In India, public spheres and civil societies have not manifested themselves primarily in political terms though in the public sphere itself participants had access to political rulers.[9] For Shmuel N. Eisenstadt (2005), this contrasts with the Islamic public sphere which was driven by a primacy of the political. In Islamic public spheres and civil societies, a notion of political community was quite at the centre but this community though autonomous was still much more tightly controlled by the ruling political formation compared to the case of state and civil society in the modern West. But what is striking is that though in Islamic civil society political community and its autonomy was a key concern, in actual terms in India without sharing this key preoccupation with the political people had a 'relatively widespread access to the political arena' (ibid.: 21) which makes the situation 'very close to the ideal model of European civil society' (ibid.: 19).

But unlike both the modern European and the Islamic case, in Indian engagement with civil society, politics was not at the core. For Eisenstadt,

> The political arena, the arena of rulership, did not constitute in 'historical India'—as it did in monolithic civilizations or in Confucianism—a major arena of the implementation of the transcendental visions predominant in this civilization'. (ibid.: 20)

Such a conception of the political was closely related to the theory and practice of sovereignty that developed in India. It emphasized

> the multiple rights—usually defined in terms of various duties—of different groups and sectors of society rather than a unitary, quasi-ontological conception-real or ideal—of 'the state' or of 'society'—giving rise to what can be defined as fractured sovereignty'. (ibid.: 21)

In the pregnant phase of Eisenstadt, this was a condition of 'non-ontologization of the political arena' (ibid.: 22).

The non-ontologization of the political and work of fractured sovereignty in Indian engagement with civil societies challenges us to rethink the primacy of the political and cult of sovereignty in our dominant conceptions of state and civil society. Instead of looking at the Indian case as an aberration, this challenges us to make our conceptions of civil society a multiverse. It also challenges us to rethink our bondage to a cult of sovereignty that dominates European modernity. Transforming Eisesntadt's perspective of fractured sovereignty we can say that civil society is not only a place of fractured sovereignties but also of shared sovereignties and sacred 'non-sovereignty' (cf. Giri 2007b; Dallmayr 2005). In order that civil society can be helpful in being a space of self-development and social transformation, the cult of absolute sovereignty at the level of state, society and self have to be transformed to a condition of shared sovereignties where all the interacting parties are interested to learn from each other in a spirit of mutual listening, co-labouring experiments, mutual interrogations and transformations. In this space, the interacting parties do not want to dominate each other with a will to power and mastery, they wish to serve each other for mutual growth and transformation. This second aspiration and activity makes this space a space of 'sacred non-sovereignty' (cf. Dallmayr 2005) animated by a will to serve, nurture, share and co-create rather than a will to dominate.

Towards a New Understanding of the Activities and Aspirations of Civil Society

If civil society is a multidimensional space of autonomy and interpenetration what are some of its activities, works and aspirations? I suggest that these are: love, labour, language, rules/law.[10] To begin with the work of love in the sphere of civil society, Uberoi (1996) urges us to realize how loving self-sacrifice of the martyrs is crucial to the work of civil society.[11] For Uberoi, it is the martyr, rather than either the heroes or the victims, who constitute the universal foundation of civil society. Though Uberoi has not discussed the barbaric misuse of ideology of martyrdom for annihilating men and women in religious traditions such as Sikhism and Islam, his emphasis on 'loving self-sacrifice' is an important contribution to rethinking the modernist emasculation of civil society. For instance, one cannot understand the work of martyrs like Shankar Singh Guha Niyogi of Chhattisgarh Mukti Morcha[12] without understanding the dimension of loving self-sacrifice in civil society, not only as a space of association and mediation but also as a site of struggle. As Chandhoke writes about Chhattisgarh Mukti Morcha,

> Despite the fact that CMM used only non-violent means of protest, such as peaceful demonstrations, *dharnas*, strikes, *morchas* and petitions—all of which are permissible in civil society—their protests were savagely put down. During a conversation with one of the CMM's leaders, I wondered whether it was not legitimate to use violence in a society where the regime virtually used violence against its own people. His answer was an emphatic no; violence, he argued, would impoverish the movement and denude it of any spirit of commitment'. (Chandhoke 2003b: 206)

Here, the struggle is both a political struggle of democratization of state and society and the spiritual struggle of realizing 'power free' existence (cf. Dallmayr 2001), i.e., not being a slave to the logic of power and using the instruments of power to oppress other people. This struggle is animated by a hope that the subaltern would embody a different subjectivity and intersubjectivity and would not try to imbibe the same logic of dominant hegemony (Chakraborty 2002). It is no wonder then that Chhattisgarh Mukti Morcha strives for a new meaning of 'what it means to be a Chhattisgarhi citizen. According to CMM, a Chhattisgarhi citizen is one who works in the region and who does not exploit either the resources or the people for his or her personal benefit' (Chandhoke 2003b: 238).[13]

The relationship between the work of love and work of civil society becomes clearer in an interesting essay by Veena Das (2003) titled, 'The small community of love'. For Das, 'One cannot base the little community of love on an appeal to law—you cannot wait, as Cavell says, for the perfect larger community before you form the smaller communities of love. Thus, the constitutional promise about life, liberty, and pursuit of happiness has the public face of what it is to claim this in law and the private face of what it is to ask that human society contain the room for these small communities to be built'. Elaborating this, Das further writes: 'In a conference I attended recently, someone asked if a song like, '*Tu Hindu banega na Musalman banega—Insaan ki aulad hai insaan banega* from *Dhul ka Phul* was still possible. I thought of Mr. Insaniyat (humanity) and how he learnt that the claims of building small communities of love was also a way of learning to be Indian'. In his article, 'Romantic Archives: Literature and the Politics of Identity in Bengal', Dipesh Chakraborty (2004: 682) also writes:

> [...] What politics can we reconstitute out of our romantic investment in language? The politics I have in mind, however, is not programmatic. The making of a romantic literary legacy into a political archive is not something we can call into being. Romantic thoughts no longer furnish our analytical frameworks, but the inheritance of romanticism is built into the Bengali language. Our everyday and unavoidable transactions with the poetry of language may thus be compared to the practice of vigilant waiting. This vigilant and active waiting can itself be political–listen to the romantic voice of a Bengali communist poet who captures its spirit:
>
> [...] When the rains depart
> We will put out in the sun
> Everything that is wet
> Woodchips and all
> Putout in the sun
> We shall
> Even our hearts

Continuing our exploration of the relationship between the work of love and work of civil society, from a philosophical and theological perspective, Giani Vattimo (1999) tells us that we are all in need of forgiveness not because we have fallen in love but because we have failed in love. Such a recognition of failure in love helps us to be repentant for our lack of inability to transform situations of conflicts and avert many social tragedies. Given the significance of the work of reconciliation and forgiveness in many societies such as South Africa or India after the violence of apartheid or communal conflicts, the work of love is quite central in civil society organizations working on post-conflict reconciliation.

From the aspiration and work of love in the sphere of civil society let us come to the work of labour. Civil society is not only a sphere of public deliberations and discursive argumentations, it is also a sphere of labour where labouring bodies come together and build new spaces of habitations and hopes. Gandhi's conception of bread labour helps us in understanding this link between the work of labour and work of civil society, so does Swadhyaya's (a socio-spiritual movement in contemporary India) vision and practice of *shramabhakti*—devotional labour (cf. Giri 2008). In Swadhyaya, participants come together and build foundations of collective well-being such as digging village wells through shared devotional labour. Similar is also the work of Habitat for Humanity, a Christian socio-religious movement in the US, which is working in many countries around the world, where volunteers of Habitat build houses together with prospective homeowners (Giri 2002a).

As civil society is also a sphere of institutions, rules and laws are quite central here, though it is important to acknowledge that civil society as a space of mobilization may challenge many of rules and laws within which civil society institutions may function.

Now to come to theme of language in the work of civil society, in many ways it is quite central as has been attested by theorists of civil society and public sphere such as Habermas (1989). A Habermasian perspective on civil society helps us understand the key importance of communication, especially communicative action, in the work of civil society. In history of India we find struggle for people's languages beyond the language of the elites and the *pundits*. Movements such as Bhakti movements as well as contemporary dalit movements (cf. Narayan 2001, 2011; Pandian 1998) have played an important role in creating people's languages and literatures which contributed to a new self-awareness among people as well as new themes and spaces of discursive deliberations about self, society and polity. For example, in Orissa, Sarala Das wrote the epic Mahabharata in Oriya and the Panchasakshas or the five friends such as Achyutananda Das and Jagannatha Das in 16th centuries not only translated epics such as Ramayana into Oriya but also created life-elevating literature. They also contributed to building study centres known as *Bhagabata Ghara* for studying these works in villages (cf. Das 1997). These reading spaces, though limited by caste and gender inequality, contributed to the generation of new spaces of conviviality and conversations. But while understanding the relationship between language and civil society in these manifold ways, it is helpful at the same time to acknowledge the limits of language in the work of civil society. The language of civil society may be a heritage to a dominant language of class and culture and here overcoming the limits of the dominant language calls for multidimensional cultural, political and social transformations.[14] While civil society is a sphere of critical deliberations this very work itself calls for listening on the part of participating actors, and this in turn calls for the ability to cultivate silence in discursive argumentations. Listening calls for meditation and thus civil society and public spheres are not only spaces of argumentations but also of listening and meditations.

Rethinking Public Spheres

This issue of listening can be taken as a starting point for rethinking the concept of public sphere coming from the Western tradition which gives much more importance to discursive argumentation than listening and meditation. It is important to note that Habermas himself writes: '[...] within the boundaries of public sphere, or at least, of a liberal public sphere, actors can acquire influence, not political power' (1996: 371). Listening helps in understanding the other better and thus have more influence on the other rather than just asserting one's point of view. Habermas goes beyond a strict sociologism in his conception of the public sphere[15] which helps us to rethink civil society as well and it vibrates with the multidimensional conceptualization of the civil society presented in this essay. The work of language in the dynamics of civil society discussed earlier finds a correspondence in Habermas's (1989) discussion on the role of literary public sphere in the rise of modern public spheres in Europe.

But it is one thing to talk about literary public sphere as a type of public sphere or even as a segment of public sphere and it is another thing to realize the integral literary dimension of public sphere itself. In later conceptualizations and realizations, literature becomes an integral part of public sphere through work of rhetoric, language, style of argumentation and mutual co-presence in such modes as co-walking, co-labouring and confrontations.[16] In their vision and practices, writers such as Chittaranjan Das, U.R.

Ananthamurthy and Mahesweta Devi from India embody this later realization of public sphere. They are tireless participants in public discourses and public spaces through speech, writing and, in case of Das, regular columns in newspapers (cf. Giri 2011). They not only help us realize the literary dimension of public sphere but also recreate public sphere through creative and critical literary interventions. As their works exemplify, which is not sufficiently explored in thinkers such as Habermas and Touraine, it is by cultivating the literary field on the part of self and society one can realize the post-conventional dimension of society, have the capacity to say 'no' in the face of an overwhelming compulsion for 'yes', and go beyond the logic of a priori social.[17] What Touraine and Habermas have not explored is how practice of creative literature can contribute to co-creating public sphere as a field of creative expression, co-realizations and confrontation.

To understand the role of creative and critical literature in the rise and continued work of public spheres, we can explore a bit more, the relationship between literature and society. Literature is not only a mirror of society but also a field of creative expressions and confrontations which breaks existing mirrors of society and creates new languages of self and social realizations and new landscapes of imaginations. Literature is not only a field of murmuring but of grumbling and a field of contestation and confrontations of the existing grammar of society based upon a higher grumbling of self and awakened social groups and movements. Both literature and society are not only fields of adaptation but also fields of transcendence and transformations in which individuals and groups strive to go beyond adaptation and create new conditions of self, co and social realizations. These are fields in which there is interrogation and confrontation of the existing logic of literature and society.

And in such transformative co-realizations the nature of 'and' plays an important role. If we conceptualize 'and' in a logic of juxtaposition, the terms and fields on both sides of 'and' do not get mutually interpenetrated and transformed. 'And' becomes a helpless presence repeating the logic of 'end' (which simultaneously means end of the meaning of as well as ultimate end or purpose). But if our conception and realization of 'and' is one of mutual interrogation, transmutation and mothering bridge then our inhabitation, meditation, dance, walk and work in the space of the 'and', the space of the middle, becomes a work of transformation, transforming a one-sided conceptualization, realization and organization of fields. 'And' is a space of quest for infinity from the actors and fields on its two sides rather than a reiteration of the totalizing logic of totality of either of them.[18] 'And' is a mothering ground and bridge of quest for and embodiment of responsibility. For example, in his work, *Sahitya O* (Literature and ...) Chittaranjan Das (1923–2011), a creative seeker, writer and experimenter from Odisha, who has written more than two hundred books on different aspects of literature, society, education, literary and social criticism suggests such a transformative, interrogative and mothering meaning and realization of 'and' (Das 1989a; also see Giri 2011). This also comes out in a joint work of co-creation in which the poetic critic and essayist Chittaranjan and poet Srinivas Udgata co-create poems and reflections on poetry together in the work *Ebam* which also means 'and' (Das 1989b).[19]

Public sphere helps us in realizing such a meaning of 'and' beyond the adaptive, already determined and ultimate logic of 'end'. Literature helps us to express ourselves to ourselves as well as to the others and the public. Expression in the field of literature is simultaneously self, mutual and public and helps in the creation of public spheres in societies.

The Calling of Creative Public Spheres

We usually look at literary creativity in an individualized way but now we need to link both to fields of creative public spaces and spheres. For our *tapasya* of creativity in literature and society, we need the spheres of the creative self, intimate groups of mutuality as well as public spheres. But in each of these spheres, we continue the modernist logic of linearity. Despite the language of sphere in public sphere our conceptualization and organization of it is linear. It is hardly a sphere where the spherical nature of our being is at work or finds an expression.[20]

The concept and organization of public sphere in modernity is also bound to a logic of double contingency and dualism. For example, we look at self, other and society through the logic of what Strydom (2009) calls 'double contingency' of self and the other. This double contingency is also imprisoned within dualism. But now we need to bring the concept of 'triple contingency' to each of these spheres. In triple contingency, along with self and other, there is also a public (Strydom 2009). But this public is not fixed, it is emergent, it is not only observing but also participating. Triple contingency does not lie only outside but also works inside. Triple contingency also is a bearer of transcendence as it transcends the dualistic logic of double contingency of self and the other.

In literature, spiritual traditions and creative imaginations we are familiar with the concept and reality of third eye. This third eye exists not only in Shiva, the meditative *tapaswee* and dancer, but also in all of us (see Organ 1987). Triple contingency can be linked to the work of third eye. Literature and creative public spheres can help us realize and cultivate not only the triple contingency of life thus, going beyond the arrogance and exclusionary assertion of either self or other but also develop and realize our third eyes, a challenge missing in contemporary theorization of society. Public sphere and creative meditation can help us realize both triple contingency and third eye and then move it further to the fourth, fifth and further dimensions of our contingencies, aspirations and struggles.[21]

Life Worlds and Living Words

But for this we would have to recreate the link between what is called life worlds and system worlds through the categories of lived worlds and living words. Our lived worlds everywhere are multiplex and plural but the language of life worlds and system worlds as it comes in sociology and in the works of critical theorists such as Habermas usually present a one-dimensional logic and rationality such as the primacy of rational in modernity and hierarchy in traditional societies. Life worlds everywhere are also subjected to dominant logic of the system world such as market, state, caste and gender. In this context to cultivate lived worlds with their creativity, courage, transcendence and multidimensionality is a challenge which calls for us to go beyond the existing logic of life worlds and system worlds. The challenge of creativity is simultaneous: simultaneously nurturing lived worlds of vibrancy, energy, soulful togetherness and meditative solitude and living words which move us not to hatred and annihilation but to mutual blossoming and co-realization. Both lived worlds and living words do *tapasya* for and with beauty, dignity and dialogues in the face of and in the midst of ugliness, indignity and violence.[22]

Living words work as new *mantras* of life, to put in the words of Sri Aurobindo and embody what Martin Heidegger (1994) calls 'way making movement'. They just do not mirror 'forms of life' but create new ways of life. They just do not reproduce existing language but create new languages of self and social realizations.[23] They just do not reproduce the rationality of either tradition or modernity but possibly embody strivings towards what Latin American thinker Enrique Dussel calls 'transmodernity'.[24] They are not just part of either the logic of transcendental awe in tradition or 'linguistification of the sacred' in modernity.[25] While they seek to make the Divine and Nature part of the communicative field of humans and express it in ways understandable to modern rational mind, it nonetheless does not reduce either of them only to what is comprehensible in the language of modern rationality. It seeks to cultivate the ineffable in both lived worlds and living words while at the same time making them part of our everyday conversations. Both lived worlds and living words become sites of courage, creativity and transcendence working in between and in the margins of fear, drudgery and pull towards an imprisonment in closed walls which is justified in the name of immanence.

By Way of Conclusion

In this essay, we have explored a multidimensional and multivalued understanding of civil society and public sphere going beyond many modernistic dualisms such as private and public, tradition and modernity, civil society and good society, religion and secularism, and life world and system world. In the process we have rethought some of the foundational assumptions of civil society, public sphere, life worlds and systems worlds in modernity by bringing cross-cultural considerations and putting Indian and European perspectives in dialogues as part of global conversations. Such a multivalued understanding not only helps us in a new understanding of civil society but also paths of Indian modernities in particular, and global modernities in general, in societies and histories.

NOTES

1. This essay builds upon my work on civil society, literature and public sphere over last fifteen years especially the following three essays, 'Rethinking Civil Society', 'Civil Society and the Calling of Self-Development' and 'Literature, Society and the Calling of a Creative Public Sphere: Towards a New Art of Cross-Fertilization'.
2. For Giddens (1994), sociology is a part of the post-traditional telos of modernity and for Beteille (2002), sociology is a modern, neither a postmodern nor a traditional discipline.
3. For example, following Max Weber, Shmuel N. Eisenstadt, a key proponent of the multiple modernities approach, defines the core of modernity as the deconstruction of a God-ordained world-view held by all axial civilizations. 'Since modern societies are no longer embedded in meaningful transcendental orders, they are in principle open to continuous transformation and adaptation' (Eisenstadt 2005: 10).
4. For Uberoi, 'The struggle to define and establish civil society in India during the modern period runs parallel to the rise, development and recognition of the vernaculars and vernacularism everywhere in language, labour and culture; and it is the story of religion and politics proceeding from Kabir (1440–1518) to the martyrdom of Mahatma Gandhi' (2003: 123). Uberoi himself says that civil society is not only a modernistic category and we can explore struggles for Indian modernities and civil societies from the strivings of Buddha and his social struggles to build new critical spaces.
5. For Neera Chandhoke, 'Civil society is not an institution; it is, rather, a process whereby the inhabitants of the sphere (i.e., civil society) constantly monitor both the state and monopoly of power within itself' (2003a: 57). Chandhoke approaches civil society from the vantage point of continued mobilization though she seems to be stressing more on political mobilization and less on reflective mobilization of self. Similarly, Oommen (2001a) has a mobilizational approach to civil society while Beteille (2001) has a predominantly institutional approach. This dualism between mobilization and institutionalization needs to be overcome for a fuller understanding of civil society.
6. Beteille asks: 'How far do religious movements and assemblies for moral, ethical and spiritual discourses contribute to the formation of civil society?' and answers: 'They may contribute a very great deal to the formation of the good society, depending, of course, on what one means by that phrase [...] I remain skeptical about what religious

assemblies and movements can contribute directly to the formation of civil society, although there indirect contribution may be extremely valuable' (2001: 307). But for Oommen, '... religious organizations were very much part of civil society in pre-independent India' (2001a: 229). It is interesting to note here that both Uberoi and Oommen are not following any universalizing conception of modernity. Oommen (2001b) follows a 'multiple modernities' perspective in his work while Uberoi (2002) is one of the few proponents of Indian modernity.

7. This is similar to Uberoi's (1996) argument about Sikhism that it is a product of dialogue between Hinduism and Islam.
8. As John S. Hawley writes of Bhakti poets: 'These poets' intimate involvement with their audiences—in their own life times, doubtless, but certainly down the generation as subsequent performers and their audiences—have taken up these roles—is the real democracy of *bhakti*' (2005: 332).
9. In this context what Eisenstadt writes about Bhakti movements is insightful: 'Many of the visions promulgated by those movements emphasized equality, but it was above all equality in the cultural or religious arena, with respect to access to worship, and only to some extent in the definition of membership in the political community' (2005: 23).
10. This four dimensional conceptualization can be compared with four dimensions of civil society articulated by Cohen and Arato (1992)—publicity, plurality, legality, and privacy. There are no references to love and labour in this framework though the theme of privacy may touch upon the theme of love to some extent. But the theme of love in the present model also refers to socially transforming love.
11. In his reflections on civil society, Uberoi (1996) is not within the modernist trap. He neither considers civil society as a product of modernist transition in history (though he would not discount its significance in understanding the contour that civil society has taken in modern past and present) nor does he look at it through the dominant logic of power.
12. Chhattisgarh Mukti Morcha is a multidimensional social movement of tribals and workers in the Chhattisgarh region of India fighting for dignity and rights and its leader Shankar Singh Guha Niyogi was gunned down at the behest of the contractors and industrialists of the region.
13. A critic had raised the question of how appropriate it is to use this notion of 'Chhattisgarhi citizen'. Chandhoke uses the word but the

way I understand the significance of such words is that it challenges us to realize a multi-layered conception of citizenship. We are not only citizens of our nation-states, we are also citizens of our significant communities of belonging including citizens of the world. Today, the rise of transnational civic movements and emergent discourse and practice of cosmopolitanism challenges us to realize the limits of nation-state centred discourse and practice of citizenship. This also challenges us to go beyond a purely *etic* use and understanding of categories such as citizenship and have an *emic* perspective which emerges from dialogues with people in conversations.

14. In her essay, 'Language, Translation and Domination', Neera Chandhoke (2003c) speaks about the condition of tribals and their languages in the discourse of civil society in modern India. For a tribal, a particular piece of land belongs to him because the bones of his ancestors are buried there. But this language is not easily comprehensible in the dominant language of property rights that dominate state and civil society in modern India. The agents of state and civil society may negotiate with these subaltern languages but they do so from the perspective of the dominant language. For Chandhoke, '[...] the more powerful language in civil society does not even have to practice savageness to bludgeon, club or hammer the less powerful language into insensibility, which is something that Habermas fears, and that he attempts to ward off through discourse ethics. The deliberative space of civil society has already been colonized, already saturated with power that privileges certain ideas of land proprietorship' (ibid.: 195).

15. For Habermas, the public sphere is not a social order, nor is it a social institution and 'certainly not an organization' (1996: 341).

16. While Habermasian public sphere is mainly one of sphere of argumentation I make it plural by bringing such activities as love and labour in to it (cf. Giri 2008).

17. For Touraine (2007), becoming a subject is integrally linked to have the ability to say 'no' to the existing logic if this does not allow creative self-realization. Habermas (1990) similarly talks about the need for developing 'post-conventional' morality which goes beyond the existing morality of society. Creative and critical participation in public sphere can help in such a realization.

18. This resonates with the thoughts of Emmanuel Levinas. Franson Manjali (2001) also explores such pathways in his *Literature and Infinity*. We can also note here what Deleuze tells us: 'It is not the elements or the sets which define multiplicity. What defines it is the AND, as something which has its place between the elements or between the sets. AND, AND, AND—stammering' (Deleuze and Parnet 2002).

19. So does poet and novelist Rabi Narayan Dash (2008) in his book of poems, *Ebam Kadha* (and buds).
20. Philosopher Peter Sloterdijk urges us to realize the distinction between a spherical approach and a linear approach.
21. This calls for cross-cultural dialogue and border-crossing dialogue between critical theory and religious and spiritual ways of thinking. It would be interesting to explore further dialogue between the concept of triple contingency in critical theory and trinity in Christian religious and spiritual tradition. For Raimundo Panikkar, an inspiring spiritual seeker and thinker, 'Trinity is not a number but the depth and unfolding of the riches of reality, which is a living relationship' (quoted in Pikaza 2010: 119). 'Panikkar thereby seeks to move beyond a form of dualism, following the best *ádvaita* experience (of non-dualism), opening a way to dialogue [...]' (ibid.). In the same way we can realize triple contingency not as a number but as the depth and creativity of relationship beyond the dualistic logic of self and other. But triple contingency also urges us to realize that Trinity whether it is in Christian tradition or Hindu tradition is also confronted with the challenges of public—an observant and meditative public.
22. In this context, what Margaret Chatterjee tells us about different lifeworlds that we inhabit is touching:

    On this side of the wall children have milk to drink at least once a day. On the other side, one *pawa* of milk has to stretch for glasses of tea for five adults plus children. As six year old girl told me this. Near the milk stall there are three *mithai* (sweet) shops. This is where the bulk of the milk goes. Consciousness cries out for transformation, a consciousness imbued with conscience. Such a consciousness would grow laterally, horizontally, turning the search light of attention on the endless anomalies around us, the endless injustices, the lack of any sense of priorities (Chatterjee 2005: 16). In the above paragraph, Chatterjee talks about the growth of consciousness horizontally and this resonates with Husserl's emphasis on horizontal ontology (see Mohanty 2002).
23. As expressed in the following poem:

    Oh friend
    You said
    We need a new language
    Anew *sadhana* of words and *tapasya* of worlds
    This is not a language of victory
    Nor is one of self-advertisement and aggrandizement
    Neither is it a language of doomsday

This is a language of walking our ways together
Walking our dreams, *sadhana* and struggle

II

In our co-habitations of affection
Of compassion and confrontation
Words become *mantras*
Of a new life, a new responsibility
Of wiping tears from our eyes and
Again taking each other into our laps
Renewing our strength from embrace
We create new paths by walking
We create new language
Our language is the language of walking
Stars of *mantras* leap from our lap

(a poem originally written by the author in Oriya and then translated).

24. The following quotation from Dussel (2010) helps us to understand transmodernity:

    Europe began to function as the 'center' of the world market (and therefore to extend the 'world system' throughout the world) with the advent of the industrial revolution; on the cultural plane, this produced the phenomenon of the Enlightenment, the origins of which, in the long run, we should look for (according to the hypothesis of Morrocan philosopher Al-Yabri, who we will discuss later) in the Averröist philosophy of the caliphate of Córdoba. Europe's crucial and enlightened hegemony scarcely lasted two centuries (1789–1989). Only two centuries! Too short-term to profoundly transform the 'ethico-mythical nucleus' (to use Ricoeur's expression) of ancient and universal cultures like the Chinese and others of the Far East (like the Japanese, Korean, Vietnamese, etc.), the Hindustanic, the Islamic, the Russian-Byzantine, and even the Bantu or the Latin American (though with a different structural composition). These cultures have been partly *colonized* (included through negation in the totality, as aspect A of Diagram 1), but most of the structure of their values has been excluded—*scorned, negated and ignored*—rather than annihilated. The economic and political system has been dominated in order to exert colonial power and to accumulate massive riches, but those cultures were deemed to be unworthy, insignificant, unimportant, and useless. The tendency to disparage those cultures, however, has allowed them to survive in silence, in the shadows, simultaneously scorned by their own modernized and westernized elites. That negated 'exterior', that alterity—always extant and latent—indicates the existence of an unsuspected cultural richness, which is slowly revived like the flames of the fire of those fathoms buried under the sea of ashes from hundreds of years of colonialism. That cultural exteriority is not merely a substantive, uncontaminated, and eternal 'identity'. It has been evolving in the face of Modernity itself; what is at stake is 'identity' in the sense of process and growth, but always as an exteriority.

These cultures, asymmetrical in terms of their economic, political, scientific, technological, and military conditions, therefore maintain an alterity with respect to European Modernity, with which they have coexisted and have learned to respond in their own way to its challenges. They are not dead but alive, and presently in the midst of a process of rebirth, searching for new paths for future development (and inevitably at times taking the wrong paths). Since they are not modern, these cultures cannot be 'post'-modern either. They are simultaneously pre-modern (older than modernity), contemporary to Modernity, and soon, to Transmodernity as well. Postmodernism is a final stage in modern European/North American culture, the 'core' of Modernity. Chinese or Vedic cultures could never be European postmodern, but rather are something very different as a result of their distinct roots. Thus, the strict concept of the '*trans*-modern' attempts to indicate the radical novelty of the irruption—as if from nothing—from the transformative exteriority of that which is always Distinct, those cultures in the process of development which assume the challenges of Modernity, and even European/North American Postmodernity, but which respond *from another place, another location*. They respond from the perspective of their own cultural experiences, which are distinct from those of Europeans/North Americans, and therefore have the capacity to respond with solutions which would be absolutely impossible for an exclusively modern culture. A future trans-modern culture—which assumes the positive moments of Modernity (as evaluated through criteria distinct from the perspective of the other ancient cultures)—will have a rich pluriversality and would be the fruit of an authentic intercultural dialogue, that would need to bear clearly in mind existing asymmetries (to be an 'imperial-core' or part of the semi-peripheral 'central chorus'—like Europe today, and even more so since the 2003 Iraq War—is not the same as to be part of the postcolonial and peripheral world). But a post-colonial and peripheral world like that of India, in a position of abysmal asymmetry with respect to the metropolitan core of the colonial era, does not for this reason cease to be a creative nucleus of ancient cultural renewal which is decisively distinct from all of the others, with the capacity to propose novel and necessary answers for the anguishing challenges that the Planet throws upon us at the beginning of the twenty-first century.

'*Trans*-modernity' points toward all of those aspects that are situated 'beyond' (and also 'prior to') the structures valorized by modern European/North American culture, and which are present in the great non-European universal cultures and have begun to move toward a pluriversal project.

25. Habermas (1990) talks about 'linguistification of the sacred'.

REFERENCES

Appadurai, Arjun. 2002. 'Deep Democracy: Urban Governmentality and the Horizon of Politics', *Public Culture*, 14 (1): 21–47.

Beteille, Andre. 2001. 'Civil Society and Good Society', *Sociological Bulletin*, 50 (2): 286–307.

——. 2002. *Sociology: Essays on Approach and Method*. Delhi: Oxford University Press.

Bhaskar, Roy. 2002. *Reflections on Meta-Reality: Transcendence, Everyday Life and Emancipations*. New Delhi: Sage Publications.

Chandhoke, Neera. 2003a. 'A Critique of Civil Society as the Third Sphere', in Rajesh Tandon and Ranjita Mohanty (eds), *Does Civil Society Matter? Governance in Contemporary India*. New Delhi: Sage, pp. 27–58.

——. 2003b. 'When the Voiceless Speak: A Case Study of the Chhattisgarh Mukti Morcha', in R. Tandon and R. Mohanty (eds), *Does Civil Society Matter? Governance in Contemporary India*. New Delhi: Sage, pp. 198–242.

——. 2003c. *The Conceits of Civil Society*. Delhi: Sage Publications.

Chakraborty, Dipesh. 2002. *Habitations of Modernity: Essays on the Wake of Subaltern Studies*. Chicago: University of Chicago Press.

——. 2004. 'Romantic Archives: Literature and the Politics of Identity in Bengal', *Critical Inquiry*, 30 (3): 654–683.

Cohen, Jean and Andrew Arato. 1992. *Civil Society and Political Theory*. Cambridge, Mass: The MIT Press.

Connolly, William E. 2001. *The Ethos of Pluralization*. Minneapolis: University of Minnesota Press.

Chatterjee, Margaret. 2005. *Lifeworlds, Philosophy and India Today*. Shimla: Indian Institute of Advanced Studies.

Dallmayr, Fred. 1993. *G.W.F. Hegel: Modernity and Politics*. Newbury Park, CA: Sage Publications.

——. 2001. *Achieving Our World: Toward a Global and Plural Democracy*. Lanham, MD: Rowman & Littlefield.

——. 2005. *Small Wonder: Global Power and its Discontents*. Lanham, MD: Rowman & Littlefield.

Das, Chittaranjan. 1997 (1951). *Achyutananda O Panchasakha Dharma* (Achyutananda and the Religion of the Panchasakhas). Cuttack: S.B. Publications.

——. 1989a. *Sahitya O...* (Literature and ...). Berhampur: Pustaka Bhandar.

——. 1989b. 'Ethara Udiba Neta', in Chittaranjan Das and Srinivas Udgata, *Ebam* (And ...). Cuttack: Books & Books.

Das, Veena. 2003. 'Small Community of Love'. Retrieved from: http://www.india-seminar.com/2003/525/525%20veena%20das.htm

Dash, Rabi Narayan. 2008. ... *Ebam Kadha* (... And buds). Balasore, Odisha: Samara Graphics.

Dussel, Enrique. 2010. 'Transmodernity and Interculturality: An Interpretation from the Philosophy of Liberation'. Paper presented at the International Symposium on 'Learning Across Boundaries', University of Luxembourg, June.

Eisenstadt, Shmuel N. 2005. 'Civil Society and Public Sphere in a Comparative Perspective'. Text of the Lecture at the Institute of Sociology, Warsaw, 27 October.

Faubion, James D. (ed.). 1995. *Rethinking the Subject: An Anthology of Contemporary European Social Theory*. Boulder: Westview Press.

Gatens, Moira and Genevieve Lloyd. 1999. *Collective Imaginings: Spinoza, Past and Present*. London: Routledge.

Giddens, Anthony. 1991. *Modernity and Self-Identity: Self and Society in the Late Modern Age*. Cambridge: Polity Press.

——. 1994. 'Living in a Post-Traditional Society', in Ulrich Beck et al., *Reflexive Modernization: Politics, Tradition and Aesthetics in the Modern Social Order*. Cambridge: Polity Press, pp. 56–109.

Giri, Ananta Kumar. 2002a. *Building in the Margins of Shacks: The Vision and Projects of Habitat for Humanity*. Delhi: Orient Longman.

——. 2002b. 'Rethinking Civil Society', in idem, *Conversations and Transformations: Towards a New Ethics of Self and Society*. Lanham, MD: Lexington Books, pp. 287–314.

——. 2004. *Reflections and Mobilizations: Dialogues with Movements and Voluntary Organizations*. Delhi: Sage Publications.

——. 2008. *Self-Development and Social Transformations? The Visions and Experiments of the Socio-Spiritual Mobilizations of Swadhyaya*. Lanham, MD: Lexington Books and Jaipur: Rawat Publications.

——. 2009. 'Introduction', in Ananta Kumar Giri (ed.), *The Modern Prince and the Modern Sage: Transforming Power and Freedom*. New Delhi: Sage Publications.

——. 2011. 'Chittaranjan Das: A Creative Thinker', *Social Change,* 41 (3): 359–380.

Gupta, Dipankar. 1997. *Rivalry and Brotherhood: Politics in the Life of Farmers in Northern India.* Delhi: Oxford University Press.

Habermas, Jurgen. 1981. *Philosophical-Political Profiles.* Cambridge: Polity Press.

——. 1989. *The Structural Transformation of the Public Sphere.* Cambridge, Mass.: The MIT Press.

——. 1990. *Moral Consciousness and Communicative Action.* Cambridge: Polity Press.

——. 1996. *Between Facts and Norms: Contributions towards a Discourse Theory of Law and Democracy.* Cambridge: Polity Press.

——. 2006. *Between Naturalism and Religion.* Cambridge: Polity Press.

Hawley, John Stratton. 2005. 'Bhakti, Democracy and the Study of Religion', in idem, *Three Bhakti Voices: Mirabai, Sur Das, and Kabir in Their Times and Ours.* Delhi: Oxford University Press.

Hefner, Robert W. 1998. 'On the History and Cross-Cultural Possibility of a Democratic Political Ideal', in Robert Hefner (ed.), *Democratic Civility: The History and Cross-Cultural Possibility of a Modern Political Ideal.* New Brunswick, NJ: Transaction Books, pp. 3–49.

Manjali, Franson. 2001. *Literature and Infinity.* Shimla: Indian Institute of Advanced Study.

Mitsuo, Nakamura. 2001. 'Introduction', in Nikamura Mitsuo et al., *Islam and Civil Society in South East Asia.* Singapore: Institute of South East Asian Studies, pp. 1–30.

Mohanty, Manoranjan. 2002. 'The Self as Center in the Emerging World of the Twenty-first Century: A Sino-Indian Perspective', *China Report,* 38 (1): 1–10.

——. 2003. 'Creative Self and its Enemies in the Emerging World', *Gandhian Perspectives,* X1 (1 and 2): 15–21.

Mohanty, Jitendra N. 2002. *Explorations in Philosophy: Western Philosophy.* Delhi: Oxford University Press.

Narayan, Badri. 2001. *Documenting Dissent: Contesting Fables, Contesting Memories and Dalit Political Discourse.* Shimla: Indian Institute of Advanced Study.

——. 2011. *The Making of Dalit Public Sphere.* Delhi: Oxford University Press.

Organ, Troy Wilson. 1987. *Third Eye Philosophy: Essays in East-West Thought.* Athens: Ohio University Press.

Oommen, T.K. 2001a. 'Civil Society: Religion, Caste and Language in India', *Sociological Bulletin,* 50 (2): 221–235.

——. 2001b. 'Multiple Modernities and the Rise of New Social Movements: The Case of India', *Indian Social Science Review*, 3 (1): 1–16.

Organ, Troy Wilson. 1987. *Third Eye Philosophy: Essays in East-West Thoughts*. Athens: Ohio University Press.

Pandian, M.S.S. 1998. 'Stepping Outside History? New Dalit Writings from Tamil Nadu', in Partha Chatterjee (ed.), *Wages of Freedom: Fifty Years of the Indian Nation-State*. Delhi: Oxford University Press, pp. 292–309.

Pikaza, Xavier. 2010. 'Raimon Panikkar (1918–2010)', *Concilium*, 5: 117–120.

Sachsenmaier, Dominic and Jens Reidel with Shmuel Eisenstadt (eds). 2002. *Reflections on Multiple Modernities: European, Chinese and Other Interpretations*. Leiden: Brill.

Seligman, Adam. 1995. 'Animadversions Upon Civil Society and Civic Virtue in the Last Decade of the Twentieth Century', in John A. Hall (ed.), *Civil Society*. Cambridge: Polity.

Sen, Amartya. 2002. 'Justice Across Borders', in Pablo De Greiff and Ciaran P. Cronin (eds), *Global Justice and Transnational Politics: Essays on the Moral and Political Challenges of Globalization*. Cambridge, MA: The MIT Press, pp. 37–51.

Strydom, Piet. 2009. *New Horizons of Critical Theory: Collective Learning and Triple Contingency*. Delhi: Shipra.

Tandon, Rajesh and Ranjita Mohanty (eds). 2003. *Does Civil Society Matter? Governance in Contemporary India*. New Delhi: Sage.

Uberoi, J.P.S. 1996. *Religion, Civil Society and State: A Study of Sikhism*. Delhi: Oxford University Press.

——. 2002. *The European Modernity: Truth, Science and Method*. Delhi: Oxford University Press.

——. 2003. 'Civil Society', in Veena Das (ed.), *Oxford India Companion to Sociology and Social Anthropology*. Delhi: Oxford University Press, pp. 114–133.

Touraine, Alain. 2007. 'Sociology After Sociology', *European Journal of Social Theory*, 10 (2): 184–193.

Wuthnow, Robert. 2004. *Saving America? Faith-Based Services and the Future of Civil Society*. Princeton: Princeton University Press.

Vattimo, Giani. 1999. *Belief*. Cambridge: Polity Press.

8

Is there Today Caste System or There is Only Caste in India?

K.L. SHARMA

The question about caste as a 'system' has always remained in vogue as it has been projected mistakenly as a sort of absolute institution relating to prescription and proscription of practice and behaviour of people, particularly among Hindus in Indian society. Available authentic sources indicate that caste system has always been resilient and dynamic as it has been affected by its inner logical inconsistencies and contradictions on the one hand, and it has also affected economy, polity, culture and religion on the other, and due to this dual process, it has never been a static and stagnant system.

In a comprehensive historical analysis of caste, Susan Bayly (2000: 4) rightly states that not a single static system of caste has dominated Indian life since ancient times. Though important scriptural writings have extolled generalized caste ideals. Bayly also mentions that no so-called caste society was formed out of the castelike observances of the medieval realms. Today, manifestations of caste are far more generalized than before. She observes that caste as we now recognize has been endangered, shaped and perpetuated by recent political and social developments. The elements of 'traditional' castes as we know today, Bayly says, have their roots in the early 18th century.

The main objective of this paper is to understand and analyse continuity and change in the caste system as a social force, having varying forms, manifestations and activities. Caste has always engaged people, often directly, with varied functions and obligations. Based on a set of norms, which acquired a sort of meta-legal approval, people have been grouped as *jātis*, and arranged as higher and lower entities.

As Bayly (2000: 1–24) mentions that the British rule significantly expanded and sharpened caste norms and conventions, recreated many manifestations of caste language and ideology as a source of power and authority, Nicholas B. Dirks (2003) also considers caste as a modern political phenomenon, a creation of the British colonialism. Both Bayly and Dirks consider that the powerful colonial state, supported norms and conventions of the caste system. Before the British, there were more of castelike elements rather than a rigid and static caste system. It is due to the British that caste became an effective mechanism and resource for the people across the boundaries of religion, language, faith and economic status. In view of such an understanding of caste, most of the theories of the origin of caste, and also the recent explanation given by Louis Dumont (1972) regarding the principle of pure and impure as the all-embracing theory of caste, do not stand validated. Since caste has its reincarnation in British colonialism, it cannot be explained in terms of the orientalist explanation as well.

Caste is unique in one significant manner that it refers to alliances/linkages among different caste groups in a given village or a setting, hence *jajmani* system or systemic incorporation of different castes in the organic whole. However, different castes also enjoyed a certain degree of autonomy, and this provided them a segmentary character. Caste had thus both organic as well as segmentary character at the same time. Because of this complexity and external political influences, caste has always been a 'contentious' phenomenon. Despite its unique nature, caste is akin to race in America, class in Britain and faction in Italy (Bayly 2000: 1) in terms of a system of social stratification.

Defining Caste as a System

Before we explain in somewhat detail the nature and functioning of the caste system in general, and also in some particular contexts, it may be desirable to mention that within each caste, in principle, all members are equal, but in reality, individuals and families have also been distinguished and differentiated based on their achieved status, despite equal ascribed ritual status, that is, birth in the same caste. Thus, alongwith ritual hierarchy of castes, intra-caste and inter-caste distinctions based on non-ritual criteria, were given due consideration and weightage. Clearly this implies that caste incorporated class, and the congruence of these two further implied inclusion of power in the orbit of caste. Though birth in a given caste could not be mutilated, but at the same time, it did not rule out a noticeable play of extra-caste considerations. Thus, caste was always more than a simple hierarchy based on the notion of 'pure' and 'impure' or a set of values and ideas (Dumont 1972; Srinivas 1952, 1962), which encompassed the entire matrix of socio-economic and political relations.

Even ethnosociologist like Ronald B. Inden (1990: 213–262) is of the view that castes were as political assemblages or 'subject citizenries' within medieval kingdoms. Each region had its specific schemes and groupings, hence no uniform all-embracing scheme of caste gradations. Caste was a dynamic, diverse and multidimensional reality of Indian society. Bayly argues that there is nothing like an orientalist fiction or monolithic cultural code regarding origin and functioning of the caste system (2000: 6). Caste has become a system of oppression, a scheme of social disabilities and hindrances like any other system of inequities.

Today, caste is a reality, though of a different kind. It is a means of political mobilization, of discrete use for specific goals, and more for seeking reservations in educational institutions and government services. Earlier, caste was more of a base for socio-cultural relations enacted through *jajmani* system and rules of marriage and commensality. Education, migration and mobility, secular occupations, office and political power have threatened the 'caste society' to a very large extent.

The propagation of caste system as an absolute and rigid system has done more harm to the Indian society than the caste system itself. Projection of caste as an ideology itself became an ideology of its propagators. This became so, no doubt, even before the advent of British rule in India, however, the British granted an added impetus to both caste and feudalism for the reasons best known to them. Writings by James Tod (1990), Herbert Risley (1969), J.H. Hutton (1963) and many others are a clear evidence of the glorification of feudalism and caste as institutions of highest merit and for good of the Indian people. Such a doctored blasphemy helped the British in pacifying the agitating souls against their rule and also sealed revelation of full facts relating to demerits of the caste system.

The British created two histories: (1) which they desired to create and produce; and (2) which they did not like to be written and desired to remain dormant or dead. For example, at times, the functionaries of lower castes withdrew their services rendered to higher castes when they were not paid their just dues, wages, and rewards. A barber, being dissatisfied, declined to do his job of cutting hair, and other multiple services. So was done by a potter, who refused to supply earthen pots. A carpenter denied supply of ploughs and other wooden implements required in agriculture, when he was dissatisfied with his patrons. Under a hierarchical system, these were the systemic provisions for seeking 'fair justice', if not 'absolute justice'. The concept of 'justice' as explained by John Rawls (1999) is quite appropriate here. After a tug of war, which ensued because of injustice done to the lower caste functionaries, under public pressure and because of non-availability of alternatives to the services rendered to the patrons, often the higher caste patrons acceded to the legitimate demands of their service castes.

While distinguishing between *jāti* and *varna*, R.S. Khare (1983: 85) writes that the concept of *jāti* implies the experience of caste in everyday social life, whereas the concept of *varna* refers to the 'ideal and symbolic archetypes'. Thus, caste is quite specific in its functioning; and *varna* is a loose/vague entity, being the fourfold division of society. *Jāti* identifies its members in a village or in a given specific set of villages. Because of such an identification, caste persists as caste, despite distinctions based on wealth, education and other achievements of its members. Markers of castes are distinct, and not reducible to material, racial, religious and educational differences. This is why upper and lower castes are not necessarily rich and poor classes, respectively. Caste difference is distinct, but it has never been the sole basis of differences in other domains. The following questions emanate from the foregoing discussion:

1. Is caste an all-pervading essence of Indian society?
2. How are the scriptural prescriptions found in everyday life of the people?
3. Is sanskritization not a superficial process of change?

4. What has nearly vanished the pure-impure syndrome from Indian social life?
5. Why have the caste-based occupations almost disappeared?

Despite the pure-impure dichotomy and relational matrix, caste was more than the purity/impurity contention. In caste, power emanated not just from ritualized ranks, it also originated from several other factors, including the nature of work, economic standing, numerical strength and performance of individual members. No doubt, some of the indigenous concepts provided clues for functioning of the Indian society, away from the prescriptions of the scriptural texts, but more important was the actual functioning of the caste system itself. There were always disputes about the order of castes, sometimes even in a given village, there were ambiguous ranks of people. As we have stated earlier that the lower castes, on certain occasions, challenged the upper castes, regarding their rights and claims for the duties which they performed for them as functionaries under the *jajmani* system. Claims, disputes, bargaining, denial and reconciliation were always there in everyday life.

Caste and Non-castelike Phenomena

Another point, also pertinent here, is that ritual hierarchy was not absolute even in principle as it has been made out to be, mainly because of propagation of a certain imagery of the caste system by the British. For example, certain rituals could be performed/completed, which were in the ritual purview of the lower caste functionaries, such as sweepers, shoemakers, barbers, potters, blacksmiths, etc., only when they agreed to render their services. These lower caste ritual performers were treated as 'pious' on given occasions, such as birth, marriage, death, etc., and they were paid customarily like the Brahmin priests. Harold Gould (1967: 26–55) has addressed the lower caste ritual performers as 'contra-priests'. A message of 'equality' in an inequalitarian system is quite implicit through the concept of contra-priests.

In this way, caste system was not absolutely rigid, but flexibility was considerably less than its rigidity. There were mechanisms and devices which prevented openness in the system. It became an insulated system of inter-caste relations. Endogamy and exogamy became the cardinal norms of marriage. Violation of rules of marriage, and deviation from hereditary occupations, and understanding of commensality were taken as an offence, and invited punishment, including ostracization from the caste, heavy fines and hardships. Even today, stray instances of punishment are reported from some parts of India, but the way, in which such punishments are carried out, is quite different from what it used to be. The modalities are very different and so are the motives behind such incidences of the so-called violations, and so are the agencies which take upon themselves to punish the 'offenders'.

Today, inter-caste relations, which were the bedrock of the caste system, do not persist. The hierarchy, which was an overarching phenomenon, has given a way to stratification. Caste has become one of the several other criteria in status-determination. *Jāti* (group) is being replaced by family (Beteille 1998: 435–451; Sharma 1974: 125–168) and individual. The two imply less rigidity, more flexibility, mobility and achievement. Family and individual are also not completely devoid of ascription. Caste is being devalued to a certain extent, and achievement is considered as a desired goal. Values and norms related to caste system have thus shown increasing tendency towards their decline. The system has become considerably weak, it is hardly in existence as it used to be in the beginning of the 20th century or even upto India's independence in 1947. However, caste persists, not as a system so much, but as a means of reckoning and identity-making (Sharma 2001: 17–43). Caste as a system has been 'questioned' and 'interrogated' (Gupta 2000). Then, what is caste? In our view, caste is more of a notion, being appropriated by a select few, eclectically and discretely. The so-called leaders and strongmen of a given caste, appropriate it for their specific aims and gains. It is used/misused as a plaything to have a mileage in community, politics, and to extract monetary benefit, out of the incidences of the so-called violations of the rules of marriage.

Another domain of appropriation of caste is elections at all levels, from Panchayati Raj Institutions (village civic bodies) to Lok Sabha (Lower House of Indian Parliament). Even elections of the Students' Unions are not free from the caste virus, and nor are the trade unions. In all these elections, candidates are nominated by political parties and groups based on caste considerations, particularly in terms of numerical strength of a caste in a given parliamentary/legislative constituency, and the muscle, men and money power of the contesting candidates of particular castes. Jawaharlal Nehru, the first Prime Minister of India, often argued in his public utterances that caste was antithetical to democracy and merit. On the contrary, some scholars are of the view that caste is not against democracy and development (Kothari 1970a, 1970b). It is argued that caste-based nomination has a representative character, because an elected person would care for the interests and welfare of those fellowmen who have voted for him/her.

Caste as a system needs to be seen in terms of the ideology of pure and impure, division of labour, connubiality, commensality, caste panchayat or *biradari*, intra-caste and inter-caste relations, etc. Caste as a phenomenon and as a notion of reckoning can be observed in political mobilization, atrocities, violence, exploitation, etc. In a nutshell, the journey is though several centuries old, transformation of its systemic character into a discrete phenomenon is particularly a 20th century incarnation, and that too, mainly after India's independence, in 1947. In view of these observations, K.L. Sharma (2001: 17–43) has suggested a comprehensive study of caste with a view to understand: (1) caste-class nexus: its continuity and change, (2) changing character of inter-caste and intra-caste relations, and (3) nature of practice and levels of mobility in the caste system.

Caste and the State

Caste and the Indian state have co-existed, and the latter has tried to twist and mutilate caste in innumerable ways. This was done more so by the British rule (Bayly 2000; Dirks 2003). The 1891 Census used the headings for social groups such as 'agricultural and pastoral', 'artisans and menials', 'professionals', and even 'vagrants'. Rankings were made based on local evidence of 'social precedence'. Earlier, in the 1881 Census, illustrated profiles of over 400 'races' and 'tribes' were presented. 'Orientalism' was clearly reflected in these census reports and in the 119-volume series of Imperial Gazetteers. 'Titles', 'races', 'stereotypes', and expressions such as 'civilized/uncivilized' were used in the context of caste. The Indian people were described as irrational, violent, childlike, morally underdeveloped, etc. The 1901 Census was the first one to evoke fierce controversies as it ranked all castes in terms of specific *varṇa* context. Determining caste rank in terms of ritual distance throughout the country was done with a political end in view.

Besides this, H.H. Risley (1969), the Census Commissioner for the 1901 Census, also described some other categories, such as 'casteless tribes' and 'landed, trading, military and priestly castes'.

However, such a statist view of the caste was negated by some other surveys and studies. For example, Denzil Ibbetson (2000) vividly describes diversity and historicity in the making of caste. He is of the view that no generalized view of a uniform 'caste society' could be found. The rural areas of Punjab had distinctively non-'castelike' features. Norms and values of caste were found in different ways in different regional settings. Caste was dynamic and fluid, and material and political factors shaped the differences of *jāti* and *varṇa* in different regional settings. In Punjab, half of the population comprised of landowners, cultivators and pastoralists in the late 19th century. Power and land control were the main bases of status. Society was quite open, and differences were of a fluid nature.

We have argued that caste is largely a creation of British colonialism, an instrument of British domination in terms of its policy of divide and rule. Caste was ritualized and hierarchized by the British by transforming the non-castelike elements into rigid ritualized phenomena. This was particularly done by H.H. Risley through 1901 Census. He worked out an index of ritual distance between castes/sub-castes and placed then in a rank order, assigning higher and lower ranks. This process of politicization/statization of caste was further carried forward by J.H. Hutton in the census of 1931, of which he was the Commissioner. Hutton eulogized caste by exaggerating its positive aspects (functions), which he pronounced as beneficial for the individual member of a caste, for his family, community, wider society and the entire state. The views voiced by Risley (1969) and Hutton (1963) gave credence to the caste as a system of hierarchy and social relations. The census of 1941 was not a comprehensive one due to the ill-effects of the Second World War (1939–1945).

The first post-independence census, conducted in 1951, did not include enumeration of caste, except counting of the Scheduled Castes (SCs) and the Scheduled Tribes (STs). From 1951 to 2001, six censuses have been conducted without enumeration of caste, though caste has remained at the centre of Indian politics. Caste-based reservations were given to the Other Backward Castes (OBCs) in 1993, based on the recommendations of the B.P. Mandal

Commission (1978–1980), through a decision of the Supreme Court of India, in which 'caste' was accepted as the basis of 'backwardness' of some communities, including the SCs and the OBCs. During the Mandalization process, through intense debates, opinions were expressed in favour and against caste as the basis of reservation. It took quite sometime in settling down the turmoil caused by the acceptance of the Mandal Commission recommendations by the V.P. Singh government for reservation of 27 per cent jobs for the OBCs.

The present United Progressive Alliance (UPA) government also introduced reservations in the Central government's educational institutes, including Indian Institutes of Technology (IITs), Indian Institutes of Management (IIMs), Indian Institute of Science (IIS), All India Institutes of Medical Sciences (AIIMSs), and the prestigious universities, such as Jawaharlal Nehru University, Delhi University, Banaras Hindu University, etc. Protests to this move was quite severe as it was said to be throttling of merit against the so-called caste-based social justice plank in educational institutions. Thus, it is not that only the colonial state used caste as a political instrument, this has persisted during the post-independence period as well, almost in all walks of life, including elections, reservations and socio-cultural mobilizations.

The UPA government seems to be inclined to use caste as a political tool more or less on the lines of British colonialism, perhaps under the influence of the regional parties, such as Janata Dal United (JDU), Rashtriya Janata Dal (RJD) and Samajwadi Party (SP), headed by the three Yadavs, namely, Sharad Yadav, Lalu Prasad Yadav and Mulayam Singh Yadav, respectively. The UPA government's inclination to enumerate castes/sub-castes/sub-sub-castes in the 2011 Census once again reminds us of the 1901 and the 1931 caste-based censuses and the Mandal Commission and its aftermath in 1990–93. In the aftermath of the acceptance of the Mandal Commission recommendations, several young people, particularly from among the upper castes, who protested against it, were killed and injured in police and paramilitary actions. There were also strong supporters of the Mandal Commission. Across the country, one could see a clear social and political divide on the Mandal issue.

The inclusion of caste enumeration in the 2011 Census would certainly generate more or less the similar mixed reactions, and the actors in this game are also more or less of the same sort. Why the present government has suddenly decided to consider incorporation of 'caste' in the 2011 Census? How would it be done? In what way would castes, sub-castes, sub-sub-castes in different regions, sub-regions, districts and villages be recorded? How would the similar castes with different names, and different castes with similar names across the regions be identified and recorded? Can simple caste enumeration, without relating it to each and every individual and family, economic standing, nature of occupations, assets, education, and ritual criteria, etc., be useful for accelerating the process of social justice and development? It is that caste is information in knowledge society? Can caste be an index of solidarity? We are raising these questions because some have opined these views in favour of enumeration of caste. The protagonists of these views argue that caste has power. Caste is a code of behaviour. It enforces a range of behaviour, including rules of marriage as in a khap panchayat. Caste creates the grammar of interaction (Visvanathan 2010). Caste is the grid of familiarity and of survival. Caste is an instrument of the division of labour in society. Such an admiration of caste is a contradiction in terms, when we find 'caste wars', and exploitation of the poor of the lower castes by the upper caste landowning families. The inhuman and cruel diktats of khaps, particularly in Haryana and Western Uttar Pradesh, are examples of the oppression of the weak by the self-appointed caste leaders. None of the victims of the khaps are top political leaders and the rich people, who have often violated the rules of marriage, namely, caste endogamy and clan exogamy.

In another newspaper article (Chandra 2010), the incorporation of enumeration of caste in the 2011 Census is stated as 'a way of reinventing identities', because 'a caste census can widen options for self-definition instead of narrowing them'. Kanchan Chandra also raises the questions: How to do it? How to know inequalities based on caste? These are relevant questions raised by Kanchan Chandra. But then we may ask: Why not count only the poor and then relate them to their caste/sub-caste? Does caste today determine inequalities? To what extent has caste changed since independence, despite 'caste wars' and caste-based reservations? Are all members/or a substantial section of a caste or of different castes 'backward'/poor or forward and well off? How to segregate the poor and the well off within the given castes/sub-castes? The problem today is to relate economic and social inequalities with caste/sub-caste, and not that of caste with economic and social disparities. What we need is to see several socio-economic segments in a given caste or a cluster of castes. Caste, as such, does not remain absolute or monolithic. It needs to be seen as an internally differentiated entity. Greater is the extent of differentiation, lesser becomes the relevance of caste as a determining factor in socio-economic inequalities.

Caste-based census would raise several questions and problems relating to identities, social precedence, politics and development. Kanchan Chandra (2010) rightly observes: 'The main question raised by the prospect of a caste-based census is not whether to collect census data based on caste but how to do it in a way that does not trap citizens in caste identities'. Can caste-based data be used to address inequalities based on caste? Claims and counter-claims for higher/equal ranks would be made on the one hand, and claims for the ranks which could perhaps accrue more benefits, by way of reservations/quotes, would be made on the other. As we know the British rule first created a situation of divide, and then intervened after the 1901 Census, when people questioned their ranks, and then the British granted decrees in some cases. What would the present government do in case of similar confusions, ambiguities, claims and counter-claims? Without addressing such likely problems, arising out of the caste-based census, the 2011 caste-based census would be of no use and could cause irreparable damage to the Indian society. People would be further trapped in the caste tangles. The loosening ends of caste would be rejuvenated and reinvented, if the situation comparable with the 1901 and the 1931 censuses occurs again after the 2011 Census. Chandra rightly asks: 'How can a caste-based census in India avoid setting its own identity traps? The 'caste parties', like the BSP, the SP and the RJD, have made several experiments of caste constructions/alliances in terms of 'backward' and 'forward' entities. They are now celebrating the incorporation of caste in the 2011 Census, because their gameplan for 'caste-based politics' seems to get a new life.

Dipankar Gupta (2010) says that inclusion of enumeration of castes in the 2011 Census is 'against citizens' of India, because 'the Census is in service of the future and not to serve past prejudices of sectional interests'. Citizenship needs to be valued more than caste and family, Gupta says, 'As citizens we do not need caste but we need development, growth, employment and clear air'. Caste is divisive, caste is against caste. 'Caste politicians' and 'caste academia' are on the same side of the coin. After the 2011 Census, there would be endless quarrels and claims for ranks and classifications which would suit for benefits in regard to education, jobs, and elections. It seems that the political leaders are competing with each other as patrons to seek support of the people in general, and of the rural people in particular. By supporting the inclusion of caste as an item in the census, they would project themselves as the saviors of the rural people, as particular castes would be there in the lists of beneficiary castes.

Caste and Electoral Politics: The Case of Rajasthan

A recent example of a nexus between politics and caste can be cited from Rajasthan, a north-western state in India. Amazing and bewildering scenes and situations were innumerable in the latest elections held in 2009 for Rajasthan Assembly. These tantamounted to a mockery of Indian democracy and the Indian state. In the history of elections, since independence, such a vulgar political scenario was witnessed for the first time. Let us cite some instances of the political vulgarization which were not only having devastating effects, but also had long-term and incurable imprints on Indian polity and society.

All the major political parties unhesitatingly admitted caste/casteism as the main criterion in nominating their candidates. In fact, the idea of winnability of a candidate had been mooted based on the supposed and fabricated numerical preponderance and support to a nominee in the constituency. Most of the aspirants for nomination presented the exaggerated numerical preponderance of their respective castes and communities. Neither the aspirants nor their political parties articulated and voiced the criteria for nomination such as commitment to ideology and programmes of development and change, and educational qualifications, professions, personal honesty and integrity, social work, etc.

Almost all castes and communities, including Brahmins, Rajputs, Vaishyas, Jains, Jats, Bairwas, Valmikis, Gujars, Meenas, Nais, Sindhis, Muslims, etc., had demanded their particular share in political representation through nomination. All these castes and communities expressed their resolve to mobilize support for the parties which would nominate their respective caste leaders. Issues of nationalism, democracy and secularism were not raised in the elections as it was the case in the general elections of 1952, 1957 and 1962. Issues relating to communalism, terrorism, unemployment, economic regression, corruption, and socio-economic backwardness had also been relegated to the background.

Besides casteism, considerations of kinship and nepotism were also advocated openly in nomination of candidates by the major political parties. Daughters, sons, wives, nephews, nieces and relatives were promoted based on their 'winnability'. Obviously, they were said to be 'capable' because of their ancestry and kinship ties with the political leadership of the state.

Such an electoral game has raised several questions about the Indian state and society. The state is unable to check this electoral malice, and the society, particularly the masses, due to their perennial incompetence, cannot stop this malady. The masses need leadership, and the leaders, taking undue advantage of this fact, become oligarchic, and develop greed for power.

Since India has a low level of development and asymmetrical structure of economic and cultural resources, its social base (caste and community) tends to orient itself for undeserving political acts and opinions. A caste leader becomes an oligarch, he does not delegate authority to leaders and workers down the line in his/her political party. A sort of opinion is created in favour of a leader based on his/her power, influence and social circles. Such a superimposed aura is a gross misrecognition of the masses and their capabilities. Ideology, education, honesty and integrity, etc., were not at all there in the electoral speeches and discourses in the elections held in 2009 for the State Legislature in Rajasthan. The issue of 'development' came up in a mutilated and ambivalent form, and therefore, it did not become the focal theme in these elections.

The questions which we may ask are: What is political representation? Who are represented? Can masses question political oligarchy and its material interests? Are the downtrodden united in their efforts to challenge the power elite? Answers to these questions lie in the fact that the nominees are the so-called caste/community patrons/protectors, kinsmen of top political bosses, favourites of the high commands of political parties, etc.

Caste-based political nominations would not provide 'accomplished politicians', who could create a high degree of euphemization of debates and discourses on issues of development, democracy, secularism, social justice, human rights, etc. What we have today is extreme vulnerability of political power due to uncertainty of its retention. Politicians, therefore, try to retain their power, and transform it into social and cultural resources. Further, this resource is appropriated for reinforcing the political power. Thus, a political leader is today more of a 'banker' rather than a social worker. Such a leader also gains a personal notoriety. A political party with such entrenched leaders remains with a well-filled treasury, and as such a party represents the established social/caste interests.

Caste and Rules of Marriage

The so-called purity of descent/caste or sub-caste is being reinvented by punishing the same clan marriages. A province in India, namely, Haryana, has attained notoriety in 'honour killings' of young men and women on the pretext of violation of rules of marriage. The perpetrators of such a heinous crime have become self-appointed *thekedars* (protectors) of honour of their castes/communities. Their advertent or inadvertent ignorance of the rules of marriage, namely, caste endogamy and clan exogamy is clearly evident in such barbarous inhuman acts in the mischievously assumed notion of purity of descent or blood group. The killing of Virender Singh (*The Times of India*, 28 October 2009) is thus one more instance of Haryana's cruel orthodoxy and cognitive blindness. For such a horrifying situation in Haryana, which is, otherwise not so backward, at least in the field of agriculture, proves that economic development does not necessarily result into social development and awakening. Men of letters, social workers and politicians are mainly responsible for such a grave crime. Sometimes, the 'violators' are inhumanly tortured to such an extent that they feel compelled to commit suicide. The people ought to know the meaning of 'clan exogamy' and rules of avoidance, relating to marriage. Such a tendency is today a new form of caste-related orthodoxy in rural India.

Generally, hypergamous marriages are enacted in India, in which the status of the bridegroom is higher socially than that of the bride. Such a custom is known as *anuloma*. The opposite to this type is called hypogamous marriages or *pratiloma*. Besides the consideration of higher and lower status, clan exogamy is considered as a criterion in Hindu marriages. A clan or gotra is an exogamous unit assuming descendence from a common ancestor. A given caste would have several gotras as exogamous units. Each gotra has a name, and each individual supposedly belongs to a specific gotra. Some castes/sub-castes could have common gotra names also. Often, the gotra names are drawn from the Brahmanical system and from the rishis (religious teachers), authors of sacred texts. Adherence to the rule of gotra exogamy is found among Brahmins more than the middle and lower castes.

J.H. Hutton in *Caste in India* (1963) observes that the exogamous group within the endogamous caste or subcaste is very far from being a stable institution of consistent pattern. In fact, marriage is often regulated by prohibited degrees of kinship. The actual number of prohibited degrees varies from caste to caste as it depends upon the number of gotras in a given caste. There are also single gotra castes/sub-castes and the rule of clan exogamy becomes irrelevant to such castes. Avoidance of the gotras of father, mother, grandmother, and maternal grandmother, etc., is also based on the assumed names of the gotras. What one can know is lineage, that is, the line of descendence, and nothing beyond lineage is empirically known to the people. It is almost impractical to know lineage history beyond five or six generations.

Exogamous restrictions are observed in regard to sib, totem, village, gotra or spinda relationships. These criteria clearly indicate obscurantism or unscientific thinking in mate selection. K.M. Kapadia (1986: 117–135), a well-known authority on marriage, observes that there is nothing in the sanskrit texts to object to clan endogamy. Marriage into the third generation or preferential marriage within the affines was prevalent even in 11th century A.D. Marriage was allowed within the same gotra or between those who recited the same *pravara* (mantra). Kapadia says: 'Manu did not likewise regard sagotra marriage as constituting a sin, serious or minor' (ibid.: 127). Thus, Manu's rule of exogamy was loose and elastic. Some commentators linked gotra and pravara, but its observance became a mere formality. It did not have substantial bearing on realities of life.

Based on such a mythological construction of the gotra and other related conceptions, caste panchayats, clan leaders and the bullies within the given castes in the villages have taken upon themselves to regulate rules of marriage. The law of the land has been suppressed by such ill-practised institutions and notorious individuals with a view to extract political and social mileage out of the present-day ambivalence and flux in the Indian society. Some people have made it a source of social and political power. Control over the community by hook and crook has become their creed. The so-called *thekedars* of caste and community have established nexus with politicians and bureaucrats to enhance their reputation and dominance through such acts. Thus, caste is more of a political phenomenon in the countryside than a basis of inter-group relations.

This is an opaque culturology. Continuity of conventional cultural conceptualizations or their renewed versions are antithetical to true democracy. Caste has lost its base, namely, inter-caste relations, interdependence and work ethics, but its penetration into politics or its discrete appropriation (or misuse) in social fields are clearly indicative of a disjunction and dissonance in India's social life.

As politics is becoming a 'family business', so is becoming monopoly/control or regulation of the so-called rules of marriage. An absolutely unscientific idea of the mythological *sagotra* is being projected as a pious act, simply for self-aggrandizement. Common people cannot stop this decadent practice because the rule of might prevails in the village. The state and the civil society (including social workers) may check such happenings with a firm hand. Since most of the preparators remain unpunished, they look for the so-called violations to occur for making a fortune out of such happenings.

A very recent example of politics of caste and violation of clan exogamy is the view expressed by a young Congress Member of Parliament, Naveen Jindal, from Haryana, who is a tycoon and a graduate of the University of Texas Business School (Gupta 2010). Jindal supported the Khap's diktat for prohibition on same gotra marriage. Legally, such a prohibition cannot be sustained. Scientifically, in ten generations, genetic roots would disappear. Culturally, gotra is an assumed or mythological name assigned since times immemorial to a so-called caste/sub-caste. How, then, the *sagotra* marriages can be prohibited? On the contrary, there are communities which have preferential first cousin marriages, and a lot of prestige and premium are attached to such marriages. Are politicians doing hobnobbing with such issues to get a political mileage? What is a khap? Who constitute it? How does it function? Khap is a sort of panchayat (court) of a caste or a sub-caste, whose members are the so-called elders in a given village or a set of villages (Chaukhala). The traditional caste panchayat in rural India used to help its weak and poor families, particularly in meeting expenses on marriages and in agricultural activities, including ploughing and harvesting of crops. It used to punish/ostracize the violators of caste ethics, but at the same as a champion of brotherhood, it was always there to support its members to bridge the gap between the strong and the weak. The idea of *biradari* (community) connotes *barabari* (equality). The khap as a panchayat has assumed only punitive functions, ignoring the basic tenet of community/equality. The fear of genetic disorder is falsely propagated for some ulterior motives, including power, money and social status. The khap diktat is an onslaught on freedom of individuals. It is anti-democracy and anti-social justice.

In *India Today* (24 May 2010), Dipankar Gupta, a well-known sociologist, observes: 'Sadly, some of our elected leaders who blinded us by their demonstrations of modernity, have turned out to be closet traditionalists, or just plain political cowards. Many of those who we thought were young, bright and energetic, have already thrown in the towel and given in to traditional casteists'. Gupta makes this observation on Jindal's support to the khap diktat on *sagotra* marriages. Is the khap an example of functioning of the caste system? Where is the caste system as the bedrock of inter-group social relations? Khap is not even a caste panchayat in a proper sense. Caste panchayat is a persisting and regular phenomenon. Khap is ad hoc, constructed sporadically and episodically, hence it has no systemic character. Anyway, khap claims to stand/represent as a body of a caste/sub-caste. Once again, we may reiterate that there is only 'caste', without the caste system. And we need to understand the 'caste' as it exists in this form.

Social Mobility: Individual and Family

In my study of six villages in Rajasthan (Sharma 1974: 125–168), I have analysed three levels of mobility in caste structure, that is, of a family, of a group, and of an individual. In no case, mobility of an entire group, that is, of a caste/sub-caste was evident. At none of the three levels, mobility was there in equal measure. Mobility of members of a given family was attributed to the family, but it did not engage all the members in the act/process of mobility in an equal measure. When a noticeable number of families moved upward, socially, economically or politically, it was commonly referred as caste mobility. Such a misnomer of caste/group mobility persists even today, though no efforts, by a *jāti*/group as such, are there in sight. No doubt, family facilitates mobility of its potentially capable members, concrete instances are that of mobility of individuals in any given context.

Social mobility has brought about intra-family, intra-caste and inter-caste status-distinctions and cleavages, which are neither determined by ritualistic considerations, nor they have created a new ritual hierarchy. Class-like differences of a high magnitude could be seen today in a given caste due to multifarious mobility of its individual members and families. Resultant social distinctions from mobility have significantly weakened hereditary occupations, connubiality, and commensality. Let us make it clear here that no uniform pattern of mobility is evident among different castes, families and individuals, and it is not in congruence with the traditional caste hierarchy or with the notion of pure and impure. Downward mobility of some families and groups from among the higher castes, and upward mobility of the previously disadvantaged families and *jāti*, are a stark reality of the present system of social stratification (Sharma 1974, 1997).

Increasing emphasis on the study of structural aspects of caste exposes the preeminence of caste as a unique cultural phenomenon, and brings out analytic and empiric distinctions between caste, class and power. Beyond caste, lies caste-class nexus and its ramifications, negating 'caste alone' approach to the study of Indian society. Earlier regarding caste, I have observed: 'Increasingly, caste is becoming a desideratum, a state of mind, a plastic and malleable institution. No more hypersymbolization is manifest to express caste differences and typifications on a continuing basis' (Sharma 2001: 7–8). Though, the 'essential' of caste is largely delegitimized, yet some sporadic caste-based pronouncements and religious and metaphysical interpretations of caste and its divinity pose a challenge to secularism and democracy in Indian society.

Alongwith the role played by family and individual in weakening of the caste system, political and economic factors have contributed immensely in shaping the dynamics of Indian society. Historian Irfan Habib (1995: 161–179) strongly denounces Louis Dumont's theory of caste as Homo Hierarchicus (Dumont 1972). Habib observes: 'The caste system, in its classical form, could therefore function with as much ease in a natural economy as in a market-oriented one. In either case, it helped essentially to maintain not a fabric of imagined purity (if it did, this was incidental), but a system of class exploitation as rigorous as any other'. In medieval India, caste system remained a means of a system of class exploitation, and the British colonized the caste system by their policy of 'divide and rule', and by propagating the norms of social distance. The census of 1901 by Herbert Risley (1969) and the census of 1931 by J.H. Hutton (1963) are unambiguous examples of sheer politicization of caste by the British.

Some western scholars, namely, Louis Dumont (1972), McKim Marriott (1989), Ronald B. Inden (1990) and Akos Ostor (1984) have advocated a renewed culturological approach to the study of caste in particular. Emphasis is on application of ethnosociology and use of indigenous concepts and categories, with a view to revive the understanding of caste as a cultural aspect of Indian society. Those who distance from such a rejuvenated culturology, their view is that caste needs to be studied in the context of its setting and surroundings. For example, Dipankar Gupta (2000: 224–264) pleads emphatically for an inter-subjective sociology/anthropology against typification to study the caste system. He is of the view that castes need to be seen as discrete entities, being all abiding and durable identities. Gupta also looks for 'individual' in caste, as we did look for 'family' and 'individual', and Andre Beteille did look for 'family'. According to Gupta, individuals interrogate their own social existence, reflect on it, and maximize their options. By locating 'individual' in caste, Gupta reinforces our earlier hypothesis of 'levels of mobility' in caste structure (Sharma 1974), and demythologize the rigid and closed supersymbolizations, typifications and binary oppositions as vehemently proposed by Louis Dumont. Received knowledge and socio-cultural recipes are being questioned increasingly by 'individual'.

Attempts towards Reconceptualization of Caste

The main motive behind these points is to see how and to what extent ideas and values are basic for knowing actual and observable behaviour of people. To what extent Louis Dumont's thesis of special type of inequality based on caste system is in practice? We have mentioned earlier that the idea of pure and impure is central to Dumont's notion of caste hierarchy. But in our view, caste is in class and in other systems of social stratification, hence taxonomic problem persists relating to the distinction of caste from other stratificatory systems. Elsewhere, I have stated: 'Caste is increasingly becoming a matter of interpretation rather than substantialization. Caste refers to a purposive rationality, and at the same time, it provides a description and explanation of the pathologies of modern polity and economy. It is no more an absolutized system as it was characterized by punitive acts like ostracisation and social neglect. Caste obstructs, which occur occasionally by a way of killings and torture of the violators of caste ethics, are incongruent with the dwindling of the caste system in recent times' (Sharma 2001: 7).

Secondly, cliches, such as tradition and modernity, continuity and change, hierarchy and stratification, organic and segmentary structures, have led to unfounded dichotomies/antinomies of a resilient and harmonic society. A continued emphasis on caste as a homo hierarchicus, culture-bound and change-resisting system (Dumont 1972) has undermined the very semblance of continuity and change. However, the encompassing capability of caste system has been questioned by several scholars, including Ram Krishna Mukherjee (1957), Andre Beteille (1966: 224–246; 1969: 219–235), K.L. Sharma (1974), and Dipankar Gupta (2000). Beteille has focused on the emergence of 'differentiated institutional structures of various kinds', and the role of 'interests' along with ideas, in shaping of social stratification. Further, he observes that a new 'caste-free occupational structure' and modern education have created a non-traditional basis of social relations, weaking intercaste and intracaste relations. Gupta is of the view that ultimately 'individual' matters a lot in the caste system.

A reconceptualization of caste system is clearly evident in the notions such as 'multiple status hierarchies', 'attributional' criteria of caste ranking, 'new castes', 'levels of social mobility', 'downward social mobility', 'obverse structural process of social change', 'structural criteria of dominance', 'new status images', etc. (Sharma 1974, 1977, 1980, 2010). These are expressions and articulations relating to change of the conventional constructions and orientations. Obviously, there is today a new discourse in vogue reflecting distantiation from caste as the basis of social relations and stratification by the alert and articulate sections of the upper, middle, and even the erstwhile depressed sections.

Thirdly, we also see a revival of a culturological framework (Marriott 1989) to look once again at the Indian society through caste and religious categories. Such an approach considerably underrates the relevance of structural criteria in effecting change in the caste system. Historical and contextual contexts (Singh 1994: 28–59) of change cannot be sidelined in understanding of the changing face of inter-caste and intra-caste relations and emergence of individual and family as more effective institutions and units of social stratification. When caste becomes weak, then family and individual emerge as stronger agencies of reproduction of equality and inequality. The two, separately as well as in conjunction, attack the traditional impediments to social mobility, and become significant units of status evaluation.

Thus, 'caste for itself' and caste as an everyday life phenomenon are two different aspects, generally unrelated to each other. In the first case, caste is an episodic, metaphoric and goal-oriented phenomenon; and in the second sense, it is a discrete, personalized, and family-specific behavioural/interactional phenomenon. Both the interpretations are not in tune with the 'caste model' (Beteille 1966: 224–246) of Indian society. Caste-free relations, new patterns of alliances and configurations across biradaries, levels of mobility, downward mobility, etc., are reflected in new status dynamics and power equations. However, discrete use of caste identity, as a resource in mundane personal spheres, and as a symbolic entity in not-so-essential social domains, remains a reality of our social life.

Caste as a Phenomenon and not as a System

Thus, in our view, caste is becoming more of a state of mind of an individual rather than continuing as an ideology, directing collective actions and practices. A pre-given ideology is being questioned for caste identity and mobilization. In her comprehensive analysis, Susan Bayly (2000) argues that caste has been for many centuries a real and active part of Indian life, and not just a self-serving orientalist fiction. Contemporary political and social developments have shaped it. Bayly adopts a middle path as she is of the view that caste is not reducible to the realm of imagination or discourse. Caste or caste-like identities have been there in changing and often threatening circumstances. The titles, symbols, and lifestyles of caste have proved to be remarkably durable and adaptable. Thus, according to Bayly, caste is neither an orientalist fiction nor a shameful crime to be disguised or ignored in discussing India's history. 'Caste is not and never has been a fixed fact of Indian life' (ibid.: 25).

Caste has been made and remade over a long period of time. Fluidity of caste has existed and persisted because of India's remarkable cultural diversity and physical environment, and the diversity of its states (provinces) and political systems. A sequence of complex but intelligible changes in Indian life have brought about changes in India's religion, state power and material environment. Caste is not just a coded way of communication or expression of differences in power and wealth. It is also not giving way to purely class-based social differences. It needs to be understood against the background of India's political and social experiences, that is, patterns of statecraft, religion and economic life (ibid.: 366–367).

Why caste has become for so many the core symbol of community in India? Nicholas B. Dirks (2003) addresses this question quite differently compared to Susan Bayly's analysis. Dirks explains that caste is not some single system that reflects a core civilizational value, and not a basic expression of Indian tradition. According to Dirks, caste is a modern phenomenon, that, it is, specifically, the product of an historical encounter between India and western colonial rule. Dirks writes: 'It was under the British rule that "caste" became a single term capable of expressing, organizing, and above all, "systematizing" India's diverse forms of social identity, community, and organization' (ibid.). He further states: 'In short, colonialism made caste what it is today' (ibid.). Caste has been continuously reinvented. Under colonialism, it was made out to be far more pervasive, far more totalizing, and far more uniform, and was made a fundamentally religious order.

Dirks considers caste as a political phenomenon in the British as well the post-British periods. Today, it is denied and accepted at the same time. Caste groups are asking for creation of social conditions essential for their development and progress. However, in everyday life caste has become nearly non-existent and passive. Recent incidences of the so-called violation of rules of marriage present a horrifying picture of caste in some parts of India. A couple of times, for example, in the state of Haryana and Western Uttar Pradesh, some self-appointed 'caste leaders' have punished the violators of the rules of marriage, that is, caste endogamy and clan exogamy. Obscurantism, orthodoxy, cognitive blindness, inhuman and cruel acts, emanating from the punitive actions against the so-called violators, reflect a totally blurred and opaque picture of the caste system.

Another manifestation of 'caste' is observable in congregations of *biradaris* (*Jāti Samaj*). Today, a couple of the so-called leaders of the upper castes have been engaged in mobilization of support of their fellowmen for political gains, in the name of realization of the demands, such as reservation, as it is available to the SCs, the STs, the OBCs, etc. The B.P. Mandal Commission's Report (1978–80) and its acceptance by the Government of India drastically changed the Indian political scene in 1991–92. Aftereffects of the Mandalization of Indian politics can be seen even today after two decades in the caste-based mobilizations for reservation by the upper castes, and in the demand for inclusion by some castes in the categories of the OBCs/STs/SCs.

While concluding this paper, we agree with Ishita Banerjee-Dube (2008: XV) as she observes: 'Caste, elusive yet enduring, retains a critical importance as concept and practice in India today'. Caste has really a diverse and chequered career in history of India. Caste has become an imprecise and vague phenomenon. Today, caste is an episodic expression and articulation rather than a systemic institution. It is not, therefore, seen in everyday life. Because of such a blurring nature of caste, manipulations for its appropriation have surfaced, and its social and cultural fabric has been relegated to the background. Caste as an ideology of pure and impure is redundant in the present-day India.

REFERENCES

Banerjee-Dube, Ishita. 2008. 'Introduction: Questioning of Caste', in Ishita Banerjee-Dube (ed.), *Caste in History*. New Delhi: Oxford University Press, pp. XC–LXIV.

Bayly, Susan. 2000. *Caste, Society and Politics in India*. Cambridge: Cambridge University Press (First Indian Edition).

Beteille, Andre. 1966. *Caste, Class and Power*. Bombay: Oxford University Press.

——. 1966. 'Closed and Open Social Stratification in India', *European Journal of Sociology*, Vol. VII: 224–246.

——. 1969. 'Ideas and Interests: Some Conceptual Problems in the Study of Social Stratification in India', *International Social Science Journal*, Vol. 21, No. 7: 17–31.

——. 1998. 'The Reproduction of Inequality: Occupation, Caste and Family', in Patricia Uberoi (ed.), *Family, Kinship and Marriage in India*. Delhi: Oxford University Press, pp. 435–451.

Census of India 1891. Vol. I. General Report, by J.A. Baines, London, 1893.

Census of India 1901. Vol. I, Part I. Report, by H.H. Risley and E.A. Gait, Calcutta, 1903. Risley published the volume—*The Peoples of India* (1909) based on the data of this Census.

Census of India 1931. Vol. I. Part III. Ethnographic Section, by J.H. Hutton, Simla, 1935. Hutton published the book—*Caste in India* (1948) based on the data of this Census.

Chandra, Kanchan. 2010. 'A Way of Reinventing Identities: A Caste Census can Widen Options for Self-definition Instead of Narrowing Them', *The Times of India*, 25 May.

Dirks, Nicholas B. 2003. *Castes of Mind: Colonialism and the Making of Modern India*. Delhi: Permanent Black.

Dumont, Louis. 1972. *Homo Hierarchicus: The Caste System and its Implications*. London: Paladin, Granda Publishing Limited.

Gould, Harold A. 1967. 'Priest and Contrapriest: A Structural Analysis of Jajmani Relationships in the Hindu Plains and the Nilgiri Hills', *Contributions to Indian Sociology*, New Series 1: 26–55.

Gupta, Dipankar. 2000. *Interrogating Caste: Understanding Hierarchy and Difference in Indian Society*. New Delhi: Penguin Books.

——. 2010. 'Caste against Citizens', *India Today*, 24 May.

Habib, Irfan. 1995. *Essays in Indian History: Towards a Marxist Perception*. New Delhi: Tulika.

Hutton, J.H. 1963. *Caste in India: Its Nature, Functions and Origin*. Bombay: Oxford University Press.

Ibbetson, Denzil. 2000. 'Punjab Castes', quoted from S. Bayly, *Caste, Society and Politics in India*. Cambridge: Cambridge University Press, pp. 138–143.

Imperial Gazetteers of India. 119 Volumes, quoted from S. Bayly, 2000. *Caste, Society and Politics in India*. Cambridge: Cambridge University Press, p. 123.

Inden, Ronald B. 1990. *Imagining India*. Oxford: Basil Blackwell Ltd.

India Today. 2010. 'The Caste Curse' (Cover Story Census), 24 May: 24–34.

Kapadia, K.M. 1986. *Marriage and Family in India*. Oxford: Oxford University Press.

Kanchan, Chandra. 2010. 'A Way of Reinventing Identities', *The Times of India*, 25 May.

Khare, R.S. 1983. *Normative Culture and Kinship: Essays on Hindu Categories, Processes and Perspectives*. New Delhi: Oxford University Press.

Kothari, Rajni. 1970a. *Politics in India*. New Delhi: Orient Longman Ltd.

Kothari, Rajni (ed.). 1970b. *Caste in Indian Politics*. New Delhi: Orient Longman Ltd.

Mandal, B.P. 1978–80. *The Backward Classes Commission*. New Delhi: Government of India.

Marriott, McKim (ed.). 1989. *India Through Hindu Categories*. New Delhi: Sage Publications.

Mukherjee, R.K. 1957. *The Dynamics of a Rural Society*. Berlin: Academie Verlag.

Ostor, Akos. 1984. *Culture and Power: Legend, Ritual, Bazaar and Rebellion in a Bengali Society*. New Delhi: Sage Publications.

Rawls, John. 1999. *A Theory of Justice* (Revised ed.). Oxford: Oxford University Press.

Risley, Herbert H. (1909) 1969. *The Peoples of India* (2nd ed.). Delhi: Orient Books.

Sharma, K.L. 1974. *The Changing Rural Stratification System*. New Delhi: Orient Longman.

——. 1977. 'New Introduction', in J. Murdoch, *Review of Caste in India*. Jaipur: Rawat Publications.

——. 1980. *Essays on Social Stratification*. Jaipur: Rawat Publications.

——. 1997. *Social Stratification in India: Issues and Themes*. New Delhi: Sage Publications.

——. 2001. *Reconceptualising Caste, Class and Power*. Jaipur: Rawat Publications.

——. 2010. *Perspectives on Social Stratification*. Jaipur and New Delhi: Rawat Publications.

Singh, Yogendra. 1994. *Modernisation of Indian Tradition*. Jaipur: Rawat Publications.

Srinivas, M.N. 1952. *Religion and Society among the Coorgs of South India*. Oxford: Clarendon Press.

——. 1962. *Caste in Modern India and Other Essays*. Delhi: Oxford University Press.

The Times of India. 2009. 28 October.

——. 2010. Editorial: 'Tackling Caste, Time to Swing the Pendulum towards Universalist Policies' and 'A Dangerous Step Backwards: Giving into the Khap Panchayats could Legalise Caste Divisions', by Mary E. John, 28 May.

Tod, James. (1829) 1990. *Annals and Antiquities of Rajasthan* (3 Vols). Delhi: Low Price Publications.

Visvanathan, Shiv. 2010 'Caste is Information in Knowledge Society', *The Times of India*, 16 May.

9

Between Exclusion and Exclusivity

Dalits in Contemporary India

PARAMJIT S. JUDGE

The expression 'dalit' is now synonymous with the lowest sections of the traditional Indian society, who were known by different names at different points of time. 'Untouchables', depressed classes, scheduled castes, underprivileged castes, etc., are some of the names given to them. At present, they constitute about 15 per cent of the population of India—the number which could be higher than a large number of countries of the world. With the exception of north-eastern tribal part of India, caste system is the most common form of social organization of India, which provides a broad context of thinking and conceptualizing of Indian society. Various studies suggest that caste is found among other religious communities, particularly among Sikhs, Christians and Muslims—a result of conversion of people in India. However, understanding caste and dalits is not an easy task, because there has been a great degree of complexity in the caste hierarchy largely due to variations in culture, social practices, and religious practices across the country within Hindu community. Caste system among the non-Hindu religious communities offers another difficulty in making a clear-cut generalization about the Indian society. Despite the presence of caste hierarchies in these religious communities, there have been noticeable differences among them from the Hindu caste hierarchy. For example, many of the castes that occupy upper caste status among the Sikhs are lower castes among the Hindus

(Judge 2002). Despite all these difficulties, it is possible to make certain broad generalizations about the caste system. Certain common properties/markers of caste have been succinctly delineated here. The purpose of this exercise is to situate dalits in the Indian social structure with its major specific features.

First, in virtually all regions of the country, two broad divisions exist among the numerous caste communities, namely, the separation between manual and non-manual labour. All those castes that are involved, in ideal typical sense, in non-manual occupations are bracketed as twice-born upper castes. Two occupations that come immediately to the mind as exceptions are swordsmanship and cooking, as these were performed by upper castes. However, the reason for these occupations' higher status is quite obvious. All the caste communities which were doing manual labour were regarded as lower castes. There have been two kinds of manual labour—unclean and clean. The castes involved in unclean/dirty/polluting work were considered untouchables whose touch could pollute the upper caste people. In this way, the dalits belonged to the lowest rungs of the Indian society.

Second, all the dalit castes faced discrimination and exclusion, which varied across castes and regions. One of the prevalent discriminations was that they were not allowed to touch the upper caste people. Virtually everywhere, these caste communities were living in distinct localities away from the upper caste houses. They were excluded from getting knowledge of religious texts, education, and non-polluting occupations. Among the numerous exclusions and discriminations the most horrifying in certain cases was that their women were not allowed to cover their breasts, thus, denying them the basic right to honourable living.

Third, all the dalits were internally heterogeneous and practised exclusion with each other. Caste endogamy was the way of life for Indian society and it was the first principle of division among the dalit castes. None of them intermarried and any such instance could invite the wrath of the caste community, particularly the caste of the girl in a patriarchal society. Internal divisions among the untouchables became highly functional for the sustenance of caste system.

Fourth, underlying the complex social structure was an equally powerful ideology of caste system, which justified the lowest status of the untouchables. It was the dharma/karma principle, supposed to have come from the mouth of Lord Krishna—the incarnation of Vishnu, according to which each caste member should perform his dharma righteously by taking up the occupation of his caste. The reward was promised in the next birth in the most abstract form, that is, birth in the higher caste.

The above explication of the traditional Indian social structure and the location of the dalits suffices enough to conclude that the caste status was quite similar to racial inequality. However, it should not mean that there has been no challenge to the birth-based caste inequality and its exclusivist character. The first challenge emerged as a result of the interaction between the Indian tradition and Islam in the medieval period. In the form of Bhakti movement, the plausibility of questioning the power of the upper castes within the framework of Hindu ideology of dharma/karma was realized. A large number of saints, such as Chokamela, Namdev, Tuka Ram, Kabir, Ravidas and Nanak to name few, questioned the legitimacy of keeping the untouchable castes excluded from the right to worship in temples. The dalits had never accepted their low caste position, which is evident from Deliége (1999) that they had a large storage of stories that tended to explain why they got the lowest position in the caste hierarchy. What is interesting about all these mythical accounts of origin is that these do not question the legitimacy of caste system. In a way, the medieval Bhakti movement, which in certain respects was a contemporary to the European period of renaissance, just failed to usher in modernity in India. The subsequent developments got corrupted into the mystical world by withdrawing from the social intervention. During this period Europe witnessed Copernican revolution, Reformation, Enlightenment and Newtonian revolution, which radically altered the understanding of external physical universe as well as the internal spiritual world.

Enlightenment attacked the social, political and religious oppression that fundamentally changed the intellectual world, despite the fact that most of the people remained ingrained in religion and spirituality (Bayly 2004).

Two dimensions of India's medieval period could be highlighted with regard to the dalits. First, there is no way of identifying the primacy of any of the exclusions of the dalits, because all aspects of their dehumanization seemed enmeshed with each other and secondly, the Bhakti movement demonstrated that it was possible to reinterpret ostensibly rigid and inegalitarian ideology. However, the Bhakti remained embedded in the religious tradition and could only emphasize the right to worship as the natural right of all individuals. Except for Guru Nanak, who started his own tradition which later on became a distinct religion, all others could not transcend limited boundaries of religious worship.

Renaissance and Modernity

What distinguished Indian renaissance from the Bhakti intervention was the way the caste system and untouchability were understood. Whereas, the Bhakti movement did not come out of the religious framework and tried to show the plausibility of achieving equality of worship, the Enlightenment philosophy questioned the religious basis of social inequality thereby ushering in modernity. The Bhakti perspective, though tended to alter the existing perspective, remained largely within the framework of tradition. Therefore, it was not an issue of exclusion but of social arrangements, which were patterned in a particular form and were seen as a normal life process. The limited occupations available for the members of society provided for a justification of including everybody in the economic life.

The arrival of British in India broke occupational structure in a fundamental way. We have a considerable debate on whether Marx was right in his characterization of Indian villages as stable and unchanging. Interestingly, Marx argued that the population growth did not lead to the change in the division of labour in India. Rather, the population pressure led to the formation of new village settlements, which were the replica of the original settlement. The British colonialism was essentially a capitalist imperialist rule. With British came new mode of production, western education and philosophy. The British administration required educated Indians to do the clerical work at the lowest level for which they were to be trained in the language of the rulers.[1] The response to the British rule, so far as Indian social structure was concerned, was one of introspection, which paved the way for renaissance in India. Indian renaissance, like the Indian socio-cultural and religious reality, had multiple trajectories. Starting from the beginning of the 19th century to 1947 when India got independence, the renaissance and nationalist intellectuals remained ambivalent towards social reform as well as the British rule (Chandra 1992). The major impact of the British rule became visible in the field of economic development where despite the imperialist character of British Indian economy marked by various regressive policies that only suited the British but were harmful for the people of India, there was development of infrastructure, both economic and administrative.[2] Economic development started escalating as a result of the increase in the trade and beginning of the industrialization process. All these developments created new job opportunities. Two trends began to develop and both had consequences for the dalits in the long term. First, various artisan activities began to undergo technological changes and artisan production began to transform into industrial enterprises. Secondly, new jobs were created and interestingly, these jobs were not linked with caste. Taking up new occupations, given the opportunity, implied moving away from the caste milieu. Despite the caste based discrimination, both the changes created consequences for the dalits. Intensification of leather trade, as noticed by Briggs (1975) in the 19th century, improved the economic conditions of the Chamars.

Transformation in the Indian society, however limited it might be, raised the aspirations of the dalits and other depressed castes and thus began dalit renaissance symbolized by Jotiba Phule. Phule was able to create an alternative tradition through the construction of the myth of Bali Raja—a mythic figure deceived by Lord Vishnu. The dalit's struggle began in real earnest after the arrival of B.R. Ambedkar. Ambedkar was a modernist in the strict sense of the term. Exclusionary practices emerged when the dalits were denied entry into new occupations and prevented from getting modern education. Certain forms of discrimination, which were earlier taken as part of the tradition and were depressive and exploitative in character, began to be reinterpreted as exclusionary in nature. These particularly included right to worship and entry in the temple. Dalits sought to end all forms of discrimination and exclusion by various means. They rejected sanskritization—a way of improving one's caste status by imitating the ways of life of the upper caste—and resorted to protest, collective mobilization and religious conversion. We, therefore, have certain instances in the colonial India where the dalits successfully changed their social conditions. The Nadars of Tamil Nadu (Hardgrave Jr 1970), the Ad-dharmis of Punjab (Juergensmeyer 1982), and the Mahars of

Maharashtra (Zelliot 1970) are some of the classical instances. In all the three cases the religious conversion or new religious identity was either the starting point or the culmination of their struggle.

The rising tide of dalit consciousness under the leadership of Ambedkar paved the way for their recognition as a distinct identity of the depressed castes. At the Round Table Conference he represented the dalits. He argued for a separate electorate and got it from the British Indian government. Gandhi did not accept it. There was a fundamental difference between the two leaders. Ambedkar was of the opinion that without the change in the constitutive rules of the Indian society and polity, the social inclusion of dalits could not take place. On the other hand, Gandhi was of the opinion that since the problems of the dalits are a matter of internal constitution of Hindu society, what was required was the change in regulatory rules.[3] Since Ambedkar was adamant, Gandhi decided to go on fast unto death in December 1932. The pressure mounted on Ambedkar to withdraw the demand for separate electorate to save Gandhi, which he ultimately did. Known as Poona Pact in which Ambedkar withdrew the demand and got into an agreement with Gandhi was the turning point in the history of dalit struggle for equality in India. The fundamental difference in the perceptions of Gandhi and Ambedkar was rooted in their commitment and priorities. Dalit scholars interpret that Gandhi's fasts '... not only helped him to maintain his dictatorship in demanding unquestioned obedience from the Congress but also to coerce others to fall in line as he did with Ambedkar during Poona Pact' (Gudavarthy 2008). It is essentially an interpretation which is possible, but lacks some degree of understanding of Gandhi in totality. For Gandhi caste based untouchability was undesirable, but held the conviction that reform was to be brought about from within the system. On the other hand, Ambedkar became progressively convinced that there was no hope from within the system and redemption lied in moving out of the system. Whereas Ambedkar was for non-communistic constitutive transformation of the Indian society, Gandhi hoped that reform and appeal to the upper castes' conscience would bring out the desired results.

Post-colonial Modernity, State and Dalits

The adoption of the new Constitution in 1950, three years after independence in which Ambedkar was involved as the chairman of the drafting committee, signified the beginning of a new era in Indian politics as well as society. It was based on the principle of inclusion making all citizens equal irrespective of their caste, creed and religion. Introduction of universal suffrage ended various kinds of disabilities imposed on dalits and other marginal communities in the political sphere. At the same time, the path to the achievement of the objective of social equality was not easy. To end age-old discrimination and oppression, the constitutional declaration was not enough. This was also known to the ruling elite of the independent India. Interestingly, the Indian Constitution also provided for the state intervention in the areas of social disabilities as a proactive agent by introducing the policy of preferential treatment to the dalits and tribals. A schedule of the list of the castes and tribes was annexed to the Constitution, as a result of which all these castes were labelled as scheduled castes and the tribes were henceforth known as the scheduled tribes.

What is now christened as reservation policy was based on the modern liberal principle according to which the individual has been the target of various benefits. The Indian state, through its modern liberal rationality, sought to end caste-based exclusions by improving the conditions of individuals with the perspective that such actions would automatically break the caste-occupation barriers. Modern occupations were inseparably linked with acquisition of education and reservation policy, as enshrined in the Constitution, and provided for certain proportions of the seats in the educational institutions. It was followed by the reservations in the public sector jobs. The percentage of seats was determined according to the population proportion of the dalits in the country as well as states. Besides the above, reservation in state legislatures and parliament were also provided for, subject to their review after every ten years by the Lok Sabha. The practice of untouchability in any form was made a cognizable offence subject to penal punishment. The post-colonial Indian state also undertook various development measures to ameliorate their conditions.

Since all these measures were put into effect in the first decade after adoption of Constitution, evaluative studies began to appear in the 1960s. Most of these studies clearly indicated two trends which had emerged in the implementation and consequences of the reservation policy. First, there was a poor implementation of the policy on account of the fact that owing to widespread poverty among them, the number of dalit students getting enrolled in educational institutions was far less than expected. Subsequently, they were unable to fill the quota of jobs reserved for them. The only exception was the political reservation where requisite number of the scheduled castes was always there to take benefits from the reservation policy. Second, certain sections among the dalits could benefit more than others from the reservation policy giving rise to what was subsequently known as emergence of creamy layer. Such a development was not contradictory to liberal principles as the reservation policy was individual-oriented. It could never have led to the corporate mobility of the dalits. Two trends could be observed in this context. The first was the formation of classes within castes (Seth 1981) and secondly, certain castes exploited these opportunities more than others. For example, the Ad-dharmis in Punjab benefited more than the Balmiki caste.

An unintended consequence was the collective reaction of the non-dalits against the reservation policy in 1970s (Bains 1997). Two categories of upper castes began to protest and form associations. The first was the students of medical colleges, particularly in Gujarat, who began the open protest. The second category comprised of government employees. The dalit employees who got jobs under the reservation policy were called 'sons-in-law of the government' by the upper caste employees. Various state governments introduced carry over system under which the unfilled post were to be added in the next year's quota. Such a policy was resented by the upper castes everywhere. It was during this period that the dalit students and employees were constructed as inefficient, incapable and incompetent. The argument was that the dalit employees did not work and were getting salaries without any work. In many states the dalit employees were also ghettoized in one department, namely, the social welfare department, of the government, whereas the rest of the government departments would have very few dalit employees. Against those dalits who would be admitted to the medical colleges against reserved seats were also constructed as dull and unintelligent and there would invariably be an argument that when these people would become doctors, they would not be able to do justice to their profession. Nobody asked such constructionists that they had to go through training and also clear all examinations.

It becomes clear that the post-colonial modernity, fundamentally rooted in the liberal principle of justice, failed considerably with the exception of one important and permanent contribution which was destined to make an impact when the arrival of postmodernity was announced in the west through the seminal work of Lyotard (1986), who argued that the grand narrative of the modernist discourse had broken down. This exception was the creation of dalit intellectuals. A section of educated dalits kept their commitment to the cause of dalits, whereas many dalits tended to hide their dalit identity (Guru 2008). The failure of modernist project of the Indian state was also accompanied by a radical shift in the dalit politics. Ambedkar had a project of bringing various dalit castes at par with upper castes for which he waged struggles and also made an attempt to realize this goal through state intervention. A casteless society was the desirable and cherished goal for an egalitarian system to exist and function.

Postmodern Twist and Dalit Assertion

It is not necessary that economic development and cultural superiority would go together. Pluralism may not necessarily be the sole privilege of post-industrial societies, as it may characterize the traditional society, which may be interpreted as multicultural reality. Indian subcontinent is a mosaic of myriad social formations ranging from archaic to postmodern. In this time and space convergence and divergence, the dalits are located in every part of the social landscape. The trajectories of emerging dalit consciousness have been multidirectional and engage the discourse of caste hierarchy in a number of ways. At the aggregate level, there is a paradigmatic shift in the way they have begun to handle the entire question of dalithood. Our following discussion is aimed at mapping this shift.

From Equality to Power

In the decade of 1980s it began to emerge that various steps undertaken by the Indian state for caste equality had not been succeeding to the extent it was expected. The hegemony of the upper and dominant castes in every part of the social and political life remained largely unchallenged. Caste-based associations had emerged among the upper and middle castes to articulate their interests in the political sphere and some of them, as it happened in Haryana, began to intervene in social affairs. The social and political resurgence of the Yadavs and the Kurmis in Bihar and Uttar Pradesh had further strengthened caste-based solidarities. Not only that, these castes started demanding reservation for the other backward classes (OBCs) to which many of them belonged. Seeking OBC status, something unheard of earlier, was a function of the emerging competition for public sector jobs in an economy that was developing at a slow pace. In other words, caste seemed to be emerging as a more powerful entity rather than an extinct category.

Kanshi Ram, who emerged as the undisputed leader of the dalits in the 1990s, shifted the paradigm from equality and castelessness to political power. One of the major defects in modernist discourse was that it was state enforced and was confined to the end of exclusion of dalits in public sphere only. The upper caste people could be persecuted if they discriminated on the basis of caste in the restaurants, educational institutions, utilization of common facilities, entry into religious places of worship, job market, etc. However, a person could not be punished, on the basis of the liberal principles if he refused to invite people on account of their caste. Somehow Gandhi's regulatory rules had a meaning in the sense that caste as an ideology existing in the mind/consciousness of the upper castes could not be erased through enactment and affirmative policies. It never meant that these policies did not produce any desirable result. As a matter of fact they enabled the dalits to cross the most crucial barrier in their march forward. It empowered them to get educated, organize and agitate.

Kanshi Ram understood it well and shifted the emphasis to acquiring of political power by creating a discourse of anti-Brahmanism. After establishing the Dalit Soshit Samaj

Sangharash Samiti in the 1981, he was quick to realize the available political space and organized Bahujan Samaj Party (BSP) in 1984. Dubey (2001) has analysed the emergence of Kanshi Ram as the major leader of dalits. He used anti-Brahmin rhetoric to its extreme in his public addresses. His protégé, Mayawati became the chief minister of the largest state (in terms population size), Uttar Pradesh, in 1995. In view of the fact that the BSP depended on the caste identity for coming to power, it reinforced caste with one difference. It challenged the hegemony of the upper castes, particularly the Brahmins, and designated them as Manuwadi forces.[4]

The influence of the BSP spread to other states, but it never reached the level of attaining power on the pattern of Uttar Pradesh. However, the discourse and practice of the BSP are not fundamentally different from the other political parties. The charisma of Kanshi Ram and after him, Mayawati has assured the success of the BSP. How do we make sense of the caste appeal of the BSP? Is it a retrogression and promotion of caste identities? The BSP, in fact, has changed the paradigm of caste equality. By emphasizing the fact that castes are going to stay in India, it has moved the trajectory of discourse to the plausibility of the existence and prevalence of caste differences without necessarily having caste system. Such a possibility, according to its perspective, exists through the capturing of formal power. The success of such a perspective requires some time for which one has to wait and see. However, there is a reasonably successful case of the Ad-dharmis of Punjab, which we shall discuss in the next section.

Identity Assertion

Punjab is a small state of India, but almost 30 per cent of its population belongs to the scheduled castes.[5] There are two major castes in the state which constitute three-fifth of the total population of the scheduled castes, namely, Ad-dharmis/Chamars and Balmikis/Mazabis. The Ad-dharmis/Chamars have experienced tremendous change in their conditions, as they were the first to exploit the opportunities made available to the dalits under the reservation policy. In the third decade of the 20th century they also organized a successful movement to be recognized as distinct religious community. Despite the fact that they have been supporting Ambedkar's philosophy of social change, they have never resorted to conversion to Buddhism. Most of them continue to be professing the Ad-dharm and worshipping Ravidas—a medieval dalit saint—as their Guru. In one of his recent stories, Rasoolpuri (2008) has highlighted the tension within the Chamar caste on account of religion. In the process he has been able come out with an answer to the question why Buddhism had not struck roots among the Punjabi Chamars.

Punjab is a Sikh-dominated society and among the Sikhs the Jats constitute an overwhelming majority.[6] The Jats are traditionally the landowning peasants, whereas most of the Chamars live in villages and used to be artisans-cum-agricultural labourers. Punjab experienced high rate of agricultural growth in the late-1960s as a result of the introduction of high yielding varieties of seeds (wheat), chemical fertilizers, institutional credit, and irrigation. The phenomenon of high agricultural productivity is popularly known as the green revolution. The consequences of the green revolution were economic in the sense that the Punjab peasantry experienced unparalleled prosperity. Same thing happened to the peasants of Haryana, Western Uttar Pradesh and coastal Andhra Pradesh a little later. Before the trickle down effect could really benefit the dalit agricultural workers, the influx of migrant labour from Uttar Pradesh began which did not only depress the wages of the local labour but also partially displaced them from agricultural labour. The Chamars responded to the emerging situation by moving out of the agricultural labour by learning emerging skills thus reducing their dependence on the upper caste landowners.[7]

The development in agriculture ran parallel to the emergence of the Chamar middle class through education, modern occupations, and international migration. According to an estimate of Juergensmeyer (1982), in the initial years in late 1950s and 1960s, 10 per cent of the total emigrants to various countries of the English-speaking west belonged to the dalit castes. Predictably, the Chamars constituted an overwhelming majority among the emigrants. The third aspect of the development among them has been the intensification of the trade in which they were traditionally involved, namely, rawhides and leather. Boota Mandi, near Jalandhar, became the major centre of trade in rawhides with its connections with rest of India. Some of the Chamar traders became rich and they began supporting the politics and religious institutions through funds. The rich Chamars of Boota Mandi have been consistently supporting all mobilizations of their caste people to the extent that all protests now set off from this place.

The Chamars have begun to assert their caste identity—a trend that was not only absent in the 1970s, but there was also a tendency to hide their caste status. Three interesting features could be witnessed in recent times so far as the Chamar identity is concerned. First, there is an obvious trend in publicly displaying their identity. It is evident from the fact that one finds graffiti on personal vehicles signifying the caste identity of the owner. For example, 'Putt Chamaran De' (sons of Chamars) could be seen scribbled on the back side of motor vehicles. It is not simply an identity assertion, but an effort to create counter-structure, because such a trend was exclusively found among the dominant Jats. Secondly, the Chamars seek to maintain their caste identity by sticking to caste endogamy.[8] The third trend is a corollary to the above-mentioned developments, that is, they are moving towards an exclusive caste group. Instead of fighting exclusion the Chamars have begun to emerge as a socially exclusive group, which has enabled them to exclude themselves from the other dalit groups for which they had to pay political costs. Unlike Uttar Pradesh where Mayawati has moved towards dalit unity, the Chamars in Punjab have continued to align themselves with either of the two major political parties, namely, the Congress and the Akali Dal. The Chamars constitute an interesting case of confronting caste inequality by maintaining caste identity. However, they are also an illustration of how an upwardly mobile caste could exclude other lower castes in the social world.

Social Science Theory and Dalit Intellectuals

Postmodernity of the dalit discourse is evident from the way they have confronted the exclusionary character of social theory in India. For the first time it has been shown that the dalits have been excluded from history and recent works also show that the dalits were also denied their anthropological past so far as the dominant discourse was concerned. Anthropological construction of the dominant upper castes remained confined to the construction of justificatory models of caste hierarchy. Guru (2002), Ilaiah (2004) and Prasad (2006), to refer some of the writers, have questioned the way the dalit identity and Indian history have been articulated in the social sciences in India. Besides the emergence of a distinct area of dalit literature, recent years have witnessed a popular trend in the publication of autobiographies on the part of the dalit intellectuals belonging to different parts of India. The trajectory of dalit consciousness is multidirectional articulating an attempt to recover what has been missing in the dominant upper caste discourse. As we shall see, the dalit discourse has created a paradox, which may trap them in casteism, and in order to come out of it, they require a politics of inclusion. However, before examining the how of this paradox, it is important to outline various trajectories of dalit consciousness.

Let us begin with the social science theory and the egalitarian discourse. Guru (2002) argues that social science theory does not take cognizance of the dalit experience. In other words, he strongly argues in favour of the construction of society as a subjective reality. Treating society as a subjective reality, for Guru, would amount to situating dalits at their rightful place, because only the dalits are capable of articulating their experience into theoretical discourse. He is not the only one among the dalit intellectuals, who claims the exclusive nature of the dalit experience. Predictably, there is more than one assumption implicated in such an argument. First of all, it assumes that Indian social inequality is unique in its form and content. Here comes the important paradox. Recently, at the Durban conference on racism, the dalit intellectuals made all efforts to show that caste is equivalent to race.[9] If we accept, for a moment, the argument that caste and race are not different, then the dalit experience loses its unique character. The second assumption is that all experiences can be theorized. However, it is important to mention that theorization needs concepts, propositions, and on top of that, language with semantic and semiotic universe. The construction of theory would occur in the given language frame (that is, a set of vocabulary and grammar). Can we say that dalit experience would be theorized in a language, which could only be understood by the dalits? At the outset it becomes clear that for such an enterprise the first precondition is either the existence of a distinct language or the emergence of a new language. So far this has not happened. Since the distribution of dalits in India is such that they are multilingual, to go for an exclusive linguistic innovation is far from practical. Obviously, Guru (ibid.) would not accept such an argument regarding the distinctness of language. Then, it should be reminded that social reality is not subjective, particularly when we are dealing with collective life-world such as that of dalits, we need to remind that it is an inter-subjective reality.

The inter-subjective social world assumes the existence of common stock of knowledge among the members of the society and their biographically determined situations enable them to understand each other's actions. If this is the theoretical logic, then arguing for the exclusive nature of theoretical discourse of a particular group is presumptuous without any base. Interestingly, all dalit castes do not undergo common experience, because of the nature of empirical reality. Numerous dalit castes are occupationally divided and hierarchically ordained endogamous groups. Their caste-based exclusion makes them one unit only in a situation of their relationship with upper castes in particular contexts. Or the Indian state has identified them as scheduled castes. The similarity ends there. What emerges as a result is an aggregation of groups who have been put together by virtue of their exclusion from social interaction, history and anthropological past.

We may now turn to dalit autobiographies which have recently come up in great numbers covering most of the regions of India. An autobiography is again a realm of the subjective and the memory. In the case of dalits, narrative of life experiences is not a simple depiction of one's life story, which is representative of the caste to which the author belongs, but also a mode of praxis. Most of the autobiographies have been authored by well-known dalit writers in their respective fields. Madhopuri (2004) and Malagatti (2007) are poets and Valmiki is a writer, whereas Moon is known as the editor of Ambedkar's collected works. The dalit writers in Maharashtra have extensively written on their life experiences. Besides Moon from the earlier generation, Gaikwad's (1992) autobiographical account makes an interesting reading, because it depicts the life-world of caste whose traditional occupation is stealing. There are many other autobiographies in vernacular languages and all of them have been noticed, discussed and translated in other languages.[10] All these works share certain common features. The first is that these provide a vivid account of the childhood of the writers. The early age was also marked by the overwhelming presence of caste-based discrimination. Whereas Moon's childhood provides us the knowledge of post-Poona pact times in Nagpur, all others largely narrate the periods of 1950s and 1960s. Interestingly, all of them become successful after getting education and their narratives either become selective or terminate at such a moment. It implies that these autobiographies are selective and purposive, but they carry valuable sociological information about the Indian society and caste-based discrimination.

What these autobiographical narratives depict is life lived in deprivation, humiliation and discrimination. All of them struggled and became successful through education and taking up of new occupations. In a way, their personal accounts turn into the description of the life conditions of their respective castes. An autobiography is the account of one's life narrated in the form of story, which the author writes when he has passed all these stages. Thus, the role of memory becomes important in the autobiographical discourse. It is because of this reason that most of these narratives are episodic in form. These works have added to our understanding of the social reality considerably, but at the same time, these works have further contributed to the overemphasis on the personal experience as the basis of the construction of social theory.

Autobiographies have added to the already growing literature which has carved out a niche as dalit literature. It began from Maharashtra (Zelliot 1992) in the form of a distinct identity of dalit literature, but has now spread to different parts of India. As a matter of fact, dalit autobiographies are a part of the broad category of dalit literature. It has evolved as a powerful voice of the dalits. Kumar (2010: 124) makes the following comment on dalit literature:

> Serious critique is sine qua non for any literary work of significance. Dalit claims that literature of the dominant group or so-called upper castes is petty and false and overpowered by romanticism. It ignores the social reality of appalling poverty and oppression of the dalits. Stating that high-caste literature is artificial and false, 'like a paper flower', Wankhade notes that 'a Marathi writer's understanding of life is restricted by his birth and upbringing in a particular caste and class and he is unable to come out of his own pond …'.

Similarly, the dalit writers, according to Kumar (ibid.), have highlighted how they have built critique of 'traditional structures of the Indian society such as caste village, and religion'. Literature provides unlimited possibilities of explorations into the world of subjective experiences, but at the same time, the existence of the term dalit literature is also a result of either exclusiveness or exclusion. Sensitizing human perceptions regarding sufferings and oppression of certain sections of the society is important and necessary also. It may however be seen whether such classified forms of literature remain within the parameters of the given genre.

Conclusion

Widely located at different social spaces between tradition and postmodernity, the dalits of India are facing two kinds of challenges. The first is emerging from outside the milieu of dalithood. We may call it the challenge of inclusion. Till today, they have remained excluded in various ways. Despite the state intervention through various policies, the overall social location of the dalits remained at the fringe of the Indian society. Prevalence of caste differentiation among them has prevented them to make collective efforts for various inclusionary strategies. Still, majority of them remain a part of the poor sections of the Indian society. There are certain pockets in India where a caste has been able to overcome certain forms of exclusion, as is the case of the Chamars of Punjab. Other castes in the same regions have failed to do so. Evidence and stories of atrocities on dalits can still be read in newspapers. Even if oppression on dalit comes to an end and all of them achieve certain level of development, there is no guarantee that they would not face exclusion. As we noted, inclusion of dalits is taking place in the public sphere of Indian social life. We generally ignore the private sphere, which involves inter-family relations and interactions, friendship and socializing. It requires change in stereotypes, prejudices and consciousness of the upper castes to abandon the caste perspective in interpersonal relations. Such a state of affairs may not be realized in the near future. The relevance of Gandhian approach could be realized in such a context, where individuals are not acting in accordance with the rules of the state in public sphere as citizens, but as autonomous individuals with rights in the liberal framework. The state, thus, cannot pass the law whereby a percentage of invited guests is reserved for certain caste groups in the marriage ceremony/celebration, as it would infringe the rights of the individuals as citizens. Encapsulation of social groups gets reinforced when hierarchical order is threatened by the egalitarian principle of the liberal state. There are parallel instances of such a process in other parts of the world where immutable differences of race and ethnicity have led to the recognition of multiculturalism, which is nothing but a form of mutual and consensual separation despite the equal rights guaranteed by the liberal state.

The second challenge is emerging from within the dalit discourse. We may call it the challenge of exclusiveness. The dalit discourse is multi-vocal and covers different aspects of the existential conditions of the dalits. There is a history of protests of dalits, largely caste-based instead of being a collective mobilization of dalit castes, against their exclusion, discrimination and oppression. In most of such cases the character of mobilization implicated the assertion for better treatment, equality and end of exclusion. In most of these cases the upper castes reacted sharply and sometimes clashing with dalits. All these mobilizations helped them to improve their conditions without necessarily ending their servitude. Frustrated by the failure of achieving desirable results after independence, a section of the dalits moved away from their religious milieu by following the path of religious conversion. They considered Hinduism as the ideological basis of the perpetuation of their continuing oppression and exclusion. Normatively, such a perspective cannot be regarded as wrong or right, but such a movement that took them away from their religious milieu also led to their emergence as exclusive groups without necessarily changing the material conditions of their existence.

The argument for the exclusive nature of the dalit experience and the construction of social science theory is again an effort towards demonstrating exclusive identities of the actors. Can diverse experience be the basis of exclusive identity? It is important to know how the experience is posited on the existential conditions. Unfortunately, all human experiences are articulated through language which is shared by all members of the society. Therefore, the dalit exclusivity cannot be theoretically positioned in the context of experience. Whereas, the construction of history and invention of tradition simultaneously accompany the discovery of historical and anthropological past, arguing for the exclusive character of identity in the historical sense seems a little far fetched. Thus, buffalo nationalism and cow nationalism are equally divided and could not be associated with the secular and egalitarian Indian society. However, if the trend continued towards the emphasis on the distinct and unique life experiences, which others cannot understand, the dalit assertion would continue to be ambivalently located between exclusion and exclusiveness.

NOTES

1. There has been a controversy over the introduction of the English language in India. However, it may be pointed out that the language of the rulers has been imposed in general. Even in India, Persian was the court language in many regions.
2. Permanent settlement, destruction of indigenous production, commercialization of agriculture for imperialist needs, etc., harmed the people of the country.
3. The help of my friend, Professor Satya P. Gautam is gratefully acknowledged with regard to the distinction between the perspectives of Gandhi and Ambedkar.
4. Ancient/medieval Hindu sage who authored *Manusmriti*—a text that codifies the caste system covering all aspects of social life of the Hindus.
5. As a matter of fact, after the state notification according to which Mahatam/Rai Sikhs have been included among the scheduled castes, the percentage has already gone up to approximately 35 per cent.
6. According to the estimates based on the data of Census of India, 1931, they should be about 65 per cent of the total Sikh population.
7. See Judge (2010).
8. See Judge and Bal (2009) for detailed discussion on the issue.
9. See Thorat and Umakant (2004) on the issue of race and caste.
10. We are referring five autobiographies for the sake of convenience. However, it may be added that these five works fairly represent the writings of this genre of literature.

REFERENCES

Bains, Ravinder Singh. 1997. 'Reactionary Mobilization against Change from Above', in Paramjit S. Judge and Satish K. Sharma (eds), *Dimensions of Social Change: Essays in Honour of Professor P.N. Pimpley*. Jaipur: Rawat, pp. 122–152.

Bayly, Christopher A. 2004. *The Birth of the Modern World 1780–1914: Global Connections and Comparisons*. Oxford: Blackwell Publishing.

Briggs, Geo W. 1975 (1920). *The Chamars*. Delhi: B.R. Publishing Corporation.

Chandra, Sudhir. 1992. *Oppressive Present: Literature and Social Consciousness in India*. New Delhi: Oxford University Press.

Deliége, Robert. 1999. *The Untouchables of India*. New York: Berg.

Dubey, Abhay Kumar. 2001. 'Anatomy of a Dalit Power Player: A Study of Kanshi Ram', in Ghanshyam Shah (ed.), *Dalit Identity and Politics*. New Delhi: Sage, pp. 288–310.

Gaikwad, Laxaman. 1992. *Uchchaka*. Delhi: Radhakrishan (Hindi).

Gudavarthy, Ajay. 2008. 'Gandhi, Dalits, and Feminists: Recovering the Convergence', *Economic and Political Weekly*, XLIII (22), May 31: 83–90.

Guru, Gopal. 2002. 'How Egalitarian are the Social Sciences in India', *EPW*, XXXVII (50), December 14: 5003–5009.

——. 2008. 'Understanding Multiple Images of B.R. Ambedkar', in Manu Bhagvan and Anne Feldhaus (eds), *'Speaking Truth to Power': Religion, Caste and the Subaltern Question in India*. New Delhi: Oxford University Press, pp. 205–220.

Hardgrave Jr, Robert L. 1970. 'Political Participation and Primordial Solidarity: The Nadars of Tamil Nadu', in Rajni Kothari (ed.), *Caste in Indian Politics*. New Delhi: Orient Longman, pp. 102–128.

Ilaiah, Kancha. 2004. *Buffalo Nationalism: A Critique of Spiritual Fascism*. Kolkata: Samya.

Judge, Paramjit S. 2002. 'Religion, Caste and Communalism in Punjab', *Sociological Bulletin*, 51 (2): 175–194.

——. 2003. 'Hierarchical Differentiation among Dalits', *EPW*, XXXVIII (28), July 12: 2990–2991.

Judge, Paramjit S. and Gurpreet Bal. 2009. *Mapping Dalits: Contemporary Reality and Future Prospects*. Jaipur: Rawat.

Judge, Paramjit S. 2010. *Changing Dalits: Explorations across Time*. Jaipur: Rawat.

Juergensmeyer, Mark. 1982. *Religion as Social Vision: The Movement against Untouchability in 20th Century Punjab*. Berkeley: University of California Press.

Kumar, Vivek. 2010. 'Different Shades of Dalit Mobilization', in T.K. Oommen (ed.), *Social Movements: Issues of Identity I*. New Delhi: Oxford University Press, pp. 116–136.

Lyotard, Jean-Francois. 1986. *The Postmodern Condition: A Report on Knowledge*. Manchester: Manchester University Press.

Madhopuri, Balbir. 2004. *Chhangia Rukh*. Chandigarh: Lokgeet Parkashan (Punjabi).

Malagatti, Aravind. 2007. *Government Brahmana*. Hyderabad: Orient Longman.

Moon, Vasant. 2001. *Growing Up Untouchable in India: A Dalit Autobiography*. New Delhi: Vistaar Publications.

Prasad, Chandra Bhan. 2006. *Dalit Phobia: Why Do They Hate Us?* New Delhi: Vitasta Publishing Pvt. Ltd.

Rasoolpuri, Bhagwant. 2008. 'Jarhan', *Parvachan*, 30, January–March: 61–69 (Punjabi).

Seth, V.N. 1981. 'Sociological Study of Harijan Protest'. Ph.D. Thesis (Unpublished). Department of Sociology, Panjab University, Chandigarh.

Thorat, Sukhdeo and Umakant (eds). 2004. *Caste, Race and Discrimination: Discourses in International Context*. Jaipur: Rawat (in association with Indian Institute of Dalit Studies, New Delhi).

Valmiki, Om Prakash. 1998. *Jooth*. Ludhiana: Chetna Parkashan (Punjabi).

Zelliot, Eleanor. 1970. 'Learning to Use Political Means: The Mahars of Maharashtra', in Rajni Kothari (ed.), *Caste in Indian Politics*. New Delhi: Orient Longman, pp. 29–69.

——. 1992. *From Untouchable to Dalit: Essays on the Ambedkar Movement*. New Delhi: Manohar.

10

Indian 'Modernity' and 'Tradition'

A Gender Analysis

MAITRAYEE CHAUDHURI

There is always some truth in stereotypes, however skewed, however exaggerated. The image of India as a land of contrasts is one such. There is probably no nation in the world which is marked by greater internal inequality, diversity and plurality. Great wealth co-exists with abysmal poverty. There is no dearth of confident, assertive women in various facets of India's public and corporate life.[1] There is no shortage of women who have never gone to school, who have been married as children, who have neither experienced nor likely to experience the basic requirements of nutrition, health care and education.[2] Newspaper headlines carry stories about 'honour killings'[3] and sex trafficking with a depressing regularity, reflecting the state of a large section of women in India. A large number of women are simply 'missing' because of technology-driven selective termination of female fetuses.[4]

This paper will, however, not delve into either the systematic cases of violence and discrimination of Indian woman nor of her many achievements. Instead, it will explore how the language of tradition and modernity has been the dominant idiom that has sought to capture the 'essence' of both the Indian nation and the Indian woman. Tourist brochures capture pictures of women in colourful, 'traditional' attire alongside visuals of 'modern', professional women in western attire 'manning' the various flourishing sectors of a globalizing India. I use the two terms 'traditional' and 'modern' with care.

The reasons why I use the terms in quotes is that both within commonsense everyday discourse as well as a reasonably influential intellectual current in Indian sociological literature on women there are some ready characteristics that tend to be associated with the idea of 'traditional' or 'modern' women. Though men are not always described as either 'traditional' or 'modern' it is significant that very often a man's likelihood of being described as 'modern' or 'traditional' rests on his purported attitude towards women. A cursory examination of matrimonial advertisements in newspapers searching for brides would show a recurrent emphasis on desiring women with a blend of the 'traditional' and 'modern'. The ideal woman would be a judicious blend of traditional qualities of domestic skills, knowledge of religious rituals and practices and modern abilities acquired through education and employment opportunities. In more common parlance the perfect Indian woman ought to be smart but not too smart, traditional but not too much.

For most urban middle class Indians this is a discourse that they are a product of and which they reproduce in turn. Issues of inequality and exclusion, which I refer to in my introductory paragraph, appear to disappear within this overarching discourse of the modern and traditional woman. The salience of this discourse demands a critical enquiry to understand both its emergence and perpetuation. Unfortunately, to a large extent, these ideas have been accepted as unproblematic, given the stock of knowledge with which we navigate ourselves in our society. Even within the dominant sociological tradition in India this has been largely taken as given. Only the task of operationalizing the concepts with ready indicators was seen as the task for us to map just how modern, and just how traditional Indian women are. Many seminars have spent long hours through the 1970s, therefore, figuring out whether a sari clad women who drives a car is modern or not? Or is she like Milton Singer's Madras industrialists simply compartmentalizing different spheres of their life. Singer's argument was that the Madras industrialists 'ritually neutralized' their work sphere, that is relatively free from customary norms and ritual restrictions. This made it easier to experiment with new experiences, processes and products (Singer 1972).

The examples of the sari wearing woman driver and Singer's idea of compartmentalization may help examine more carefully the Indian debate on the women's question and nature of Indian modernity. The first example indicates that the idea of the modern in India is deeply gendered. In other words the query whether a western suited Indian man is modern or traditional is unlikely to be either raised or decided by his clothes. The second example that Milton elaborates points out that modernity changes the functioning and meaning of public and private spaces. Common to both examples, however, is the fact that the idea of the modern is necessarily entangled with the idea of the western. This, of course, is no surprise given the history of a modernity that emerged in the west and therefore was necessarily culturally constitutive of the western context. That a western modernity sought to speak in the universal mode, of a rationality that transcended all cultural specificities cannot however brush aside the defining fact that western modernity rested on the culture and legacy of the west. This association of the 'modern' with the 'western' was compounded by the fact that the 'western' was inextricably linked with the 'colonial'. The 'modern' Indian, a product of western education in a colonial context, was therefore at once envious and critical of the west. This ambiguity defined the 19th century middle class social reform movement that emerged and was constitutive of the colonial context. Most importantly for this paper, the women's question was central to the reform attempts. Any attempt to fully comprehend the making of the dominant discourse of the 'modern' and 'traditional' Indian women will have to return, therefore, to the past.

This colonial past was one wherein India witnessed a whole mix of ideological influences from the modern west and a return to the traditional but forever marked by an interpretative framework that was an unintended consequence of colonialism. This would be equally true of Orientalist celebration of ancient India as much as it would be that of an arrogant rational dismissal of India's past. This paper will attempt to present a synoptic account of these trends. A return to the past will also afford us a perspective to understand why in the matrimonial advertisements the desired Indian woman is a combination of the 'traditional' and 'modern'.

It is in this context that this paper will look at the sources, the content of the ideas and their selective appropriation by the emergent Indian middle class in colonial India which led to a certain fashioning of the notions of the 'traditional' and 'modern' and also implied a certain making of the public and private—a theme that is linked crucially to the gender question. These lines of enquiry which this paper hopes to pursue will strengthen my broad contention that a history of the women's question offers us a vantage point to understand the story of Indian modernity.

A Colonially Mediated Modernity and the Women's Question

Cultural representations are crucial in the making of modern nations. Central in the making of the national imaginary has been the figure of the woman.[5] India has been no exception (Chaudhuri 1996). Women are often projected as cultural emblems of the Indian nation and society. Changes in her attire and demeanor are therefore hastily condemned as threats to culture and tradition. Such responses have been witnessed in many parts of the world and at one level can be read as a response typical of patriarchal societies. At another level, this essentially patriarchal response has to be conjoined with the specific historical experience of colonial societies. Changes to 'tradition' had to be condemned on two grounds—one, that they ran counter to 'natural' patriarchal norms and two, that they are alien and western. It is well known that India experienced a colonially mediated modernity. However, so many years after the end of colonial rule, at a time when post-colonial presence within the western academia is overtly conspicuous, the actual trauma that a colonized people underwent has retreated perhaps from public awareness. The humiliation and denial that marked the colonial experience, therefore, needs reiteration to fully appreciate how a colonially mediated modernity paved an uneasy and contentious relationship to the west, necessarily involved a difficult link to the modern. This ambiguous connection with both the modern and the west persists as a strong and deep feeling in the 'modern' Indian mind.

The experience of western colonial rule left an indelible impression on the Indian consciousness and led to a set of paradoxical responses. For the emerging Indian western educated middle class that slowly made its presence felt in 19th century colonial India, the west was at once a world to be emulated and yet at once disparaged. India's long years of colonial rule in a very fundamental way shaped her present. Some of the first issues that were debated in the colonial public discourse were gender questions. Explanations for this were many. The more oft quoted ones were that the Christian missionaries scoffed at the dismal state of Indian women and zeroed in on practices like sati, child marriage and maltreatment of widows, in particular the large number of high caste child widows. Liberal views in Britain too were of the opinion that the status of women indicated the status of a nation. Sir Herbert Risley wrote that while education had produced a class of Indians interested in political advancement it was unlikely that they could attain it for:

> A society which accepts intellectual inanition and moral stagnation as the natural condition of its womankind cannot hope to develop the higher qualities of courage, devotion and self sacrifice which go to the making of nations. (cited in Chaudhuri 2011: 15)

Goaded by such attacks, the new Indian middle class sought to reinterpret traditional institutions and culture. Understanding this middle class is important, for much of contemporary debates on gender and culture embody the tensions of this class that emerged under the aegis of colonialism. 'On the one hand they ...' were products of an English education introduced by the colonial masters and therefore victim to a Eurocentric view of modern society. On the other, they were victim to the 'feeling of historical denial' (ibid.: 12–13).

> While Hindus remembered the glories of an ancient Hindu past, Muslims recalled the might of pre-British Muslim India. Since the Muslim memories of the recent past were stronger, the Muslims had less of the new class in their ranks; so their sentimentality was mainly that of restoration. (ibid.: 13)

The point that is being sought to be made is that in this recasting of what constitutes 'tradition' and 'national culture', colonialism had a significant role to play. There are two aspects to what one refers to as the making of the traditional and modern culture. The first, pertains to women and its significance in the presentation of the 'national' culture. The second, relates to the fact that in a diverse and multicultural society like India this invocation of the 'national' entails projection of the dominant cultural community and marginalization of the other communities who in turn tends to affirm sometimes discriminatory gender practices as cultural emblems of the community. Debates on practices such as *purdah* and child marriage in the 19th century suggest that once a custom was seen as belonging to the 'other' community, there was greater willingness to relinquish it. For instance, some Muslim social reformers opined that *purdah,* as was practised in 19th century India, was influenced by Hindu practices and that child marriage too was a Hindu custom. Reform in such a context was possible. Significantly some Hindu social reformers felt that *purdah* was an Islamic custom and could therefore be dispensed with.[6] More recently, a rich body of writings on gender and caste has emerged contesting the exclusionary and discriminatory cultural notion of the traditional Indian woman which was constructed (Rege 1998).

What one is arguing is that a colonially mediated modernity of a society marked by diverse religious traditions, the gender question got doubly implicated. The women's question became a site of many contesting processes. One, the status of women became one between 'tradition' and 'modernity'. Two, the process got compounded because the conception of 'tradition' itself was contested. Central in the 19th century was an effort to critique, reinvent and valorize 'tradition'. We shall see this in the debate on sati, way back in the early 1800s. Three, since India has been marked by distinct religious, linguistic and ethnic communities, there was a contestation between the communities about whose tradition, whose culture ought to be the model on which the 'national' Indian woman had to be imagined. The gender question thus became a potent site of conflict. We shall see this manifesting itself almost 160 years later after the abolition of sati in 1829 in 1985 and 1986 with the Shahbano case and Deorala sati case. We discuss this later in this paper. Four, models of the modern bourgeois domesticated woman and the modern normative family of the west also made its impact felt in the cultural reconstruction of what the Indian traditional woman was all about. The following paragraphs explicate these lines of confluence and contestation.

Culture, Tradition and the Re-casted Woman

The manner that colonialism shaped the relationship between culture and women are deep and complex. The middle class desire to change the traditional family pattern stemmed not from an exposure to western liberal ideas alone but to the strains that developed in the families of the newly educated men. Modern education and urbanization introduced a new barrier between men and women of such of families. The common practice for men who came to study and stayed to work in the cities was to leave their families behind in the villages. The tremendous gap of experience became a formidable barrier for close companionship between husbands and wives, mothers and sons. The only class of women who could supply such companionship was the courtesans who were accomplished women, trained in the finer art of social interaction. With increased urbanization, sex work became more commercialized. The demand could not be met by daughters of the traditional courtesan castes alone. The large number of young high caste widows, helpless victims of family neglect and even torture was an obvious recruiting ground.

Middle class social reformers concerned with the threat posed by this for both the family and society, raised questions about the ill-treatment of widows, the denial of remarriage, child marriage and polygamy in the newspapers and journals of the time. The women's question became a central issue in some of the most controversial debates over social reform, arguing whether reform would strengthen or weaken the social structure. The advocates of reform argued that ameliorative measures would strengthen the family—the chief unit of Indian social organization. Education would not turn the women away from their traditional familial roles but improve the efficiency of wives and mothers, and strengthen the hold of traditional values on society, since women were better carriers of these values. Thus, came about the curious mix of traditional and modern attributes of the normative Indian woman which the title of this paper alludes to. Herein, we find an affirmation of the recast Aryan woman, of the Victorian faith in the sanctity of the family, of middle class propriety and respectability.

The process of nation making for India with its diverse communities, languages and religions was bound to be contentious. In the construction of 'national' culture (however defined) women play a particularly important role as cultural emblems. Thus, practices like sati or child marriage or prohibition of widow remarriage or purdah or denial of right to divorce could be read as cultural emblems. One has already alluded to this earlier in the paper. To find discriminatory practices against men portrayed as cultural emblems will not be easy.

Accompanying the process of recasting women as emblems of culture, was a process of refashioning of gender norms also in the name of 'culture' and 'refinement' by the new Indian middle class. Driven by the idea that Victorian upper class culture and gender norms were a desirable model to aspire to, efforts were made by reformers and nationalists later, to 'refine' Indian women. What it translated into often was imposition of codes of dressing and behaving that would 'train, improve and nourish the gentler and nobler qualities of heart', 'genteel norms' and 'domestic virtues' (Chaudhuri 2011: 31–32). Various colonial laws were brought in place to decree various practices of Indians, particularly of the lower castes obscene. For instance, performing women who danced and sang in traditional Bengal were legally banned from performing. A complex process thus got underway which created a new upper caste, middle class 'culture' that defined norms for the typical Indian 'woman'. The new, however, became 'traditional', the old an anomaly, inconsistent with true 'tradition'. I am tempted at this point to mention that the iconic sari worn by the modern middle class Indian women is a style, more 'modern' than 'traditional'. Significantly, it is worn along with a 'blouse' and 'petticoat', terms clearly originating elsewhere.[7] In the 1960s, one often heard the use of the term 'chemise' by middle class Bengali grandmothers. That of course offers another take on our complex social histories, which we cannot pursue here.

A quote from an early reformer captures both the paradox of tradition and modernity as well the divide between private and public realms, so central to modern western philosophy (Benhabib 1987). The desire of middle class Indian males to refashion conjugal life and 'home' has often been seen as a propelling reason for the early reform attempts.

> ... (India's) need is to devise such a system of education for Hindu females as will make her an agreeable companion, a good mother, an intelligent and loving wife, and an excellent housewife. We want her to possess those mental accomplishments which enable the wife to serve as a solace to her husband in his bright and dark moments, the mothers to undertake, or at least to superintend the early instruction of her child, and the lady of the house to provide those sweet social comfort, *idealized in the English word—Home* (Chaudhuri 2011: 51 emphasis mine).

The paradox in the formulation is that while the idea of the 'Home' English style is new, it soon acquires an invocation of timeless tradition to legitimize it. But that indeed is the style of nationalism itself, at once modern, at once invoking of traditions stretching to an immemorial past. We thus notice how colonially mediated modernity led to a rethinking of tradition and culture. Gender norms underwent change. This change was compounded by the fact that in a diverse and culturally plural India what constitutes traditional gender norms became a key site of contestation between different communities. Both statements concealed more than they revealed. But importantly such gendered rhetoric became part of community identity discourse.

Indian nationalism has to be, therefore, understood also as a cultural critique of colonialism and an assertion of 'national culture'. In this, assertion the image of 'Indian womanhood' was significant. And this has had serious long-term implications. Many were detrimental to women's democratic rights. Yet the assertion itself propelled an early visibility of the women's question itself and a certain legitimacy of women in the public sphere. I cannot enter into this aspect but not mentioning it at all would not do justice to the long tradition of women in public life and a significantly a long 'tradition' of debating 'feminism' (Chaudhuri 2005).

Contesting Identities and Jurisdiction: Community, Gender, State

To return to questions of culture, community identity and scriptural sanctions, they have been very much part of the manner in which the women's question emerged in India. One of the first issues, where this comes up, is the sati dispute. While the Brahmo Samaj marshalled enormous *shastric* evidence to show that sati is not mandatory, the Dharma Sabha pleaded with the British to disallow those, who knew nothing of their customs and religion, from speaking. It petitioned 'that in a question so delicate as the interpretation of our sacred books, and the authority of our religious usages none but Pundits and Brahmins and teachers of holy lives, and known learning ought to be consulted—not men who have neither faith nor care for the memory of their ancestors or their religion' (Chaudhuri 2011: 20–22). The Age of Consent Bill that raged through India in the end of the 19th century further argued that the natural and nationalist right of a community to decide when and how to reform, rejecting the right of an alien and unresponsive state to legislate on the private matters of Indians (ibid.: 72–77).

While the establishment of an independent state in a way altered the terms of discourse, the problem of differing identification of communities to the state persists. The majority community 'naturally' identifies with the 'nation–state' while degrees of discomfort persist with the other communities. That India attained independence with the partitioning of the country and unprecedented killings on 'communal' grounds have marked the discourse of state and communities till date. So far as women are concerned, the questions that persist are: Who decides who speaks legitimately for a 'community'? Who decides what constitutes the 'culture' of a community?

Western ideas had a great bearing on the manner that the ideas of early social reformers, nationalists, socialists and communists were shaped. As mentioned already, these ideas entered India through a colonial encounter which meant an abiding paradoxical relationship with the west (and the modern)—at once admiring and envious, at once suspicious and superior. The harking back to the ancient Hindu past and the purported high status of women thereof, which forms a necessary trope of modern Indian historiography has to be located within this colonial state. This eulogy of a Hindu past was an assertion both against the colonial west and the Muslim 'other'. Likewise the Muslim community developed a narrative of a pristine Koranic past that had got sullied by contamination with the many suspect Hindu practices in India. This attempt by the two major communities to distinguish themselves from the 'other' often rested on gendered practices. Indeed, scholars have contended that the very construction of monolithic and apparently internally homogeneous communities, namely the Hindu and Muslim gave the lie to a longer tradition of syncretism and overlapping identities. In that sense, the contemporary form of the communities themselves are modern, not traditional. The shift from *gemeinschaft* to *gesselschaft* did not quite happen. An assertion of fixed bonded communities, a deeply gendered process, has had very severe and often tragic implications for South Asia. The next section seeks to capture a persisting pattern of contesting gender and community rights that has played out from the colonial period right into the contemporary present.

While the establishment of an independent state in a way altered the terms of discourse, the problem of differing identification of communities to the state persisted. The majority community 'naturally' identified with the 'nation state' while degrees of discomfort persist with the other communities. That India attained independence with the partitioning of the country and unprecedented killings on 'communal' grounds have marked the discourse of state and communities till date. So far, as women are concerned, the questions that persist are: Who decides who speaks legitimately for a 'community'? Who decides what constitutes the 'culture' of a community?

The Shahbano case dramatically brought all these questions to the fore. On 23 April 1985, the Supreme Court of India passed a judgment granting maintenance to a divorced Muslim woman Shahbano (AIR 1985). The court awarded Shahbano maintenance of ₹ 179.20 per month from her husband and dismissed the husband's appeal against the award of maintenance. The judgment of the Supreme Court sparked off a nation-wide controversy. The principal argument put forward by conservative Muslim opinion was that the Muslim Personal Law was based on the Shariat, which is divine and immutable. Though sections from the Muslim community defended the judgment the state was more willing to listen to the voice of conservative spokespersons of the community. Shahbano herself was pressurized to such an extent that in an open letter she denounced the Supreme Court judgment:

> ... which is apparently in my favour; but since this judgement which is contrary to the Quran and the *hadith* and is an open interference in Muslim personal law, I, Shahbano, being a Muslim, reject it and dissociate myself from every judgement which is contrary to the Islamic shariat. I am aware of the agony and distress which this judgement has subjected the Muslims of India today. (*Inquilab* 1985)

The state passed the Muslim Women's Bill and the Hindu communal forces saw this move as an appeasement of the state to the minorities. The question that arose is who exactly the Bill was seeking to protect—community leaders, divorced husbands or women (Pathak and Rajan 1986)?

It is important to emphasize that the tendency for the conservative leadership of a community to affirm gender discriminatory practices as authentic culture is not confined to any one community. Soon after the Indian state passed the retrogressive Muslim Women's Bill on 4 September 1987 an eighteen year-old widow Roop Kanwar was burnt alive on her husband's pyre in the full gaze of about 3,000 spectators, accompanied by the full panoply of Rajput valour. Despite Rajasthan High Court's directives to the State Government to prevent the celebrations in honour of Roop Kanwar, it was celebrated in a very big way. About two lakh people assembled and paid obeisance to the place where the sati had taken place, the 'sati-sthal'. Many leading politicians participated in the celebrations. The women of the Rani Sewa Sangha, a voluntary social movement to preserve India's 'ancient traditions' dressed as brides marched through the streets of Delhi to commemorate 'the historic act of self-immolation'. Sati was projected as the highest ideal of female spirituality and renunciation, the highest achievement of 'naridharma' (the duty of women) and '*pativrata*' (devout wife). This was imbued with the aura of sacrifice associated with Rajput history (Sangari 1988: 26). The sentiments expressed at the sati case were widely perceived in consonance with the 'natural cultural' and 'national' sentiments of the people. The 'nation' perceived no threat while the Shahbano case was widely projected as an instance of a minority community's disloyalty to the state and nation. Quite clearly women to be cultural emblems of the nation have to conform to a particular culture.

Most recently, we have had a steep rise in 'honour killings' of young men and women who chose to marry outside their caste and community, which once again are being defended in the name of tradition and culture of specific communities. Though it is increasingly becoming a public issue, we have to wait and see how this develops, for major political parties have either kept a careful silence on this or are slowly veering around to a defense of the traditional *khap* panchayats (the traditional village councils), the moral police of the community that has been overriding the constitutional provisions of the state to assert their 'traditional' patriarchal control. A young modern industrialist Navin Jindal, also a Congress MP has come out in support of the *khap* panchayats, once again invoking 'time immemorial' tradition (Joshi and Naqshbandi 2010). Rhetoric apart, it is a straightforward defense of violent assertion of patriarchal control over women's sexuality and a matter of control of power for 'modern' political leaders rest their base and support on 'traditional' village councils. This I argue is a break from the early years of Indian politics which did seek to break oppressive social practices whatever be their customary legitimacy. (Chaudhuri 2011) For national politics was imbued with the democratic vision of the nationalist movement. In such a context serious attempts to engage critically with 'tradition' and 'modernity' were attempted. This one would aver is no longer the case.

Conclusion

Today, in a globalized era, politics is emptied of its egalitarian content and disengaged with democratic aspirations of the ordinary woman and man. Politics is reduced to power blocks and smart moves, reflective of corporate deals rather than engagement with democratic ideals and practices. Tradition in such a context thus becomes a pawn to promote 'consumption' or a ploy to win 'electoral support'.

The new era has also seen dramatic transformations in the Indian media. A new public discourse in India began to be articulated from the 1990s with the new liberal economic policies. Accompanying this was also a marked change of the state and nation's approach to the gender question (Chaudhuri 1996). In an earlier era the poor and dispossessed occupied an ideologically central place in the state vision. In the new globalized developmental frame, the state retreated from many of its welfare functions. The market increasingly occupied a central space. This has been accompanied by a major ideological shift in public discourse in which an advertisement-driven media has had a significant role to play (ibid. 2001). In the images that the media projects the dispossessed classes have virtually disappeared. Significantly, the domestic space, the private realm of women, has returned in a globalized India but with some changes. Thus, just as we have a redefining of middle class virtues at home, the household is actively redrawn as a site of consumption and the Indian woman learns that 'thrift' is no longer a virtue and shopping a legitimate pleasure (ibid. 1998). And Indian men learn that looking good is not only a woman's privilege, as new images of groomed Indian men flood the electronic and print media. Simultaneously, 'tradition' appears to become a key site for promoting consumption. Each traditional ritual, once a localized practice, has now become potent forums for national celebration and conspicuous consumption. The 'Big Indian Wedding' has become a site for conspicuous consumption and celebration of 'traditions'—often very recently invented. The rhetoric of tradition and modernity now gets appropriated by a market keen to promote its goods and services.

In this new phase of globalization, even as dominant and visible sections of the Indian society move forward to what may appear as an unmarked consumer society, deep lines of contestation between the modern and traditional play themselves out even as basic questions regarding what constitutes 'tradition' and whose 'tradition', remain unresolved. In the entire story of India's modernity, a gendered perspective offers us a critical look into how patriarchal power whether of class or caste, of state or community plays out in issues pertaining to gender. As this paper sought to show the rhetoric of 'tradition and modernity' within which the status and role of Indian women were sought to be understood hid more than it revealed.

NOTES

1. The largest state in India, Uttar Pradesh is governed by not just a woman Chief Minister who is single, but a woman coming from the most oppressed dalit community. The list of powerful women CEOs of major corporations is long, and the media covers their achievements in a major fashion. Even as I write the media reports that Dr Kiran Mazumdar-Shaw has entered the elite ranks of the Indian business world as India's richest woman. She is the Chairman and Managing Director of Biocon Ltd. (www.mapsofindia.com, 6 May 2010).
2. Female literacy was at a national average of 53.63 per cent whereas the male literacy was 75.26 per cent in the 2001 census. India's maternal

mortality rate stands at 450 per 100,000 live births according to UNICEF (Dhar 2009).

3. A young woman journalist working in Delhi was found dead in her native home. Her parents were opposing her desire to marry a young woman who belonged to a 'lower caste' (Deo 2010). A number of honour killings, executed at the behest of khap panchayat, traditional village councils, to punish defiant young adults for marrying outside society's norms, grab media headlines (Bharadwaj 2010).

4. The 2001 census showed 933 women for 1000 men. The sex ratio in more prosperous and developed states of Punjab, Haryana and Delhi was 874, 861 and 821 respectively.

5. Yuval-Davis and Anthias (1989) has summed up the ways in which women have tended to participate in ethnic and national processes and in relation to state practices. These are:
   (a) as biological reproducers of members of ethnic collectivities;
   (b) as reproducers of the boundaries of the ethnic/national groups;
   (c) as participating centrally in the ideological reproduction of the collectivity and as transmitters of its culture;
   (d) as signifiers of ethnic/national differences—as a focus and symbol in ideological discourses used in the construction, reproduction and transformation of ethnic/national categories; and
   (e) as participants in national, economic, political and military struggles. In practice these would tend to blur into each other.

6. See Chaudhuri 2011, Chapters 2 and 3.

7. With the rise of Indian nationalism, self-conscious attempts were made to fashion what would constitute visible signs of Indian tradition and culture. There were also attempts to develop a dress style that would draw on the tradition of different regions. In the late 1870s, Jnanadanandini Devi, wife of Satyendranath Tagore, the first Indian member of the ICS, returned from Bombay to Calcutta. She adopted the Parsi style of wearing the sari pinned to the left shoulder with a brooch, and worn with a blouse and shoes. This was quickly adopted by Brahmo Samaji women and came to be known as the Brahmika sari. This style gained acceptance before long among Maharashtrian and Uttar Pradesh Brahmos, as well as non-Brahmos.

REFERENCES

Benhabib, Seyla. 1987. 'The Generalised and the Concrete Other', in Seyla Benhabib and Drucilla Cornell (eds), *Feminism as Critique*. Oxford: Blackwell and Minneapolis: University of Minnesota Press, pp. 1–15.

Chaudhuri, Maitrayee. 1996. 'Citizens, Workers and Emblems of Culture: An Analysis of the First Plan Document on Women', in Patricia Uberoi (ed.), *Social Reform, Sexuality and the State*. New Delhi: Sage, pp. 211–235.

——. 1998. 'Advertisements, Print Media and the New Indian Woman', *Social Action*, July: 239–252.

——. 2001. 'Gender and Advertisements: The Rhetoric of Globalisation', *Women's Studies International Forum*, Vol. 24, No. 3/4: 373–385. Reprinted in Joseph Turow and Matthew McAllister (eds), *The Advertising and Consumer Culture Reader*. London: Routledge, Ch. 11.

——. (ed.), 2005. *Feminism in India*. London: Zed.

——. 2011. 'The Concept of Gender: Its Travels and Travails', in Maitrayee Chaudhuri (ed.), *Sociology of India: Intellectual and Institutional Practices*. Jaipur: Rawat, pp. 381–399.

——. 2011. *The Indian Women's Movement: Reform and Revival*. New Delhi: Palm Leaf.

Inquilab. 13 November 1985. Open Letter to Muslims, reprinted and translated in *Radiance*, November 24–30.

John, Mary. 1996. 'Gender and Development in India, 1970s–1990s: Some Reflections on the Constitutive Role of Contexts', *Economic and Political Weekly*, November 23.

Natarajan, Jayanthi. 1996. 'A Political Hypocrisy', *The Hindu*, December.

Pathak, Zakia and Rajeshwari Sunder Rajan. 1989. 'Shahbano', *Signs*, Vol. 14, No. 3: 558–582.

Rege, Sharmila. 1998. 'Dalit Women Talk Differently: A Critique of "Difference" and Towards a Dalit Feminist Standpoint', *Economic and Political Weekly*, October 31.

Sangari, Kumkum. 1988. 'Perpetuating the Myth', *Seminar*, No. 342, February.

Singer, Milton. 1972. *When a Great Tradition Modernizes: An Anthropological Approach to Indian Civilization*. New York: Praeger.

Yuval-Davis, Nira and Floya Anthias (eds). 1989. *Woman-Nation-State*. New Delhi: Palgrave Macmillan.

Websites

Deo, Digvijay Singh. 2010. 'Mystery Surrounds Delhi Journalist's Death'. 3 May 2010, http://www.ibnlive.in.com, accessed 7 May 2010.

Bharadwaj, Ajay/DNA. 2010. 'Khap Gets Rap: 5 Sentenced to Death for Honour Killing'. 30 March 2010, http://www.dnaindia.com.india/report_haryana-honour-killing-case, accessed 3 April 2010.

Dhar, Sujoy. 2009. 'Indian Grapples with High Maternal Mortality Rates'. 26 January 2009, http://in.reuters.com, accessed 11 May 2010.

Joshi, Vishal and Aurangzeb Naqshbandi. 2010. 'Navin Jindal, Chauthala Join Hands, Lobby for Khap Panchayats'. 11 May 2010, http://www.hindustantimes.com, accessed 12 May 2010.

http://dance.www. withshadows.com, 24 March 2010, accessed 3 April 2010.

www.ahmedabadmirror.com, accessed 7 April 2010.

11

Technology Growth in India

Some Important Concerns

DURU ARUN KUMAR

The Government of India, since its independence from British colonial rulers in 1947, has supported and promoted science and technology through its various national policies. India was one of the first countries to adopt a Science Policy Resolution in 1958, which stated, 'The key to national prosperity, apart from the spirit of the people, lies, in the modern age, in the effective combination of three factors, technology, raw materials and capital, of which the first is perhaps the most important, since the creation and adoption of new scientific techniques can, in fact, make up for a deficiency in natural resources, and reduce the demands on capital. But technology can only grow out of the study of science and its applications'. As a result of this, a number of science and technical educational and research institutes and laboratories were set up on government initiative in different parts of India.[1] Further, acknowledging the widespread core competence and innovation in a number of areas in the country and to make India a self-dependent and advanced nation, the Technology Policy Statement, 1983 was introduced to give technological development a clear direction for the growth of indigenous technology and the acquisition of technology from outside.[2]

The Government of India constituted the Technology Development Board (TDB) in September 1996, as per the provisions of the Technology Development Board Act, 1995. The Act enables creation of a Fund for Technology Development and Application to be administered by TDB. The Fund receives grants from the Government of India out of the cess collected by the government from industrial concerns under the provisions of the Research and Development Cess Act, 1986, as amended in 1995.[3]

Thus, it may be ascertained that there has been a consistent patronage and political support for science and technology activities in India. This is also indicated by a huge science and technology institutional structure and several programmes created under various government departments and ministries to promote and support research and development in various fields such as Department of Science and Technology, Department of Information Technology, Department of Electronics, Indian Space Research Organization and several others.[4]

As a result of these sustained efforts through various funding schemes, significant progress has been made in certain technology sectors, particularly in strategic industries such as space sciences,[5] nuclear technology, defence technology, aviation and information technology. India's defence research laboratories have successfully developed light combat aircraft, ballistic missiles, satellite communications and several other technologies of strategic importance.

Looking at some of the examples mentioned above, we notice that most of these developments are in highly specialized and niche areas, with long gestation periods and far removed from scope for immediate application for direct public domain, but have been internationally acclaimed. These fields are highly capital intensive and depend on continuous government support.

Another important development has been that of IT and IT-enabled services sectors in India, recognized globally as highly competitive sectors. The IT-ITES industry has two major components: IT services and business process outsourcing (BPO). The growth in the service sector in India has been led by the IT-ITES sector, contributing substantially to the increase in gross domestic product (GDP), employment, and exports. The sector has increased its contribution to India's GDP from 1.2 per cent in financial year 1998 to 7.1 per cent in financial year 2011.[6]

India's progress in Information and Communication Technologies (ICT) is also accompanied by many challenges. There is a perception that the Indian economy as a whole has not benefited from the ICT industry because of the high regional concentration of

ICT activity and low diffusion of ICT to other sectors of the economy. A large part of the IT sector is involved in export-oriented services and products. It helps provide employment and earns foreign revenue for India but adds limited value addition to India's technology requirements. The IT and ICT boom is visible only in special regions and locations mostly in southern India, and the concentration of skilled human resources in the IT and ICT sectors is adversely affecting other sectors of the economy.[7]

Consumer Market

In the last few decades India has emerged as a huge consumer market. This can be traced to a shift in the economic policy from socialist to market economy to tide over the balance of payment crisis in 1991. As a part of the bail out plan under the International Monetary Fund, India made certain structural economic reforms. The main thrust of the 1991 economic reforms in India was to allow for the operation of a free market, where the forces of demand and supply could freely compete and the local and the national economy could be integrated into the global economy (Kothari 1997). The elaborate structure of licences, controls and regulations was abolished to help increase production, efficiency and demand and decrease prices. Import restrictions were relaxed and steps were taken toward the liberalization of foreign trade and investments, a reduction in custom duties, an increase in incentives and policy changes to attract foreign capital. As a result of this, there was an upsurge in import of mass produced goods in the Indian markets.

A wide array of products such as foreign cars, televisions, electronics, washing machines, air-conditioners, processed foods, perfumes, and other consumer goods, became freely available and have become symbolic of new status-conscious Indians. Incentive for industrial production has come primarily from these changing demands. Thus, as pointed by Kothari, it is not the availability of essential commodities, improved access and control over productive resources, low-cost and decentralized conventional and alternative energy sources, but rather products and services that are mostly beyond the means of the majority of the low income groups of people.

Even though a large number of imported consumer products are available in the Indian markets, most do not cater to the essential needs requirement of the poor people, there is an increasing demand for such products for different reasons. There is 'indigenization' or 'domestication' of the meaning attached to possession of these consumer products. It is considered as a symbol of higher status by the bourgeoning urban middle class and those aspiring to higher social status. The concept of domestication of foreign products and brands has been studied by other scholars too. As pointed out by some, even the most 'global' brands, such as McDonald's or Coca Cola, have different cultural connotations and are consumed quite differently in different places.[8] Arjun Appadurai argues that 'as rapidly as forces from various metropolises are brought into new societies, they tend to become indigenized in one way or another' (Appadurai 1996: 32). The following years have seen most of the imports and fresh investments in the productive economy, oriented not toward meeting the basic needs of a majority, but primarily toward satisfying the consumption patterns of the elite.

Besides policies of free market economy adopted by India there has also been a preference for imported products as they are believed to be of superior quality than the locally manufactured ones. Except where it is entirely unavoidable, as pointed out in a vision document, Indian administrators (whether in the public or in the private sector) avoid local designs. They consider that well-worn imported designs alone are risk free. For instance, it is the official policy in the Department of Telecommunications (and in others too) not to procure any equipment unless it has been used for a minimum of two years. As a result, Indian designs face a Catch-22 situation: They will not be accepted unless they have been in use, and they cannot be in use until they are tried out (Indiresan 2001)!

As a result of the above developments, even though there is a large influx of technology products available in Indian markets for a price, it is not clear that they play a role in India's technological capacity building. Do they fulfil the technological needs of the society at large in an equitable and inclusive manner? We illustrate our point by discussing the revolution caused by the introduction of mobile technology in India in the last two decades.

Mobile Phones

Mobile phones are the first form of electronic communication technology to be widely used in India. Since mobile networks are cheaper to build than landline networks, and communication by phone does not require literacy, mobile phones are now increasingly adopted in regions with no extensive prior form of communication technology. The rate of mobile phone sales in India has been phenomenal ever since the introduction of mobile technology in 1995. With a subscriber base of more than 851 million, the mobile telecommunications system in India is the second largest in the world and it was thrown open to private players in the 1990s.[9] According to the International Data Corporation's Q3 2011 Mobile Phone Tracker release, the Indian mobile phone market grew 12 per cent in units shipped, over the previous quarter, to clock 47.07 million units.[10] According to a market survey company, mobile user base had increased to 407 million users by 2011. And interestingly, it also claims that there has been higher increase in penetration and tele-density in the rural mobile connections compared to urban India.[11]

Modern media communication technologies have been developed and essentially tailored to fulfil the needs of the high-income, literate people of the developed countries. According to some studies, '... technologies ... are a part of a matrix of global relations that has historically placed the developing world in a derivative relationship' (Kavoori and Chaddha 2007: 227). This relationship has been reiterated in earlier histories, of television, radio, newspaper and the Internet (ibid.: 2007). Cell phone is also one of them. Since introduction of mobile phones in the Indian market, it has found many users for many reasons. As pointed out by these studies, a majority of low-income, low-literacy populations have a fluid and temporary identity. They lack any form of permanent identification and are under the radar of governmental and institutional surveillance. For a migrant population, the mobile phone could even be their only fixed point of reference. Further, it is observed that, the so-called emerging market has by-passed technological, physical, educational, amongst other barriers to creatively use mobile phones to uplift themselves.

Mobile telephony like cinema, in an earlier era, seems to be a great social leveller. Further, mobile technology probably helps rural farmers decide which market to go, to sell their produce at the highest possible price. Even in the case of the urban poor such as craftsmen—electricians, plumbers, etc.—the mobile phone directly gives them access to customers. Previously, they were dependent on contractors and shopkeepers to point them to work. Now they can function independently as free lancers and peddle their skills without relying exclusively on contractors and shop-keepers who have land lines and were the only means of contact between the craftsman and his customer. All this is a direct result of the easy availability of mobile phones. So it is not at all surprising that India is emerging as one of the biggest consumers of mobile telephony.

Discussion

Looking at the various government policy measures with regard to science and technology we may argue that a technologically deterministic approach is adopted on the belief that based on the developed countries' model, introduction of science and technology institutions can bring about growth of science and technology. Government legitimated its policies in terms of the technological imperative. It was implied that by supporting important technology areas of research there will be a trickle-down effect that will eventually lead to technological development of the society at large. However, the advanced technology efforts have remained confined to areas sponsored by government funding and infrastructural support.

While on the one hand, there are regions in India which are called 'cybercities' and 'silicon valleys' of India with state of the art technology development centres in Information Technology (Kalra 2006), on the other hand, a large part of India's population lives in poverty and remains untouched and unaware of these technology achievements. There are several regions which do not have access to electricity, potable drinking water and basic health facilities. Provision of these basic facilities would probably require a small fraction of the budget spent on the so-called sophisticated technology development programmes. How do we reconcile India being a technologically advanced nation on the one hand, while on the other, more than thirty per cent of its population lives in poverty with no access to basic amenities for a dignified life?

The consumer markets, ruled by free market forces, have been inundated with secondary goods, with a higher profit margin and catering to the middle and upper classes of the country. Among these, mobile phones are one of the few imported technologies which have found ready acceptance by the rich and the poor alike because of its small size, portability, user-friendly features, affordability and most importantly, fulfilling a need caused by increasing urbanization and migration of people in search of livelihood and absence of any reliable and affordable means of communication available to people based in underdeveloped parts of India. However, a large number of mobile phone users in non-urban areas use it only for basic communication and are not able to use several other features such as text messaging and Internet access because literacy rates in these areas is very low. Poor infrastructure and erratic or no power supply create other logistics problems. Lack of English language knowledge also poses limitations to their optimum use.

Exploring the complexities in what she calls 'schizophrenic India', Rama Bijapurkar suggests that 'the holy grail of the Indian market lies in understanding its plurality' (Bijapurkar 2007). India is not one homogenous society, but a collection of many different communities defined by language religion and ethnicity, each with its distinctive cultural ethos, social pattern, and demography. To be successful in the Indian market, it is not sufficient to create 'no-frills' cheaper versions of feature-rich expensive products but to invest effort in understanding use requirements and developing appropriate models (Bijapurkar 2001).

The current experiences have shown that people who do not use ICTs are willing to accept technology and put in the effort to learn to use it. But for the products to become successful, they must be designed to suit the users' real needs.[12] India presents several obstacles for widespread adoption of information and communication technologies, but perhaps the most persistent problem of all has proved to be the problem of text input in Indian languages.[13] Computer usage in India has been almost entirely in English and is restricted to the English-speaking, upper-class and middle-class people. Mobile phones have recently proved to be an exception to this rule, with a significant number of models becoming available in Indian languages, however text entry in Indian languages continues to be a rare phenomenon.

Important sectors such as manufacturing technologies, infrastructure development, electronics and power generation industry have made significant progress with regard to scale of production, quality and competitiveness, but the most frequently voiced concerns relate to lack of skilled manpower and poor infrastructure, specially, power shortages in the country, as important limiting factors in their progress.

As of 2011, there are 1,522 degree-granting engineering colleges in India with an annual student intake of 5,82,000, plus 1,244 polytechnics with an annual intake of 2,65,000. However, these institutions face shortage of faculty and concerns have been raised over the quality of education[14] (Mitra 2008).

According to industry estimates 'only a quarter of all gradùates are employable and about 80 per cent of job seekers in employment exchanges are without any professional skills. India is suffering from a massive shortage of skilled manpower' (Duggal 2005). But employability here refers to the management skills in marketing, finance and operations, and not technology and engineering skills, as is apparent from this report which pointed out, 'Businesses in India have started spreading their tentacles in towns, cities and semi-urban areas in search of newer markets. These are seen as future markets for telecommunications, FMCG and retail sector among others. As companies expand their operations, they are not finding enough trained people to fit into different positions' (ibid.). Further, it reports, 'Retail, insurance, finance industry are booming. The recently released KPMG report on retailing in the country titled as 'Consumer Markets in India, the next big thing?' has revealed that plans are up for at least 150 new shopping malls by 2008. Also, the number of department stores has been growing at 24 per cent annually. Such growth would again aggravate the demand for trained man power in organized sectors dramatically.

Following the services sector concentration, consumer services have been a focus area for the Business schools which include financial, banking, retail, consulting, telecom, IT, etc.

Because of the increase in the jobs available in the service sector many young engineering graduates prefer to join non-technical service oriented and managerial jobs. As a result of this, manufacturing industries and other technology sectors are not able to get technically qualified manpower. More than 90 per cent of the engineering graduates prefer to join management professions (Arun-Kumar 2008).

How does this state of affairs impact the technology development in India? On the one hand, we have a large infrastructure to support science and technology education and research activities. We also have an ever-increasing demand for growth of various industrial sectors. But, on the other hand, there is a steady decline of a willing and technically qualified manpower because of preference for lucrative jobs in the service sector. This problem is further compounded by the poor quality of technical and engineering education in many privately funded engineering colleges due to lack of good teaching faculties and infrastructural support. At the same time, due to increasing investment in the market economy, the demand for the service sector and management professional has increased manyfold with the corresponding disenchantment with the core technical jobs. Science and technology qualified manpower forms the backbone of this sector. In the absence of this it may be challenging for India to sustain a broad-based technological development, and subsequently to become an integral part of social change. This needs to be explored further with respect to different technology sectors in India with the help of empirical studies.

NOTES

1. http://www.dst.gov.in/stsysindia/spr1958.htm
2. http://www.dst.gov.in/stsysindia/sps1983.htm
3. http://www.dst.gov.in/stsysindia/sps1983.htm
4. http://www.tdb.gov.in/
5. National Centre for Astrophysics, a centre of the school of natural sciences of the Tata Institute of Fundamental Research, has set up a unique facility, the Giant Meterwave Radio Telescope for radio astronomical research at metre wavelengths. GMRT is a very versatile instrument for investigating a variety of radio astrophysical problems ranging from nearby Solar system to the edge of observable universe. http://gmrt.ncra.tifr.res.in/

6. http://www.indianembassy.org/indiainfo/india_2000/chapters/chp07.pdf
7. http://www.nasscom.in/indian-itbpo-industry; http://www.digital-review.org/uploads/files/pdf/2009-2010/chap-21_india.pdf
8. Daniel Miller's (1998) work on consumption practices in Trinidad and Marie Gillespie's (1995) ethnographic study of young Punjabis in Southall, West London are some of the examples of this 'domestication' of meaning.
9. http://en.wikipedia.org/wiki/Communications_in_India
10. http://www.idc.com/getdoc.jsp?containerId=prIN23230811
11. http://indiatechonline.com/juxtconsult-india-mobile-phones-study-2011-545.php
12. International and national standardization bodies such as ISO, UNICODE, World-Wide-Web Consortium (W3C) and BIS (Bureau of Indian Standards) to ensure adequate representation of Technology Development for Indian Languages (TDIL) Programme initiated by the Department of Electronics and Information Technology (DEIT), Ministry of Communication (http://tdil.mit.gov.in/).
13. Technology Development for Indian Languages (TDIL) Programme initiated by the Department of Electronics and Information Technology (DEIT), Ministry of Communication & Information Technology (MC&IT), Government of India has the objective of developing Information Processing Tools and Techniques to facilitate human-machine interaction without language barrier; creating and accessing multilingual knowledge resources; and integrating them to develop innovative user products and services. The Programme also promotes Language Technology standardization through active participation in international and national standardization bodies such as ISO, UNICODE, World-Wide-Web Consortium (W3C) and BIS (Bureau of Indian Standards) to ensure adequate representation of Indian languages in existing and future language technology standards (http://tdil.mit.gov.in/).
14. *The Education Race,* special report by *Newsweek*, August 18–25, 2011 issue.

REFERENCES

Arun-Kumar, Duru. 2008. 'Impact of Globalization on Core Engineering Education in India', *Perspectives in Global Development and Technology*, Vol. 7, No. 1: 55–68.

Appadurai, Ahmad. 1996. *Modernity at Large: Cultural Dimensions of Globalization*. Minneapolis: University of Minnesota Press.

Appadurai, Ahmad and C.A. Breckenridge. 1995. 'Public Modernity in India', in C.A. Breckenridge (ed.), *Consuming Modernity: Public Culture in a South Asian World*. Minneapolis: University of Minnesota Press, pp. 1–20.

Bijapurkar, Rama. 2001. 'New Markets, New Rules', *Business World*, July 30.

——. 2007. *We Are Like that Only*. India: Penguin Books.

Duggal, Sanjeev. 2005. 'Is Lack of Talent Pool Affecting India Inc's Growth? India is Suffering from a Real Shortage of Manpower', Posted online: Friday, 4 November 2005 *The Financial Express*, http://www.financialexpress.com/old/fe_full_story.php, content_id=107542.

Gillespie, Marie. 1995. *Television, Ethnicity and Cultural Change*. New York: Routledge.

Indiresan, P.V. 2001. 'Technology Policy in a Vision for the Future', http://planningcommission.nic.in/reports/sereport/ser/vision2025/tech.pdf (accessed 23 May 2012).

Jackson, Peter. 2004. 'Local Consumption Cultures in a Globalizing World', *Transactions of Institute of British Geography*, NS, 29: 165–178.

Joshi, Anirudha et al. 2008. 'Rangoli: A Visual Phonebook for Low-literate Users' (Conference)/Mobile HCI 2008.

Kalra, R. 2006. 'High Technology and Urban Development in Bangalore', *GeoJournal Library*, Vol. 86: 71–81.

Kavoori, Anandan and Kalyani Chaddha. 2007. 'Cell Phones as a Cultural Technology: Lessons from the Indian Case', in A. Kavoori and N. Arceneaux (eds), *The Cell Phone Reader*. New York: Langenscheidt Publishing Group.

Kothari, Smitu. 1997. 'Whose Independence? The Social Impact of Economic Reform in India', *Journal of International Affairs*, Vol. 51, No. 1: 85.

Kumar, Anshuman Holambe et al. 2011. 'Saral: Devanagari Text Input System in Mobile Phones', E-Book, Freetechbooks.com.

Manzar, Osama and Syed S. Kazi. 2009–2010. 'India', *in Digital Review of Asia Pacific*. New Delhi: Sage Publications, pp. 192–200.

Miller, D. 1998. 'Coca-Cola: A Black Sweet Drink from Trinidad', in D. Miller (ed.), *Material Cultures: Why Some Things Matter*? London: UCL Press, pp. 169–187.

Mitra, Sramana. 2008. 'How to Save the World's Back Office?', *Forbes*, March 14.

12

Story of the Clashing Images of the Country

The Case of India's Image at Home and in Poland

PIOTR KŁODKOWSKI

The main objective of this paper is to demonstrate the complex process of creating a country image. It consists of two parts, being interrelated with each other, however not in a direct way. In part one, I focus on the image of India which is partly a result of the grand economic transformation initiated in the beginning of the 1990s, and partly a heritage of much older cultural and political tradition. The selection of texts that I have made to analyse this complex process of image creation, may appear to be a subjective one, but I tend to believe that the selected texts faithfully reflect a wide and popular spectrum of opinions and convictions. I dare to think the phenomenon of 'clashing images' is a never-ending story, as nowadays a country image is always in *statu nascendi*. In part two, I deal with the history of India's image in Poland. In other words, I attempt to present the case of a country which, unlike other European states, never ventured to establish its own political presence overseas, so it was not able to use the powerful state-machinery to acquire the knowledge very much needed to control a subjugated territory, but nevertheless, it could build a complex structure of various images of the civilization it hardly had any direct political contact with. The accuracy and intensity of this image-building process often depended on genuine interest in the culture of 'a distant land', on the creativity and sensitivity of the local elite and political circumstances which could positively or negatively affect its receptivity. By the end of the 18th century, Poland was probably the most religiously, linguistically and culturally diverse country on the European soil, located—and Poles often emphasized the fact—between 'the West and the East' (with its own diversity the pre-partition Poland resembled, *toutes proportions gardées,* the most culturally diverse Indian subcontinent). No wonder, Poles drew inspirations for their own cultural identity both from the countries in the West (mostly France and German-speaking princedoms/kingdoms) and the East, which had a bit more obscure location in their minds but generally comprised the Russian and Ottoman empires plus Persia, although the latter one had probably more mythical dimension for Poles as they hardly ever had a chance to visit it. India gradually started to occupy a very important place, first in their poetic imagination, then in their scholarship and art. The process of building various images of India in Poland was somehow different from the one in Western Europe, as it was, at least in its early stages, mostly founded on imaginary concepts, poetic association with Polish folklore or extremely brave religious comparisons, and much later, on common striving for freedom, both spiritual and political. I assume that the phenomena of image-building of India in the Western countries, especially in the ones that played the global game in the 19th and 20th centuries, have been described and analysed quite satisfactorily; whereas, the same process in Central European states, i.e., in the ones that had very limited direct contacts with South-East Asia yet gradually developed their interests in this region, has not been dealt with sufficiently. It is my intention to fill in the gap in a history of Indo-European contacts, with focus on Poland, the country that has constructed its own versions of clashing images of India. As in part one, the selection of texts (or persons) I refer to may seem to be subjective, but I am convinced these adequately illustrate the attitudes, impressions, concepts and ideas which have greatly contributed to the process of making the image (or, in fact several images) of India in Poland. In part two, the phenomenon of 'clashing images' is hardly visible, as this stage of an image development is not yet present in our part of Europe. I generally refrain from commenting on the veracity of analysed images, because I think each of them contains a few particles of the perceived and experienced ground-reality and a few particles of the imagined and projected reality. Therefore, the final product is usually a combination of intentionally selected facts, their interpretations and our own vision of justice, success and truth.

There is little doubt in today's world that innovation, creativity and conducive cultural and political frameworks are the key drivers of business, economic or social success. Modern national companies, multinational corporations, centres of higher education, NGOs, selected teams of scientists do their best to project an attractive image of their own organizations and their own activities, which should be externally perceived as being deeply rooted in the realm of practical innovation, unlimited creativity and strong corporate culture. In other words, to promote its various products and services a company, especially one operating internationally, desires to be positively branded. The concept of branding is not only limited to commercial, social or scientific entities, it is also applicable to nations and countries. It is quite reasonable to assume that a well-conceived and well-managed country image has a significant role in branding countries. As a result it helps the country to brand its own products, services, its own culture—which may serve as the half-independent soft-power globally—or its policies in the international arena. While USA has been known for long as 'the country of liberties', Great Britain has projected its own image as 'cool Britannia' and India's slogan is internationally recognized as 'incredible India'.[1] The tangible and less tangible profits of positioning the country can be easily discovered in the stereotyped attitude towards available products and services. Plenty of customers worldwide declare their trust in 'German cars', 'French perfumes', 'Italian/Chinese/Indian cooking', although 'German cars' may be assembled in Shanghai, 'French perfumes' made in Thailand and the taste of Chinese dishes prepared in Europe might be miles away from the original one.[2] Nevertheless, this stereotyped perception of 'national products' still prevails and it is very unlikely it will be totally replaced by branding of international products whose origin is often not disclosed to potential customers. According to Simon Anholt and the company GMI (cited as Anholt-GMI) these nation brands are far more important than a Nike or Nestlé. It is their vision that with globalization, 'countries compete with each other for the attention, respect and trust of investors, tourists, consumers, donors, immigrants, the media and the governments of other nations'. It is thus clear that for a country's government or organization it is essential to know where it should position itself and what it plans to achieve while projecting a nation brand. And it is not less important to ask how to define the branding of a country, how to measure its strengths, how to project its real advantages and finally how to persuade others into accepting its own positive image. Anholt-GMI propose their own Nation Brand Index which is based on people's perception of a country in six selected areas: tourism, exports, governance, people, culture and heritage, investment and immigration.

After accumulating the collected data each country is ranked in the six selected areas and the result is indicated by a hexagon. The country with the highest overall score becomes the country with the best branding but there are also winners for each selected area.[3]

Making of a New Modern Country Image at Home and Abroad: India's Case

All the proposed tools which can be applied for measuring the brand of a country are certainly very useful but unlike in the case of multinationals which appear to be extremely flexible in their pursuit of profits and therefore in reshaping and projecting its own image and—to some extent—its own economic reality (e.g., by changing or expanding sectors, in which they may operate), the limits of a country branding are clearly visible, or at least they are less prone to modifications. Promoting a country as a whole image is inevitably subject to where the reality is. This perceived reality seems to be inescapable; the geographical location of a country, its history and economy or cultural values, in other words: hard facts cannot be mere fiction. However, this is not to deny that every country is able to create its own narration which may refer only to 'positive' facts selected from the national treasury of history. This 'positive fact selection' can hardly become dominating, as the process of creating a national image is partly a spontaneous activity, in which a role of the State, especially the democratic one, is limited. In case of national branding, various images of a country may emerge at the same time or at different times so the final product is likely to have changeable shades, several layers, or clashing interpretations. Projecting a carefully planned country image, which by definition should be more static than dynamic, will always pose a threat, because the historical reality and subjective perceptions can vary very quickly. This sort of image is a very complex structure, so it is not perceived in the same way globally. For example, an image of India in Europe would differ significantly from her image in Pakistan or China. The issue is even more complex, as a centrally projected image may or may not be accepted on the domestic ground, which in turn may produce the phenomenon of 'clashing images': a few images, being at variance with each other yet existing within one broad image. This image game is becoming an inspiring challenge as it is being played both internationally and domestically; it is hard to conclude which one is more rewarding or more frustrating.

Branding India

Shashi Tharoor, an Indian politician and a Member of Parliament, who previously served as the United Nations Under-Secretary General for Communications and Public Information and as the Minister of State for the Ministry of External Affairs, is a prolific author and journalist who takes credit for promoting a new inspiring image of India for the international audience. In his oft-commented books, especially *Nehru: The Invention of India* (2003), *India: From Midnight to the Millennium* (1997) or *The Elephant, the Tiger and the Cell Phone: Reflections on India in the 21st Century* (2007) he projects a great Indian leap into the 21st century, the experience of 'the unimaginable transformation of the country' so far portrayed as having been deeply rooted in its tradition and ancient culture. Tharoor's vision of a 'New India' appears to be shared by many readers, both domestic and foreign. In the chapter 10 of *The Elephant* ... he observes:

> We all know India has changed dramatically in recent years: the country I left when I first went abroad as a student in 1975 would be barely recognizable to the young Indians of today. To those who remember the old India, there's visible evidence of change around, from the variety of makes of cars on the roads to the number of channels on my mother's television set, not to mention the malls now sprouting like mushrooms in chic suburbs that used to be dusty and forlorn mofussils. But what about the invisible evidence of

> change? How does one capture the transformation of attitude that's essential a part of what India has become? [...] Sreesanth's extraordinary hit over Nel's head for six (both are cricket players, representing India and South Africa respectively—PK) encapsulates for me all that is different about the new India: courage, assertiveness, a refusal to be intimidated, a willingness to take risks and ultimately the confidence to stand up to the best that the outside world can fling at us. This goes well beyond the cricket field. [...] India is the land that throws out the intruders of Kargil, that acquires Europe's largest steel conglomerate in the face of taunts about 'monkey money', that exports more films abroad than it imports, that challenges the traditional assumption of superiority by others, that wins Booker prizes and Miss Universe contests.[4]

Tharoor perfectly understands the value of a well-presented image of a country, or an appealing narration on modernity and antiquity in one which easily captivates the reading audience. He is the author of a catchy phrase that in today's world it's not the size of the army that wins, it's the country that tells a better story. Since India has always been extremely good at telling stories, the modern version of the 'narrative branding' does not pose a real challenge for creative intellectuals, national brand managers and inquisitive observers. They may refer to ancient history or to more recent developments to give substance to their new vision of the country, and we assume that very few foreign critics would be capable of challenging a proposed line of reasoning. The fact that India, as a multi-linguistic, multi-religious and multi-ethnic state, has been functioning successfully for more than 60 years, and this, in spite of the pessimistic analyses and gloomy views expressed by a plethora of European and American journalists, academicians or statesmen, mostly in the 1960s and 1970s, is per se the most visible proof of a success story. Ramachandra Guha, the author of the opus magnum on the modern history of India, 'India after Gandhi: The History of the World's Largest Democracy', aptly delineates the intellectual divisions between Western and Indian politicians and ideologues in their perception of democracy, cultural coherence and the concept of the state.[5] He reminds us that for the Americans and for many European nations a shared language and mostly shared faith worked in tandem with animosity towards the colonists or foreign oppressors which was the case especially for the Poles, the Czechs or the Lithuanians. He says:

> Behind every successful nationalist movement in the Western world has been a certain unifying factor, a glue holding the members of the nation together, this provided by a shared language, a shared religious faith, a shared territory, a common enemy—and sometimes all the above.[6]

By contrast, the Indian nation in its official stance does not privilege a single language or religious faith. Although the majority of Indian citizens declare to be Hindus, India is not a Hindu state and there is no one national language spoken by all the inhabitants. Guha illustrates this secular and linguistic vision of the modern India with a few examples:

> Like Indian democracy, Indian secularism is also a story that combines success with failure. Membership of a minority religion is no bar to advancement in business or the professions. The richest industrialist in India is a Muslim. Some of the most popular film stars are Muslim. At least three presidents of India and two chief justices have been Muslim. In 2007, the president of India is a Muslim, prime minister a Sikh, and the leader of the ruling party a Catholic born in Italy. Many of the country's most prominent lawyers and doctors have been Christians and Parsis. [...] The pluralism of religion was one cornerstone of the foundation of the Indian republic. A second was the pluralism of language. Here again, the intention and the effort well pre-dated Independence.[7]

The globally projected success story of India, a state proud of both its ancient history and very promising future, is being retold by external observers, fascinated by the process of economic and social transformation which has produced, strong in number and assertive in attitude, a new middle class, combining dynamism and creativity with attachment to more traditional values. This frequently retold success story is set in a densely-populated country characterized by the most unimaginable ethnic, religious, linguistic diversity and coexisting cultural identities; in a country that has managed to create pan-Indian sentiments and pan-Indian pride, and that in spite of the not-so-old conflicts painfully experienced along the divisive lines of a language, religion and caste. The story is based on the economic achievements, mostly in the advanced technology sectors: IT, nano- and bio-technology, or pharmaceutical industry which have reshaped and modernized the business structure in India. On the global scale the story was widely publicized by Thomas Friedman in 2005 when his mega-bestseller *The World is Flat: A Brief History of the Twenty-First Century* was released. In the book, Friedman recounts a journey to the Indian IT-centre in Bangalore, when he realized globalization has changed core economic concepts. One of his most inspiring interlocutors, Nandan Nilekani, the former CEO of Infosys, made a statement on 'the flattening world' and that later was used by the author as the title of the book. Friedman's view that the phenomenon of flattening is a product of a convergence of personal computer with fibre-optic micro cable with the rise of work flow software has often been criticized (Nobel's laureate Joseph Stieglitz presented quite an opposite opinion: not only is the world not flat: in many ways it has been getting less flat) but his message nonetheless reached the global reading audience who learned about the fundamental role of India in the process termed by the writer as Globalization 3.0.[8]

The Clashing Images

In the first decade of the 21st century more success stories appeared. American, British, German, Russian or Polish journalists, academicians, business persons or politicians with better or worse literary skills shared their impressions, analyses and opinions on the 'Rising India'. Some of them have been focused on India for years and have kept the readers updated on the changing image of the country. In 2008, Dietmar Rothermund released a book: *India: The Rise of an Asian Giant*.[9] It summarizes his research on the transformation process in India and discloses to a reader an impressive spectrum of challenges the country has had to face since its independence. The author is, as he puts it himself, 'a witness who has watched India for nearly half a century'. He first visited the place in 1960, and managed to interview Jawaharlal Nehru, India's first prime minister, twice. The image of India globally, as portrayed in the book, has undergone an astonishing number of changes and modifications, reaching a stage of an undisputed Asian giant ready to play a long deserved role of a superpower. It is the superpower with almost unlimited potential to be utilized in the near future. The book must have contributed to strengthening an already positive image of India in Europe, but not all the readers shared the author's optimism. A good illustration of a more skeptical view on the future of India and her globally projected image comes from a review by William Leith, representing The Spectator Book Club. Although he does not hide his very limited knowledge on the subject, his remarks and conclusions may reflect a common perception of the country abroad. The perception more focused on the negative implications of the economic growth, he perceives as being still generated by the Western nations. In fact, he is quite far away from the economic reality because India is not as much dependent on the pro-export policy as other Asian countries, including China.

> Does all of this make you, along with Professor Rothermund, convinced that India has a great future? I'm not as confident as the Professor. Just looking at Rothermund's facts, you can see the problem immediately. It's that India, with its vast, cheap workforce and Westernised elite, depends on First World business cycles for its wealth. This gives it great business opportunities, but also makes it terribly vulnerable. As recently as the 1990s, there was a wave of suicides among cotton farmers when the cotton price took a dive, courtesy of the global market. The main point about the rise of India, it seems to me, is that it's not based on the rise of Indian things, but on India's ability to sell stuff to the uncaring, treacherous West. And that can't be good.[10]

It should not come as a surprise that in every truly democratic state any sort of a positive branding is usually contested by those who may as well share the optimistic views on their own country but who are also aware of all the deficiencies, like commonly experienced injustice, social inequalities, or legal and cultural constrains in economic activities which are daily reported by the free media. They demand 'a much better balanced' image of the country so that its citizens (and foreign observers too) can see the surrounding reality in the right proportions. Patwant Singh, one the most respected Indian thinkers, in his *The Second Partition: Fault-Lines in India's Democracy,* paints a gloomier picture of the Rising India. He does not deny that India is the world's second-fastest growing economy but admits that one in every four of its citizens lives on less than a dollar a day. He repeats a well-known mantra that the nation is proud of having more dollar millionaires and billionaires than the United States but stresses the fact it also has the highest number of maternal deaths in the world. Patwant Singh strongly argues that there are two countries and two nations existing side by side. The First India, whose image is being globally projected; and the Second India, whose plight is not the most favourite theme of Bollywood filmmakers. In the preface he states:

> But somewhere along the way India got partitioned a second time without the world—or even Indians themselves—knowing it. So what we have now is two Indias. First India, the prosperous power with global aspirations, includes the country's top stratum and the middle classes; Second India comprises the rest of the population: starving, malnourished, subject to untreated disease, often unemployed and homeless, with infant and maternal mortality daily realities.[11]

Patwant Singh's critical stance on the recent development of India, reflects a much wider discussion on the social and economic implications of the twenty-year transformation process. Or better said: it is an illustration of a plethora of debates held on a regular basis by representatives of political, academic and business communities. Although his book does not reveal new facts on the social ground reality which has been analysed and interpreted frequently both in India and abroad, he manages to impose his own interpretation on a nation's modern image which started to prevail on the global scale quite recently.

An image of any country being strongly divided economically and socially appears to be quite universal and may be applicable to several dozen nations. The essence of these divisions in the Indian context is nonetheless much more significant internationally as it differs from what we are able to discover in other parts of the world. The two clashing images have already emerged and that will gradually catch the attention of the interested global audience. In the case of India, a democratic country with huge economic and social potential, this clash of images will likely have an international resonance given her size, global role and aspirations.

In the domestic arena, the wave of criticism of the selected social phenomena is quite powerful in the vernacular press. The special *Independence Day* issue of the biggest Hindi daily *Dainik Jagran* (2011), with a readership exceeding 55 million, is almost fully dedicated to presenting the views and impressions on contemporary India, expressed by a few historians, academicians, students, members of various social and religious communities. Their views, both pessimistic and optimistic ones, should be regarded—we tend to believe—as the samples of the nation's satisfaction and depression, successes and failures, ambitions and illusions. Pushpesh Pant, a Jawaharlal Nehru University professor, comes up with the classical list of grievances against the state, against politicians and the world of local customs, traditions and rituals. The priority in criticism is given to the poor machinery of the state in the context of the social movement against corruption as initiated by a Gandhian, Anna Hazare plus the consequences of the two widely media-covered 2G and CWG scams. According to Pushpesh Pant the reactions of the state to civic anger resemble the ones of the British Raj government interested only in 'keeping law and order' and certainly not in 'upholding the liberties of individual citizens'. Painfully felt divisions between those who are privileged in the society and those who are considered inferior, the phenomena of child marriage, dowry, caste system and female foeticide can be found on the list of grievances as well. Professor Pant concludes his essay with the extremely emotional appeal to his readers, with the request to ponder on the true meaning of freedom and liberty: *Yah kaisi aazaadi! Bol ki lab aazaad haim tere! Ab tak.*[12]

His conclusions as well as the negatively projected portrait of India may stem from the 'structural impatience'—a popularly imagined yet immaterialized vision of a democratic country, a type of a welfare state with the dynamic economic growth and developed civic society in which social injustice and crippling corruption is minimal. It is the vision of a country which has always existed, although in various avatars, in the imagination of the Indian intelligentsia. That sort of vision, as Sunil Khilnani suggests in his book *The Idea of India,* seems to be more a product of the planned or intended social engineering than of an objective analysis of the transforming reality which, as we have come to know after studying the history of the 20th century, may become extremely resistant to the bravest and the most revolutionary social reform projects.[13]

Balancing the Reality

These extremely gloomy images of the country are challenged by Patrick French, a British writer, the author of an acclaimed book *India: A Portrait*. He is perfectly aware of all the Indian success stories circulating in Europe and America, but also of the tendency to criticize the present state of affairs in India after the great economic reforms were introduced in 1991. This wave of criticism, contrary to what French says, is visible not only outside of India but very much at home as well. The writer seems to be slightly irritated by the extremes of that criticism and therefore he makes every effort to recreate a much more balanced image of the country in which global success stories are combined with local failures. His essay 'A Tryst with Change' appeared in *The Times of India*, a special *Independence Day* issue focused on changing perceptions of the recent history and the challenges the country will have to face in the coming years. Patrick French presents his own, as he wishes, balanced vision of India's image deeply set in the historical ground reality:

> Today, there's a widespread tendency, particularly in foreign publications, to look at the downside of the Indian history. During a recent lecture in Mumbai, I was told India was now divided between haves and have-nots. My reply was that in the 1970s, when per capita GDP was rising at less than 1 per cent per annum, it was divided between have-nots and have-nots. A conclusion that India is today in a terrible state ignores not only the period before economic reform, but the conditions in the country immediately after Independence. In the year of India's first general election, American diplomat Bill Bullitt wrote in *Life* magazine: 'An immense country containing 357 million people, with enormous natural resources and superb fighting men, India can neither feed herself nor defend herself against serious attacks. An inhabitant of India lives, on average, 27 years. His annual income is about $50. About 90 out of 100 Indians cannot read or write. They exist in squalor and fear of famine'. In 2011, while poverty remains a chronic problem for many in this country, it exists alongside swathes of middle-class wealth. An Indian's life expectancy today stands at 67 years and is rising. The changes of the last 20 years cannot be reversed. The hundreds of millions of people lifted out of poverty cannot be told they should return to their villages.[14]

The phenomenon of the clashing images of India crosses easily her borders, although the final combination of these two is likely to have various proportions in different countries. An image of India abroad, as it is the case with other nations, may have been gradually stereotyped or, given the impact of Indian soft power recently, may have become 'Bollywoodized'. Some elements of Edward Said's concepts of *Orientalism* can be traced in this stereotyped image as well. These reflect the simplified knowledge about the 'mystical or mysterious East' (of which India is seen as a part), which is generated from preconceived archetypes that envision all 'Eastern' societies as fundamentally similar to one another, and fundamentally dissimilar to 'Western' societies.[15] Most of the preconceived archetypes on India are much more likely to be found in those countries which made their presence on the subcontinent through centuries-long commercial and political activities, religious or missionary initiatives, long-lasting cultural bonds and—last but not least—military interventions. Fortunately the archetypes coexist with much more modern concepts and images of contemporary India.

The Image of India as Created in Poland

Poland, unlike many other European countries, never ventured to build its colonial or imperial status in Asia or Africa. From 1795 to 1918 it did not exist as a sovereign state so it could not play any role in the Big Game of the 19th century. Poles had quite limited access to many Asian countries under control of the old European superpowers and therefore their imageries of India were, to a large extent, founded on the available reports on 'the grand voyages' (mostly produced by the British or French), selected pieces of literature and philosophy (whose authors were mostly the Germans) or simply by word of mouth. What strongly attracted Polish 19th century poets, philosophers, the well-educated members of the intelligentsia and the academic community to 'the European discovery of India' was a spiritual message of classical Hinduism and Buddhism. With Max Mueller's translations of the most sophisticated Sanskrit works, Schopenhauer's philosophical zeal for the Upanishads, Goethe's admiration for Kalidasa's Shakuntala, publications by August Schlegel, Alfred de Vigny or Paul Deussen and the Buddhist treatises rendered into English by the Pali Text Society, the metaphysical richness of India became a true source of inspiration for Poles who yearned for freedom of their own country and reflected upon the glorious past and spiritual dimensions of the present.

Ex Oriente Lux

Adam Mickiewicz in his letters discloses a growing interest in Indian culture which he perceives as very close to the tradition of the Slavonic peoples but emphasizes even more strongly the affinity between ancient India and Lithuania. He refers to widely popular comparative studies on the similarities of mythological symbols and explains the philosophical link between the concept of Atman/Para-Brahma and Lithuanian Pražimas, who, in its active incarnation, is named 'Devas'. Mickiewicz's poetic drama *Dziady*, considered one of the greatest works of European Romanticism, may partly reflect his extensive studies on Indian classical literary antiquities. The essence of the *Dziady* ritual which is an ancient Slavonic and Lithuanian feast commemorating the forefathers, could resemble an Indian sacrifice, although it seems to be doubtful whether it was the poet's intention to bring out that resemblance. Mickiewicz endeavours to discover more cultural, social and metaphysical Indo-Slavonic bonds which could illustrate a popular belief in the common origin of these peoples and their common ideal of moral values. He comes up with the idea of the 'perfect Indo-Slavonic synthesis' he discovers in a Slavonic peasant, 'the Brahmin and Christian, the most splendid'.[16]

The great Mickiewicz's passion for Indian civilization was shared by another one of the 'Three Bards' of Polish literature, Juliusz Słowacki. He may have been inspired by the Upanishads, available at that time in various translations, especially by the most revealing formula 'tat tvam asi' (Thou art that) and by the message of Buddhism. The former inspiration, as Juliusz Kleiner suggests, can be found in Słowacki's poetic prayer 'Genesis out of Spirit', while the latter in his poem 'King-Spirit'. A Polish Indologist, Maryla Falk in her study 'Indian Element in Słowacki's Thought' presents quite a daring conclusion on the literary and philosophical structure of the poem. She declares the 'King-Spirit' to be not less than 'the first Boddhisatva-epic in Western literature'.[17] This conclusion may appear somehow disputable to a few, however it rightly directs our attention to the original source of poetic and philosophical inspiration. For the Polish poets, India was the promised land of ancient spiritual wisdom and her universal message, they believed, should be heard and meticulously interpreted. This idealistic image was shared by many like-minded intellectuals in Europe, but in Poland it was even more glorified by adding the elements of common cultural and spiritual heritage of Slavonic (plus Lithuanian) and Indian peoples.[18]

The true light of spiritual freedom must come from the East—*ex Oriente Lux,* that widely-accepted phrase did not cease to exist by the end of the 19th century when romanticism lost a part of its literary and spiritual appeal. It retained its popularity in the first decades of the 20th century in several European countries, and Poland was no exception. Wincenty Lutosławski (1863–1954) was probably the first intellectually prepared propagator of yoga in Poland. A philosopher and an expert on Plato's works, he studied the treatises of Vivekananda and Yogi Ramacharaka (the pseudonym of William Walker Atkinson) which became the basis of his own philosophical version of yoga, popularized later in Poland. Lutosławski shared his views with Indian readers, publishing articles in magazines including *East and West, Vedic Magazine* or *Young India.*

Antoni Lange, a talented poet, polyglot and translator, discovered for himself 'the land of spirituality' through Annie Besant's and Madam Blawatska's books on Theosophy. He was also a keen student of Sanskrit and acquired a good command of the language which made it possible to translate a big portion of the ancient Indian masterpieces. Lange, himself a master of the poetic phrase, rendered into Polish the selected parts of the 'Mahabharata' and 'Ramayana', then the 'Panchatantra', 'Hitopadesha' and 'Gitagovinda'. His fame as a translator rests mainly on the renditions of *Savitri* (1910) and *Nal and Damayanti* (1906), and especially the former is still regarded as the best ever translation of the poem into Polish. Lange's works deeply influenced another poet, Jan Kasprowicz whose literary achievements owe a lot to philosophical tradition of India and Rabindranath Tagore's poetic vision of the world. Kasprowicz, one of the greatest bards of Polish literature, concentrates on the beauty of nature, and the structure of his poetic narration, as suggested by Jan Tuczyński, to some extent reflects the metaphysical attitude of ancient Indian sages. The poet was inspired by the teachings of the 'Brihadaranyaka-Upanishada', 'Bhagavadgita' and the tenth book of the *Rigveda* (hymn 129). He is also the author of two poems: 'Savitri' and 'Sita', obviously referring to their Indian archetypes, which deal with the universal concept of liberating love.[19]

The list of Polish poets or writers who drew upon Indian literary and philosophical tradition is much longer: Kazimierz Przerwa-Tetmajer, Leopold Staff, Wacław Sieroszewski, Witkacy and Stanisław Maria Saliński, to name but a few. Various interpretations of the formulas 'Tat tvam asi' or 'Aham Brahma asmi' (I am Brahma), the teachings of the Vedanta and Buddhism, the literary richness of the Mahabharata and Ramayana, and finally the poetic vision of Tagore in the widely translated 'Gitanjali'—all these elements, artistically processed by men of literature, contributed to forming the spiritual image of India, prevalent among the well-read representatives of the Polish intelligentsia. This image was much strengthened at a later time by two prominent Poles who declared India to be their second motherland. These were Wanda Dynowska, known under her Indian name as Umadevi, and Maurycy Frydman, also known as Swami Bharatananda. Both of them were very close to leaders of the Indian independence struggle and offered their services and hearts to the Dalai Lama. Dynowska and Frydman started in 1944 the Indian-Polish Library (Biblioteka Polsko-Indyjska), translating Indian classics (mostly religious and philosophical works) into Polish. Their books were available in Poland in the 1960s and 1970s and the Library was at that time probably the most popular source of information on the spiritual dimension of India.[20]

The image of India in Poland would not be complete without the remarkable contribution of Polish Indology which deserves its own very high position among the European scholarship centres. The first Sanskrit Chair was founded as early as 1893, at the Jagiellonian University and the Indology Department of the Oriental Institute at the University of Warsaw was established in 1932, and is now the biggest centre for Indian studies in Poland. A very long list of Indological publications had probably a relatively limited resonance (due to their scholarly methods of analysis, specific topics dealt with etc.) in the process of shaping the more general image of India, nonetheless a few of these works (e.g., Stanisław Schayer's *History of Indian Literature* or Krzysztof Byrski's translation of *Kamasutra*) did impress the wide reading audience who were able to draw their own inspiring conclusions, later developed, modified and used in the popular press.[21]

Polish Refugees and Maharaja Jam Saheb

World War II was probably the most traumatic period of history for Poles. They were the victims of genocide, ethnic cleansing, imprisonment and deportations on a scale never experienced before. For a few of those children who had been deported to Soviet Siberia, India—after the Sikorski-Mayski Agreement in 1941—became their second home. Joseph Stalin granted 'amnesty' to thousands of Polish citizens, out of whom approximately 5,000 children, mostly orphans were transported to India. The successful cooperation between the Red Cross, the British Army, the Polish II Corps Command, the Consulate General of Poland in Bombay and the Indian local authorities resulted in establishing 'Little Poland' in the western part of the country. The first group of children arrived in Balachadi, near Jamnagar (Gujarat) in July 1942, and since then until 1946 about 1,000 of them lived there. At the end of 1942, construction began on a new settlement in Valivade, next to the town of Kolhapur. The first group of refugees, mostly children and women, arrived in 1943. In the beginning there was naturally a shortage of teachers, textbooks or the needed equipment but in spite of that, all the young people in settlements were required to attend school. Very efficiently the whole educational and cultural infrastructure was completed. In Valivade, for example, there were three Polish kindergartens, four elementary schools, a secondary school, a lyceum and a teachers' training centre. The children and their guardians could also attend Sunday mass, play soccer or organize Christmas carol evenings. Daily activities did not leave much space for reviving traumatic memories.[22]

The image of a new children's home in India has been depicted in several publications. India is portrayed as an extremely tranquil and colourful place, with very warm and friendly people; it is a safe haven where young Poles, after experiencing terrible Soviet ordeals, finally found peace, protection and loving care. Maria van der Linden, in the book *An Unforgettable Journey* recounts warmly her arrival to India and her stay in Jamnagar:

> The ship sailed into shallow waters near Jamnagar until it could proceed no further. At that point an anchor was dropped and its

> engines switched off. One by one we were then lowered over large jute nets suspended down the side of our stationary ship. We were assisted by Indian soldiers who carried the small children on their shoulders, into the waiting barges below. Two tugs were employed to tow each barge towards the coast, again as far as the sea depth permitted. The Indian soldiers then carried us on their shoulders individually into extremely shallow water where we waded bare-footed ashore towards the adjacent sandy beach. Here by the sand dunes a train awaited our arrival. This train brought us to Jamnagar, one hour later. [...] Our new camp was 25 miles from the town of Jamnagar. The camp had been constructed by courtesy of the Maharajah of Jamnagar who also paid for all the daily expenses connected with the running of this new orphanage. Our camp site was on hilly land overlooking the sea some three miles away and near the Maharajah's summer residence, which occupied another hill site terminating in a high cliff, by the sea. We had an excellent view of our benefactor's holiday resort from the camp. Here we were safe as his honoured guests .... The Polish children's camp at Balachadi-Jamnagar was in the Indian state of Gujarat. The camp's hilly situation provided a panoramic view of the surrounding landscape. Golden sand on the beach glistened in the tropical sun and the clear blue sea beyond it reflected hot sunrays. The sunsets were a magnificent sight to behold. The crystal clear moonlit sky was illuminated by numerous twinkling stars. It was full moon when we arrived. The tranquillity of the night was invariably interrupted by the eerie howling of wild hyenas and jackals which roamed the wide arid expanse around the camp .... [23]

A very special role in the whole 'Polish Project' in India was played by the Maharaja Jam Sri Digvijaysinhji Ranjitsinhji Jadeja (Jam Saheb), the ruler of Jamnagar. He extended his hospitality to young Poles, bore the costs related to running the settlement and actively participated in cultural life of the Polish community in Jamnagar. He is credited with saying to the children: 'As you have no parents I shall become your father, here in India'. In the interview for the weekly *Tygodnik Polaków 'Polska'* (Poles' Weekly, Poland), published in November 1942, he made an official declaration to provide the young refugees with all the necessary assistance and finances. He also stressed his deep interest in the history of Poland and recounted a memorable meeting as a youngster with the world-famous Polish pianist and Prime Minister Ignacy Jan Paderewski.[24] Jam Saheb became a symbol-figure in the Polish-Indian relations, especially after 1989. His role as the guardian of the Polish orphans in India has been often emphasized and the story of his life narrated in many publications both in Poland and abroad. There is a very popular and much respected Bednarska High School in Warsaw whose Honorary Patron is Maharaja Jam Saheb, very warmly yet unofficially referred to as 'our Polish Maharaja'. This extremely positive image of hospitable India was also revived by the Polish Prime Minister, Donald Tusk on his official visit to New Delhi. In the conversation with the President of India, Pratibha Devisingh Patil, he said, 'at the time of World War II when others were killing our children you were able to save the lives of many of them'.[25] This particular part of the general image of India, the country that extended hospitality to Polish children at the time of need, would probably get even more solidified if the story were translated into the language of a feature film, or at least, a well-promoted documentary.

'Indian Art Deco': Stefan Norblin

The hard times of the War generated another remarkable link connecting Poland and India. It could be best described as an inspiring combination of Polish artistic creativity with Indian cultural heritage. An introduction to the story comes from the Luxury Travel Magazine which promotes one of the most unique and luxurious hotels in India, and probably in the world:

> Designed by the renowned Edwardian architect Henry Lanchester and embellished with exotic murals of the self-exiled Polish artist Stefan Norblin, the palace is a blend of Eastern and Western architectural influences. Set amidst 26 acres of lush gardens, perched above the skyline of Jodhpur, rises the imposing facade of Umaid Bhawan Palace, the last of the great palaces of India and one of the largest residences in the world, now a Taj Luxury Hotel. Named after Maharaja Umaid Singh Ji, the grandfather of the present Maharaja of Jodhpur, Maharaja Gaj Singh Ji, this golden-yellow sandstone monument was conceived on the grandest possible scale in the fashionable and grand Art-Deco style. It was completed in 1943 and has served as the principal residence of Jodhpur's Royal family since then ....[26]

Umaid Bhavan has become the symbolic place of Polish artistic presence in Asia. It was Stefan Norblin, who contributed significantly to decorating, embellishing or, better said—creating the grandeur and majesty of the palace interior. Norblin (1892—1952) was a well-known artist in Poland before World War II who earned his fame as a world-renowned portrait painter, having done work for much of the royalty in Europe and the Middle East. When the Nazi army invaded Poland in September 1939, Stefan and his wife Lena immediately fled, picking their way across Europe and the Middle East until they could land in their new home, India. It is not quite clear why the Norblins decided to stay over there, as initially they had been planning to travel to a completely different destination which was America. They must have been fascinated by the cultural charm of the country and this fascination somehow may have coincided with their financial problems which made their travel plans difficult or impossible. Fortunately, Norblin was able to secure special commissions by the Maharaja of Morvi and the Maharaja of Jodhpur. The task he was given by the royals turned out to be the most unusual and most challenging in his professional career and unfortunately it was also the last one (of that scale) in his life. Claus-Ullrich Simon in his publication 'Stefan Norblin, a biography that should be rewritten' highlights the artistic style and Norblin's creativity which was fully materialized in the process of embellishing the grand Indian palaces:

> Because this palace which was just completed in 1944 and was not accommodated for the reigning Maharaja but his modern minded son, the Maharaj Kumar Mehandrasinghji of Morvi, Norblin created many paintings in the Art Deco style: wild tigers lurking in tress watching the guest dine, Hindu gods guarding his sleep and half nude ladies winding themselves around trees watching whoever is in the swimming pool. There is also an erotic cabinet with a round bed: hidden behind mirrors there can be found clearly erotic paintings, which can only be illuminated from inside, and are depicting European lovers in daring poses, pursuing their pleasures. The main part of Norblin's work for this palace is made up of paintings portraying Hindu gods drawn from the infinite sources provided by the Hindu religion. [...] Norblin also worked as a court painter at the design of the Umaid Bhavan Palace in Jodhpur. He created many paintings which in contrast with the works of art designed for Morvi, appear somewhat heavier, even warlike. During this time paintings and interior perspective drawings were made for the furnishing of the Royal Hunting Lodge, Sadar Samand which was built around the same time as the palace. One of Norblin's last accomplishments was a series of six murals, applied directly on plaster, in the Oriental

Room, the Throne Room of the palace which depict themes of Indian mythology.[27]

By the end of the 1990s almost all the murals were in a terribly bad state and needed very careful and professional restoration. The Polish Ministry of Culture and National Heritage in collaboration with the Ministry of Foreign Affairs initiated the process of the long-awaited restoration works which could officially start after signing the agreement with the Maharaja Gaj Singh II of Jodhpur. Once it was done all the necessary finances were allocated and a group of the most experienced Art Deco restorers was selected to commence the work. By the end of 2010 the six murals slowly began to regain their past glory and almost at the same time Stefan Norblin, somehow half-forgotten in Poland until then, began to regain his position in the Art Pantheon. In September 2011, the Regional Museum in Stalowa Wola, a town located in the Podkarpackie Province and known for its Art Deco architectural design, organized the Stefan Norblin Exhibition, the first of this kind in Poland. In a close cooperation with the Maharaja of Jodhpur and the Ministry of Culture, the Museum was able to display Norblin's works which were otherwise inaccessible for the Polish art-lovers. The whole event was not only dedicated to the artist, his life and artistic achievements, it was a promotion festival of Indian heritage, Indian dance and Indian cuisine as well.[28] India was portrayed as a land of the sublime art which combines the elements of her cultural richness with Polish and European vision of universal creativity. That new element added to India's image was, to some extent, reflected in the decision made by the Government of Poland to promote officially the selected Norblin-related cultural events during the Polish Presidency of the Council of the European Union in 2011.

Norblin's story in India, is however best known through his paintings and murals (very few written materials on his life there have been retrieved so far), and may appeal strongly to various segments of Polish society, up till now only mildly interested in the subject. There are attractive and fascinating elements in the story which are likely to enrich or at least influence to some degree the present image of India in Poland. It cannot be denied that one will come across slightly stereotyped, or referring to Mircea Eliade's terminology, archetypal parts of this image: Norblin's adventurous grand voyage to India, majestic maharajas' palaces as if created by dreams, the most unimaginable pastimes of the royals, the gods of Hindu pantheon depicted in the most unusual way by the painter, then his life in India full of mysteries, and finally his dramatic suicide in America.[29] India, in this new avatar, may reappear as the land which resembles more of Kipling's literary imageries than the subcontinent's reality of the 1940s. It should not, however, become a source of worry, because we have always lived on cultural archetypes while projecting our new images or recreating the old ones, and—as Eliade points out—we shall need them to constantly activate our creative imagination without which, I reckon, we may lose a part of our own collective personality.[30]

Gandhi after Gandhi: The Concept of Non-violence

Poland's romantic vision of history, full of bloody self-sacrifice and freedom myths, was gradually modified and finally transformed in the 20th century. At the time when the myths clashed with the most brutal reality, and when the contemporary history of Europe produced millions of victims, a totally new philosophy of action had to be devised in order to save—as it was defined—'the national substance'. Adam Zamoyski in his book *Poland: A History*, explains the historical and psychological circumstances of this fundamental shift in thinking on the present and the future:

> It was the events of 1918—1921 and the horrors of the Second World War that turned the issue into a moral one for thinking Poles. The consequence was a wide-ranging discussion on the whole question of what a future Poland's attitude to Russia, Lithuania, Belarus and Ukraine should be. This discussion was carried on during 1970s and 1980s, in word and print, in smoke-filled rooms and over radio waves, both within Poland and in émigré circles, mostly in London and Paris. It was in many ways the kind of reassessment that former colonial powers were forced to make during the 1950s and 1960s, and it had three fundamental consequences. The first one was that the Poles came to accept the necessity of taking territorial disputes out of the argument. The second was that they grew used to treating other new potentially independent nations as equals and their aspirations as legitimate. The third was an acceptance that the only way forward was through cooperation, at any cost. No formula for adopting any form of violence could be approved of.[31]

The concept of non-violence was, first of all, applicable in the broad area of domestic affairs, especially in the struggle against the Communist regime, which by the end of the 1970s was opposed by a growing number of politically active Poles. This concept was sometimes combined with the idea of civil disobedience, based on the position that laws can be unjust, and that there are human rights that supersede such laws. The whole philosophy of non-violence and civil disobedience, perfectly embodied in Gandhi's satyagraha movement, became a trademark of Polish opposition which must have drawn its inspiration from many sources. One of them was undoubtedly the Mahatma and his formula of a non-violent fight against the oppressors in South Africa and the British colonial rule in India. Gandhi's autobiography had already been translated into Polish and was widely read not only by lovers of the Indian civilization. It was followed by many other publications that shed more light on the historical context of the satyagraha movement. Probably the most politically significant promotion of the non-violence philosophy was Richard Attenborough's film 'Gandhi' screened in 1982, in fact only a few months after the Martial Law was imposed in Poland. Mahatma Gandhi became a symbolic figure for many Poles, an archetype of a non-violent freedom fighter, frequently invoked by the organized Opposition, Academia members, journalists or workers. Ashis Nandy, an Indian political psychologist, comes up with an interesting interpretation on the link between this archetypal Gandhi and Polish workers who rejected violence in their political struggle:

> When the Polish workers rose against their authoritarian regime in the late 1980s, they talked of Lech Walesa as their Gandhi. [...] But the Polish labourers were not interested in the historical, verifiable similarities or dissimilarities between the two; they were making a different statement. They were saying something about what they themselves wanted and about how Gandhi with his weapon of militant nonviolence, had become in our time a symbol of defiance of hollow tyrants and bureaucratic authoritarianism backed by the power of the state and modern technology. For above all, this Gandhi is a symbol of those struggling against injustice, while trying to retain their humanity even when faced with unqualified inhumanity.[32]

After 1989, when the Communist system collapsed and the democratic, free-market transformation commenced, this political archetype of Gandhi began slowly to fade away. He is certainly remembered as the founding father of contemporary India, a deep thinker and a history-changer whose universal message is still recognized worldwide. However, as history has its unpredictable twists and turns, I would not rule out the possibility that a new archetype of Gandhi will one day appear again.

Bollywood and Global Business: The Latest Avatar of India in Poland

Classical Bollywood movies, unlike in Romania or in the former Soviet Union, had not been screened in the cinemas or telecast in Poland prior to 1989. Only the narrow circles of Indology students or best-informed Indian cinema lovers had very limited access to a few films, mostly with Amitabh Bachchan starring. That started to change gradually by the end of the 1990s; however, a true breakthrough in accepting 'the Bollywood message' took place only in 2004 when *Kabhi Khushi Kabhi Gham* was screened in the biggest cinema halls in Poland. Mira Nair's 'Monsoon Wedding', although not a Bollywood movie itself, had generated earlier a discussion on the Indian film industry in the Polish media, but it was Karan Johar's mega-hit that showed to a local audience the emotional, artistic and commercial potential of the Indian soft-power. The film, with Polish subtitles was available soon on a DVD version and almost immediately found its way to the top 10 best-selling films in the Empik chain of shops located in all the big cities and major towns. The same year, one of the most popular film festivals, ENH Cieszyn focused on classical Bollywood movies: *Kuch Kuch Hota Hai, Dil Se, Devdas, Kal Ho Naa Ho, Main Hoon Na,* and in Warsaw and Cracow the first edition of the 'Ticket to Bollywood' Festival was organized. In 2006, the top Polish winter spa, Zakopane, became a location for the film *Fanaa* in which the Polish Tatras played the dramatic role of the Indian Himalayas. Both of the superstars, Aamir Khan and Kajol appeared on Polish TV and probably were slightly amazed after realizing how popular and easily recognizable they were, and that in a country which they had come to for the first time and knew very little about. The growing interest in Indian cinema was somehow reflected by the book market. Shashi Tharoor's controversial book on Amitabh Bachchan was translated into Polish and a young film-scholar Urszula Woźniakowska published her academic study *Bollywood: Yearning for Truth and Longing for Myth*.[33] In the popular press, the phenomenon of Bollywood was often analysed, although in a rather superficial manner. The well-known clichés of escapism and social problems illustrated by a film narrative or archetyped struggle between good and evil appeared, sometimes accompanied by colourful biographies of Shakh Rukh Khan, Aishwarya Rai, Aamir Khan or Big B. For the most committed Bollywood fans and for Bollywood 'beginners' a special Internet forum in the Polish language www.bollywood.pl has been created, which is believed to be a very reliable source of information on latest films, events, stories or books on the subject.

Another event which strengthened the Bollywood message in Poland was the visit of Amitabh Bachchan to Cracow in April 2011. He was the chief guest of the Off Plus Camera Festival during which the European premiere of his film 'Paa' took place. Amitabh Bachchan was officially welcomed by the president of the city, recited publicly in the theatre 'Teatr Stu' his father's poetry, Harivansh Rai Bachchan's 'Madhushala', and participated in the ceremony of disclosing his father's portrait in the Jagiellonian University. All these events were widely covered by the popular media in Poland, and later he shared his impressions on the visit with thousands (or millions) of his fans on the blog http://bigb.bigadda.com/

The Bollywood presence in Poland is a recent phenomenon, but it has already exerted an impact on the process of shaping India's image. Some stereotyped perceptions may have got even stronger, like the ones emphasizing traditional family values and father-son relations (*Kabhi Khushi, Kabhi Gham*) but there are new elements not visible before. Terrorism as a serious threat to India's stability (*Fanaa* being quite popular, due to the fact the film was partly shot in Poland), the concept of modern patriotism cutting across the social divisions of religion or caste (*Lagaan*) and the attitude towards Islam (*My Name is Khan*)—these 'filmed' and popularized problems were hardly mentioned or referred to in the context of India's image in Poland in the 1990s or prior to 1989 but gradually started to occupy its space in the popular imagination during the first decade of the 21st century. It should be stressed however, that this impact has its own limitations and can generally be discerned in a big metropolis where cultural or academic centres and all kind of activities related to them contribute fundamentally to discovering new areas of inter- and cross-cultural interactions.

The recent Bollywod phenomenon in Poland coincides with another one, which is the arrival of powerful Indian companies interested in huge investments and diversification of their global business. In fact, it was Mittal Steel, producing 80 per cent of the country's steel, that opened the gates wide for other companies to follow. Lakshmi Mittal and his family drew the attention of the local media which narrated extremely colourful success stories on his global enterprises, with a quite understandable focus on his daughter's costly wedding in the Versailles palace. A story of another Indian company, Infosys generated slightly less colourful but more business-oriented interest in the global capabilities and ambitions of Indian IT and BPO, especially when the decision was made to shift the company's European headquarters from London to Łódź. This relatively new wave of Indian business activities was perceived as a herald of the far-reaching transformation of world economy in which the Asian players are very likely to play a big, if not dominating role in the near future. That was somehow being proved by the sheer amounts of money the new big players allocated for their large-scale acquisitions, green-field investments or joint-ventures. Only in Poland have Indian-global companies invested more than 2 billion dollars.[34]

The global visibility of Indian entrepreneurs has been often reported by the Polish media, but most of these reports are based on European or American sources. It is very true that these success stories have added a valuable element to the already positive image of India in Poland, but this time the copyrights for this are not held in Warsaw or Cracow. The 'success story' message is totally an imported product, nevertheless it appears to fit well into the whole image structure.

The image of India in Poland has changed significantly since the end of the 1990s when Indian soft and economic power became much more noticeable globally and when it found its shape in the Polish mainstream media. The newest strata of this image structure coexist with the older ones, based on the stories and narrations dating back to World War II or to the pre-war period. The poetic dimension of this image, most visible in the poetry of romanticism and 'Young Poland' (Młoda Polska), should not be neglected either. There are also some stereotyped elements, as elsewhere in Europe, like social divisions (castes), spirituality (gurus and brahmins), religious beliefs (sacred cow) which often reflect the reality in a distorted form. People of Poland have their own unique image of India, as I endeavour to prove; the image that owes a lot to the historical, cultural and common socio-psychological bonds linking both countries, sometimes in the most unusual way. One may only wonder, if and when the phenomenon of the 'clashing images' of India will appear in Poland, and how it would be transmitted to the general audience. This phenomenon is already being carefully studied by a few, keen to learn more on contemporary India. At present, their number is limited mostly to the representatives of the academic community who are privileged to have much bigger access to the world of international affairs and still do not lose their interest in the problems of universal nature. However, that situation is likely to change soon, especially when the globalization process accelerates and the multipolar world order becomes the only reality.

NOTES

1. *Incredible India (Atulya Bharat* in Hindi) slogan was officially branded and promoted by Amitabh Kant, Joint Secretary under the Union Ministry of Tourism in 2002.
2. See the following: Philip Kotler, Donald H. Haider and Irving Rein 1993; Benno H. Signitzer and Timothy Coombs 1992; see also: *To Develop Country Image and National Brand Strategy to Attract Foreign Direct Investment: An Example from Central Asia: Kyrgyzstan*. The text is available on the website: http://www.bledcom.com/uploads/papers/Tunca.pdf
3. See: *How the World Sees the World*, The Anholt-GMI Nation Brands Index, Third Quarter, 2005; see also Nation Brand Index—*What Brand Image Does Your Country Have?* The text is available on the website: http://www.marketing-planet.com/surveys/nation-brand-index-what-brand-image-does-your-country-have.html
4. Shashi Tharoor 2007.

5. Ramachandra Guha 2007. It is worth mentioning that the US magazine *Foreign Policy* named the author as one of the top 100 public intellectuals in the world in May 2008. In the poll that followed, Guha was placed 44th.
6. Ibid., p. 750.
7. Ibid., p. 752.
8. See: Thomas L. Friedman 2005.
9. See: Dietmar Rothermund 2009.
10. William Leith 2008. The text is also available online: http://www.spectator.co.uk/books/752721/trouble-and-strife.thtml
11. Patwant Singh 2007, p. 15.
12. Pushpesh Pant 2011, p. 9; *Dainik Jagran* is the biggest daily in India in terms of readership, and probably the biggest in the world. No other newspaper can break so far the record of 55 million readers.
13. See: Sunil Khilnani 1999.
14. Patrick French 2011, p. 22.
15. See: Edward W. Said 1979. Said puts forward several definitions of 'Orientalism' in the introduction to the book. Some of these may have been more widely quoted and influential than others: 'A way of coming to terms with the Orient that is based on the Orient's special place in European Western experience' (p. 1); 'A style of thought based upon an ontological and epistemological distinction made between the "Orient" and (most of the time) "the Occident" (p. 2); 'A Western style for dominating, restructuring, and having authority over the Orient' (p. 3); '... particularly valuable as a sign of European-Atlantic power over the Orient than it is as a veridic discourse about the Orient' (p. 6); 'A distribution of geopolitical awareness into aesthetic, scholarly, economic, sociological, historical, and philological texts' (p. 12).
16. Adam Mickiewicz 1929, p. 156. Probably the best study on the influence of Indian literary and philosophical tradition on Polish literature, especially the literature of 'Young Poland' (Młoda Polska) is by Jan Tuczyński 1981. Jan Tuczyński refers to Mickiewicz's inspiration and interest in Indian civilization in the Chapter on Mickiewicz, pp. 63–71.
17. M. Falk 1951, p. 257.
18. J. Tuczyński, op. cit., pp. 75–96.
19. Ibid., pp. 125–154.

20. Wanda Dynowska's biography and a story of her activities is available on the websites: http://www.jkrishnamurti.republika.pl/dynowska.htm; http://www.autodydaktyka.republika.pl/ezoteryka/dynowska.htm; See the text by Tadeusz Margul, 1965. *Wanda Dynowska—Wielka Ambasadorka Kultury Indyjskiej* (Wanda Dynowska—The Ambassador of Indian Culture); see also another text: *Wanda Dynowska i Maurycy Frydman, twórcy Biblioteki Polsko-Indyjskiej* (Wanda Dynowska and Maurycy Frydman, the Founders of the Polish-Indian Library)—http://prognozy2030.salon24.pl/51965,wanda-dynowska-i-maurycy-frydman-tworcy-biblioteki-polsko-indyj; The official name of the Library in English has a few variations, e.g., *Polish-Indian Library, Indian-Polish Library, Indo-Polish Library.* In my opinion the best English equivalent of the Polish version is '*Polish-Indian Library*'.

21. There are many publications on the history of Polish Indology, available both in Polish and English. In fact these are the stories within one story as there are several Indological centres at Polish universities. The oldest one is in Cracow (Jagiellonian University), followed by Warsaw (University of Warsaw). Indological studies (traditional ones like 'Indology' or in selected academic areas) are pursued also in Poznań, Wrocław and Lublin. Indology departments publish their own works on a regular basis, e.g., 'Cracow Indological Studies' or 'Warsaw Indological Studies'. See also D. Stasik and A. Trynkowska 2006.

22. The best documented collective work on Poles in India during WWII is *Polacy w Indiach 1942—1948, w świetle dokumentów i wspomnień* (Poles in India 1942–1948 in the Light of Documents and Memories). London 2000, as well as, *Poles in India 1942–1948: Second World War Story,* 2008.

23. Maria van der Linden 1994, Chapter 8, *Journey to India*. Available also on the website: http://www.antoranz.net/BIBLIOTEKA/LINDEN/HTM/L08.HTM

24. *Polacy w Indiach…* (Poles in India), 2002, pp. 82–83.

25. I had the privilege to listen personally to the conversation held in the Rashtrapati Bhavan (President's Palace in New Delhi) on 8 September 2010.

26. The official website of the luxurious Taj Hotel Group, a text on the Umaid Bhavan Palace in Jodhpur: http://www.tajhotels.com/Luxury/Grand-Palaces-And-Iconic-Hotels/Umaid-Bhawan-Palace-Jodhpur/Accommodations.html

27. Clauss-Ullrich Simon 1996, pp. 3–5. See also in the same volume: Joachim K. Bautze 1996, pp. 8–18.

28. The official inauguration of Norblin's exhibition on 2 September 2011 was covered widely by the local media, e.g., the popular, regional edition of the *Gazeta Wyborcza*: http://rzeszow.gazeta.pl/rzeszow/1,34962, 10208138,Norblin_i_miasteczko_Indyjskie_juz_w_sobote_w_St_.html; a special press release was prepared by the Stalowa Wola Regional Museum. It is available in Polish on the website: http://muzeum.stalowawola.pl/2011/38_norblin/robocze/nornlin_info.pdf. The event was broadcast by the Radio Rzeszow and telecast by the channel of the Polish television TVP Kultura.
29. See: Mircea Eliade 1959.
30. See: Mircea Eliade 1971, see also (Mircea Eliade 1963).
31. Adam Zamoyski 2009, p. 399.
32. Ashis Nandy, *Gandhi after Gandhi*, http://vlal.bol.ucla.edu/multiversity/Nandy/Nandy_gandhi.htm; The text was first published in a slightly amended form as 'Gandhi after Gandhi', in *The Little Magazine*, Vol. 1, No. 1 (May 2000), pp. 38–41.
33. See: Shashi Tharoor 2004 (The original title is *Show Business*, published in 1992); Urszula Woźniakowska 2010.
34. Not all the economic reports, both Polish and Indian, provide the same figures on Indian investments in Poland. In case of Mittal the issue is even more complicated, as Mittal holds a British passport and Mittal's company is registered in the EU. Therefore all the investments made by Mittal's company are officially not classified as Indian. Nevertheless it is a popular perception that it is 'India Inc' (of which Mittal is a part) that has made huge investments in steel business and wields global economic power.

REFERENCES

Bautze, Joachim K. 1996. 'The Art of Stefan Norblin in India', published in the volume *Art Deco for the Maharajas: Stefan Norblin in India*. Berlin: Polish Cultural Institute, Indian Cultural Center, in collaboration with Museum of Transport and Technology.

Deshpande, Satish. 2004. *Contemporary India: A Sociological View*. New Delhi and New York: Penguin Books.

Eliade, Mircea. 1959. *Myths, Dreams and Mysteries: The Encounter between Contemporary Faiths and Archaic Realities*, transl. P. Mairet, London: Harvill Press.

——. 1963. *Myth and Reality: Religious Traditions of the World*. San Francisco: Harper and Row.

——. 1971. *The Myth of Eternal Return or Cosmos and History*. Princeton: Princeton University Press.

French, Patrick. 2011. 'A Tryst with Change', *The Times of India*, August 15: 22.

——. 2011. *India: A Portrait*. New York: Alfred A. Knopf.

Friedman, Thomas L. 2005. *The World is Flat: A Brief History of the Twenty-First Century*. New York: Farrar, Straus and Giroux.

Falkówna (Falk), Maryla. 1951. 'Indian Elements in Słowacki's Thought', published in the volume *Juliusz Słowacki 1809–1849: Księga zbiorowa w stulecie zgonu*. London.

Gerlach, Tomasz. 1988. *Indie w świadomości Indusów* (India in the Consciousness of Indians). Wrocław: Ossolineum.

Glazer, Sulohana Raghavan and Nathan Glazer (eds). 1990. *Conflicting Images: India and the US*. Glenn Dale, Maryland: The Riverdale Company.

Guha, Ramachandra. 2007. *India after Gandhi. The History of the World's Largest Democracy*. London: Macmillan.

Holmes, Fred R., Ann Newton Holmes and Aman Nath. 2008. *Jodhpur's Umaid Bhavan: The Maharaja of Palaces*. Mumbai: India Book House.

How the World Sees the World. 2005. The Anholt-GMI Nation Brands Index, Third Quarter.

Khilnani, Sunil. 1999. *The Idea of India*. New York: Farrar, Straus and Giroux.

Kotler, Philip, Donald H. Haider and Irving Rein. 1993. *Marketing Places: Attracting Investment, Industry and Tourism to Cities, States and Nations*. New York: The Free Press.

Kudelska, Marta. 2002. *Filozofia Wschodu* (The Philosophy of the East). Kraków: Wydawnictwo Uniwesrytetu Jagiellońskiego.

——. 2004. *Karman i dharma*. Kraków: Wydawnictwo Uniwesrytetu Jagiellońskiego.

Leith, William. 2008. *Trouble and Strife*, Spectator Book Club, 7 June. http://www.spectator.co.uk/books/752721/trouble-and-strife.html

Linden, Maria van der. 1994. *An Unforgettable Journey*. Palmerston North, New Zealand: Dunmore Press.

Margul, Tadeusz. 1965. *Wanda Dynowska—Wielka Ambasadorka Kultury Indyjskiej* (Wanda Dynowska—The Ambassador of Indian Culture); see also another text: *Wanda Dynowska i Maurycy Frydman, twórcy Biblioteki Polsko-Indyjskiej* (Wanda Dynowska and Maurycy Frydman, the

Founders of the Polish-Indian Library). http://www.autodydaktyka.republika.pl/ezoteryka/dynowska.htm

Mickiewicz, Adam. 1929. *Dzieła* (Collected Works), Vol. XI, edited by M. Kridl, Warszawa: Biblioteka Arcydzieł Literatury.

Nandy, Ashis. 2000. 'Gandhi after Gandhi', *The Little Magazine,* 1(1): 38–41. http://vlal.bol.ucla.edu/multiversity/Nandy/Nandy_gandhi.htm

Nation Brand Index—*What Brand Image Does Your Country Have?*, http://www.marketing-planet.com/surveys/nation-brand-index-what-brand-image-does-your-country-have.html

Pant, Pushpesh. 2011. 'Bol ki Lab Aazaad Haim Tere! Ab Tak', *Dainik Jagran*, Nai Dilli, 14 August.

Polacy w Indiach 1942–1948 w świetle dokumentów i wspomnień: Praca zbiorowa (Poles in India 1942–1948 in the Light of Documents and Memories: Collected Works). 2002. Warszawa Koło Polaków z Indii 1942–1948.

Poles in India 1942–1948: Second World War Story. 2008. Edited by Teresa Glazer, Jan Siedlecki, Danka Pniewska, Wiesia Kleszko and Joanna Chmielowska. London: Association of Poles in India.

Publicysta (pseudonym). *Wanda Dynowska i Maurycy Frydman, twórcy Biblioteki Polsko-Indyjskiej,* http://prognozy2030.salon24.pl/51965, wanda-dynowska-i-maurycy-frydman-tworcy-biblioteki-pol sko-indyj

Rothermund, Dietmar. 2009. *India: The Rise of an Asian Giant*. New Haven: Yale University Press.

Said, Edward W. 1979. *Orientalism*. New York: Vintage Books Edition.

Signitzer, Benno H. and Timothy Coombs. 1992. 'Public Relations and Public Diplomacy: Conceptual Covergences', *Public Relations Review,* 18 (2).

Simon, Clauss-Ullrich. 1996. 'A Biography that should be Rewritten', published in the volume *Art Deco for the Maharajas: Stefan Norblin in India*. Berlin: Polish Cultural Institute, Indian Cultural Center, in collaboration with Museum of Transport and Technology.

Singh, Patwant. 2007. *The Second Partition: Fault-Lines in India's Democracy*. New Delhi: Hay House India.

Stasik, Danuta. 2007. *'Kabir i Miłosz: czyli poetyckie wspomnienie o St. Schayerze'* (Kabir and Miłosz: Poetic Remembrance about St. Schayer), *Przegląd Orientalistyczny,* 1–2: 125–135.

Stasik, Danuta and Anna Trynkowska (eds). 2006. *India in Warsaw: A Volume to Commemorate the 50th Anniversary of the Post–War History of Indological Studies at Warsaw University (2003/2004)*. Warszawa: UW.

Tharoor, Shashi. 2004. *Bollywood*. Transl. by Artur Karp, Warszawa: Wydawnictwo Akademickie Dialog.

——. 2007. *The Elephant, the Tiger and the Cellphone: Reflections on India in the Twenty-first Century*. New Delhi: Penguin Books India.

Tillotson, Giles. 2011. *Umaid Bhavan Palace*. Jodhpur: Mehrangarh Museum Trust.

'To Develop Country Image and National Brand Strategy to Attract Foreign Direct Investment: An Example from Central Asia, Kyrgyzstan', http://www.bledcom.com/uploads/papers/Tunca.pdf

Tokarski, Stanisław (ed.). 1996. *Kraje pozaeuropejskie w polskich środkach masowego przekazu: Metamorfozy recepcji*. Warszawa: Wydawnictwa naukowe semper.

Tokarski Stanisław and Surender Bhutani. 2007. *Nowoczesne Indie: Wyzwania rozwoju* (Modern India: Challenge of Development). Warszawa: Polska Akademia Nauk.

Tuczyński, Jan. 1981. *Motywy indyjskie w literaturze polskiej* (Indian Motives in Polish Literature). Warszawa: PWN.

Tully, Mark. 2011. *Non-Stop India*. New Delhi: Penguin Book India.

Woźniakowska, Urszula. 2010. *Bollywood: pragnienie prawdy i tęsknota za mitem* (Bollywood: Desire for Truth and Longing for Myth). Kraków: Universitas.

Zamoyski, Adam. 2009. *Poland: A History*. New York: Harper Press.

13

Globalization, ICT Revolution and Socio-cultural Changes in India

Sociological Explorations

BINAY KUMAR PATTNAIK

The rise of Information and Communication Technologies (ICT) including software industry, in countries like China, India, Singapore, South Korea, Taiwan, Hong Kong, Philippines, etc., has become synonymous with globalization because of the timely arrival of these digital technologies and its inherent capabilities for the faster proliferation. Most conducive in this regard has been the new global economic order. The application of these new technologies in the changed global economic order has also changed the global business by promoting international subcontracting and subsequently, international outsourcing. The rise of Indian IT industry during the 1990s has been the most spectacular achievement of Indian industry. This industry in India grew at an incredible rate of 50 per cent per annum during the whole of the 1990s. Being an export-oriented industry it has earned 75 per cent of its revenue from exports alone. Subsequently, the ICT revolution in India and in other developing countries (including newly industrialized countries [NICs]) has not merely earned enough foreign currencies, but also more significantly, has brought in widespread socio-cultural changes. Apart from what I am going to analyse here in this paper, there are other ICT impact areas that have thrown new challenges to sociologists. Following are some of the socio-cultural areas where the ICT impact changes oscillate between utopian to nightmare types: (i) Building social capital through the use of Internet (Facebook, Linkedin, etc): It has been observed to be highly useful for professionals in general and academicians in particular who build up their social capital internationally and realize the benefits in the long run. (ii) Ethnocization through Internet: Apart from reinforcing ethnic ties among lose community members and facilitating the resurrection of ethnic beliefs and practices, Internet helps ethnic groups to publicize their cultural/religious ideals and reach out to potential new recruits. (iii) Internet pushing for a sexual revolution: Internet contains abundance of pornographic sites/materials, access to which is of course universal and not restricted by any law. Starting from a mere commercialization of human body (sexually), Internet is now offering experiences of virtual sex, interactive sex, through its sites. Hence, as a big source of cultural pollution, it is now posing serious cultural threats to tradition-bound cultures. (iv) Emergence of a new class of transnational capitalists: The IT revolution gave rise to a new class of capitalists who were, in fact, engineering professionals. This was true of both India and China. (v) Emergence of a new class of workers as well as a new subculture of theirs in India: The second phase of the this revolution known as the ICT revolution in India and in other developing countries (including NICs) more significantly, has created a new class of workers/professionals. Based on knowledge based technologies (being fully R&D based), it has given rise to a new class of workers/professionals and consequently a subculture of its own. The first phase of the said revolution in India known as IT revolution took place in the last decade of the 20th century, i.e., 1990s and its second phase known as the ICT revolution followed in the early years of the next decade, i.e., 2010s. This paper deals with these later aspects of the socio-cultural changes engendered by the ICT revolution in India with a concern for social equality.

The paper tries to articulate some of the socio-cultural impacts of the ICT revolution in India from sociological viewpoints. Having perceived the phenomenon within the framework of social stratification, the author tries to deal with the; (i) issues of social stratification that perpetuates itself through the use of new technologies of ICT, and (ii) the emergence of a new class of occupations and a corresponding class of new workforce that has come to be known as ICT/knowledge workers, along with its own subculture. Thus, based on secondary source observations, the paper is a study of India's techno-coolie and cyber-coolie, as a new class of elite technical workforce, the basis of its identity formation (class consciousness) and its emerging sub-culture.

Further, the paper also tries to examine the knowledge workers' perceived identity of being professionals/executives in the frame work of Goldthorpe's 'embougeoisement' thesis.

The Indian IT Revolution

India's IT revolution has been attributed to a number of socio-cultural factors including the popular propensity toward its never-ending argumentative nature, the logical structure of its generic language called Sanskrit, and the deep popular use of numbers and rudimentary arithmetic used off hand. These cultural factors were reinforced by social factors like availability of young educated manpower with English tongues.

Further, India had been the house of the second largest pool of English-speaking engineers in the world. The brilliant IIT engineers who had migrated to USA and the large number of competitive Indian young engineers at home, provided the ideal ground for an IT revolution. By now it is well known that the phenomenal growth of the Indian IT and subsequently the ITES (Information Technology Enabled Services) industry has been greatly shaped by the liberalization of policies. By the year 2002, India had acquired 24 per cent of the global IT/ITES services. And, in the year 2009, it had acquired 66 per cent of the global IT/ITES revenues (NASSCOM 2009: 2).

Foreign capital began to flow into the Indian industry after the government introduced, the then mini-scale liberalization of policies in 1984, that allowed 100 per cent foreign subsidiaries of MNCs to operate in India. That apart the pro-IT policy initiative of the then Government of India is worth mentioning. For example, the STPI (Software Technology Parks of India) had been one of the most successful initiatives of the government and it has now offices in more than 30 cities in India. It not only functioned as a 'single window', simplifying and cutting short all bureaucratic procedures and protocols, but also provided for infrastructures. The government also in partnership with private enterprise had set up a number of science parks (with all infrastructure provided) within which cyber cities grew.

The first foreign-owned export-oriented offshore software firm to be set up in India was the Citicorp Oversea Ltd at SEEPZ (Santa Cruz Electronics Exports Processing Zone), Bombay in 1985 followed by the Texas Instruments setting up at Bangalore in 1986 to do some chip designing. But to Friedman (2006: 128) the real IT revolution in India had started with the arrival of the General Electric in 1989. Following Texas Instruments many MNCs entered into India and the indigenous software industry was inspired. Through 1990s the government continued to provide subsidies through STPI, when the Indian IT industries acquired foreign collaborations to experience growth. The 'body shopping' model based on labour contract services got a boost through which low-paid Indian engineers were hired by foreign companies abroad to deliver their services 'on-site'. But by then 'body shopping' was already a known practice of contractual hiring of Indian techies by firms abroad. Way back in the 1970s, having realized shortage of IT labour in the west, the Indian companies had capitalized on it and had began to send hired technical staff to work overseas on particular projects in the USA or in Europe. This practice came to be known as 'body shopping'. This was the 1st instance of globalizing Indian IT industry. Body shopping was a contractual arrangement to work on site for a specific period with less salary, on the employer's conditions. These were all programmers who were sent on short stay visas. The practice became widespread and the industry grew around this for a while. Asma Lateef (1996–97), in her study software industry in Bangalore, noted that by 1990 over 95 per cent of Indian software firms were involved in body shopping activities. But it turned out to be an unstable system as there was no commitment either from the employer (only gives short-term employment) or the employee who was constantly looking out for a better deal. It did no value additions and offered them no better career path. However, it gave good exposure and a reputation to Indian techies. Some of them broke the contracts and got better placements in USA.

However, body shopping began to decline by mid-1990s and later got replaced with offshore outsourcing of services. Global firms began to set up export-oriented development centres close to the programmers' home. And for most global firms it meant India. By the turn of the millennium more than 185, Fortune 500 companies, i.e., two out of every five global giants, were outsourcing some of their IT requirements to India. In the early years of 2000 almost every software company in the world including Microsoft, Oracle, Sun, Adobe, etc., had set up their offshore software development centres in India. With this turn the ground was already set by some MNCs for the revolution.

By mid-1990s the Indian IT companies began to shift away from body shopping towards the offshore model with the proportion of revenue falling from 90 per cent in 1988 to only 56 per cent in 1999–2000 (Kumar 2001: 4279) and to 41 per cent in 2003. The larger Indian IT companies 'moved up in the value chain' to offer value-added services, even at times, turnkey projects. Those large Indian IT companies were born in 1980s. But the 1990s witnessed the mushrooming growth of IT SMEs (small and medium scale enterprises) in Indian metros like Bangalore, Hyderabad, Mumbai and New Delhi as many ambitious techies left the large companies to start their own SMEs. This is something akin to what happened then in Silicon Valley as 'start-up trend'. The easy availability of 'venture capital' funds after 1995 contributed handsomely to the growth of SMEs in IT sector.

The Indian IT industry then had three strong links to the global economy, such as (i) dependence on foreign contracts (order), (ii) dependence on MNC FDI as wholly-owned subsidiaries to develop software development centres, and (iii) the dependence on foreign venture capital (mid-1990s onwards).

After the legalization of the Venture Capital (VC) in India in 1988, VC funds came into existence and the most successful one was the Technology Development and Information Company of India (TDICI) at Bangalore, as joint venture of the ICICI and UTI-two financial institutions. Several of the early software firms like Mastek, Microland, Wipro, etc., were benefited from this. Noteworthy that in the year 1995, the unfolding liberalization policy allowed the entry of foreign VC funds and institutional capital to India. Further noteworthy was that a bulk (80% by 1999) of these funds came from NRIs (Non-Resident Indians) especially the US-based Indian techies who had done booming business in the USA. Glaring examples of this were the Draper International (headed by Kiran Nadkarni) 1995 and the Walden-NIKKO India venture capital company (in late 1990s). The US-based VC firms made possible the 'US-India corridor' by which many US-based IT/software firms had acquired development centres in India. In the dotcom boom period of 1999–2000, there were as many as 100 VC firms (including Indians) that were operating in India but it soon dropped. In 2002 there were 60 foreign VC firms operating in India. In the absence of official figures, unofficial figures show that by the year 2000 the investment from foreign VC was over $1 billion (Upadhya 2004). Similarly, NRI investment figures in the IT industry are not exactly available but it is claimed that half of IT companies in Bangalore since 1999 had some NRI investment component. Saxenian (2002: 43) reports of a relevant survey which had found that about 50 per cent of Silicon Valley's NRI IT firms had business relations with Indian firms as partial/wholly owned subsidiaries (37%), sub-contractors/supplier of materials/parts (28%) or some sort of joint ventures (16%).

Thus, three types of VC funds flew to Indian IT industry, such as: (i) Indian (large institutional investors like ICICI, UTI, etc. and a few private ones), (ii) exclusively foreign VC funding, and (iii) the ones known as cross-border funding through which the Indian development centres of US-based firms have been funded. A good example of this is US-IVCA (US-Indian Venture Capital Association).

Further, the case of 'TiE' (The Indus Entrepreneurs), a consortium type organization of NRI/US-based Indian techies, was an example of funding and fostering entrepreneurship among Indians. TiE was founded in 1992 but soon became successful with 8,000 members in 34 chapters spread across US, Canada, Singapore, Dubai, Malaysia, India, etc. TiE became a point of emulation to replicate the Silicon Valley magic in Europe and Asia. In the same decade, pushed by shortage of skilled workers, the USA tripled the number of visa granted to skilled personnel. This new type visa came to be known as H1-B. Nearly half of the H1-B visa granted by the USA was to Indians and most of these technical personnel were in the IT field and a majority of these went to California to participate in the hi-tech gold rush. India's golden diasporas including big achievers like, K.B. Chandrasekhar (founder of Exodus Communication), Vinod Dhan (father of the Practicum chip), Vinod Khosla (co-founder of Sun-Microsystem), Kanwal Rakhi (co-founder and head of Inventus Capital & Excelan Co.), Gururaj Deshpande (co-founder of Sycamore Networks), Rakesh Mathur (founder and CEO, Junglee), etc., looked homeward. Kanwal Rekhi became the president of TiE global. This Indian diasporas in the US, like their Chinese counterparts, linked Silicon Valley, the technology hub, with home land market (for cheap labour and business opportunities) and created transnational webs.

Hence, the 1990s witnessed an exodus of NRI technical professionals from US to India to start IT firms in India. They also funded IT industry in India directly as mentors/promoters through VC mode.

Rise of New Class of IT Capitalists in India

It is now well known that a new class of entrepreneurs have emerged out of the IT revolution in India. As noted by Upadhya (2004), most of the founders of software firms have middle class origin, those who have built on their cultural capital of higher education (usually through engineering education), acquired social capital (knowledge and business networks) through their professional careers in USA. Their social capital enabled them to make use of the trust and cooperation of their professional networks, for making innovative business advancements, because their social capital could reduce the transaction costs, bureaucratic procedures and even corruption. Thus, the combined virtue of cultural and social capital engendered a class of technological capitalists in Indian IT sector. This class of capitalists is not only driven by high need achievement orientation, but also by high level of technological innovations. They could ride innovation-driven business that has flattened the technological world, at least in the IT sector to a great extent. This class of IT capitalists is also distinguished by its global linkages. Not only that many of them had studied/worked in USA/abroad but also their business were: (i) greatly dependent upon foreign contracts (particularly USA), and (ii) most of them acquired foreign funding either directly or through foreign venture capitals (which were mostly from USA, particularly the Silicon Valley). This class of entrepreneurs is distinct from the traditional Indian capitalist class (Seth Ji's leading family business) and corporate houses (like, Ambanis, Bajaj, Birlas, Goenkas, Godrej, Kirloskars, Tatas, Singhanias, etc.). These are also first generation entrepreneurs. These IT entrepreneurs of large as well as SMEs themselves made a distinct social category by itself. Most software firms were formed by non-conventional first generation entrepreneurs who were mostly engineers by training and had long experience in IT industry as professionals, both in India and USA. 'The middle class origins of many of the entrepreneurs who have drawn upon their cultural capital through higher education and acquired social capital through job experiences have given a distinct culture and orientation to this industry' (Upadhya 2004). As most of the software entrepreneurs were from middle class families, (without business experiences) they even did not have ready capital back-up and hence had to scrape together capital from family savings, loans from friends, etc. (e.g., Infosys story).

As the offshoot of liberalization of the Indian policies and globalization of the economy, this bourgeoisie is more adaptable to MNCs. Instead of being wary of the presence of the multinationals in the IT sector, this class could find a synergy with MNCs and have learnt to benefit from their presence. Therefore, this class, first being the offshoot and later being part of the transnational IT business, is the strongest votary of globalization. By virtue of creating enormous employment and profit, this industry has influenced Indian economic and industrial policies greatly during the last two decades. Upadhya (2004) calls them the 'icons of the resurgent India'. It may also be noted that this transnational entrepreneurial class has emerged in tandem with a transnational labour regime which has also generated a new class of IT workforce in India.

Emergent New Class of Elite Workforce

In this context of impact of IT and subsequent ICT revolution in India, extremely relevant is the notion of 'techno-coolie' and 'cyber-coolie'. These derogatory terms refer to a new class of elite 'knowledge workers', emerging out of the global outsourcing and offshoring of services. This is the direct off-shoot of globalization process. Birth of this new workforce is not confined to India alone, rather is spread over several other developing and even newly industrialized countries like China, Singapore, Taiwan, Hong Kong, Philippines and Israel. Hence, both the words refer to knowledge workers not merely that of India but to all such workers of countries who have become part of the international out-sourcing services. But India has a giant share in this.

Techno-Coolie: Software engineers or other IT professionals (otherwise known as techies) of developing countries are seen as a new knowledge workforce that caters to the global informational economy. The workforce is highly flexible and mobile. These IT professionals called as techno-coolies are mostly employed in the USA and other developed countries or even many of them who are employed in home countries travel abroad very frequently for 'on-site' delivery of their services. The geographically dispersed nature of the software outsourcing business makes physical mobility as one aspect of the migration. The developed form of ICTs even enabled part of the services to be delivered 'virtually'. Software engineers even located in home countries, along with colleagues and managers spread over distant geographical locations work as 'virtual teams' to communicate among themselves and deliver to the customer abroad through computer networks. In this connection they make short, foreign visits too.

Migration of techies from India to Europe although started in late 1970s, it became significant in late 1990s, particularly due to the 'Y2K' crisis. The important routes of this migration from India by the techies were three: (1) The first one was through 'body shopping' arrangement by which Indian techies were sent on short contracts to work on the customer's site abroad. (2) The other arrangement was through outsourcing by American/European firms through Indian software service providers which had a team of techies working on the project at home and another team working onsite at the customer's venue abroad. Earlier, large IT firms like TCS, Infosys, HCL, etc., were engaged in body shopping and had offices both in India and US/Europe. (3) The third arrangement was immigration through the Indian subsidiaries of European MNCs like, Philips, Robert Bosc, Siemens, etc.

1. *Body shopping:* This arrangement was not so encouraging for the Indian techies as they were engaged on the customer's site on low-end maintenance jobs with low salaries. Their employment conditions, compensations and nature of contract are determined by the consultants (Indian agencies) and their works were managed by the customers. The techies were usually on a contract with the consultant company to be paid on hourly rate, other than the travel accommodation and maintenance allowances. The duration of the stay abroad is specified in the contract. Usually, the techie cannot break the contract with the consultant for greener pasture abroad as they had to pay back heavily for violating the contracts. The Indian consultants were basically sub-contractors suppose to provide mere 'bodies'/engineers with specifications to the MNCs.

2. *Outsourcing companies:* Those techies travelling abroad by outsourcing arrangements through Indian service providers like TCS, HCL, etc., usually have their base jobs in India but are sent abroad to the client's site for a certain period. They are managed by their Indian service providing agency and not the client; mostly they get the Indian salary, with extra money for Europe/USA. The techies could make good money out of this but again carried onerous contracts or bonds with Indian agency not to join the job of the client or anybody in the client's country. Further, on return, they were bound to work with the Indian agency for a few years, and the like. Violation of the bond invites a hefty fine that may drive the techies bankrupt.
3. *MNC subsidiaries:* A good number of Indian engineers go abroad to work through their parent subsidiary companies of US/European MNCs like Oracle, Philips, Robert Bosc, etc. These are employees of the MNC subsidiaries in India called software development centres and are in fact better placed compared to the earlier two mechanisms. They go on short-long-term assignments and are comfortably placed abroad, as employees of the subsidiaries they are provided with housing, good working conditions, allowances, etc. Even they have to make little or fewer adjustments in terms of work culture, etc. Often they are housed with employees of parent MNCs in block apartments abroad.
4. The other category of mechanism for the techies was to get employed directly by US/European companies leaving the Indian agencies' contractual arrangements behind. Although most of them had come under 'body shopping' arrangements for on-site delivery, but have shifted away. Their salaries and employment conditions are better than first three types.

Apart from predicaments related to mode of recruitments, these Indian techies are marred by prohibitive immigration laws and regulations. It is well known that for Indian techies, obtaining visas, work permits and residence permits for European countries is much harder than for the USA. Upadhya (2006) in her study among Indian techies in Netherlands, Germany and Belgium has tried to analyse their plight in terms of work culture differences, as victims of European stereotypes about Indian techies, culturally embedded communication patterns, poor time management, inability to adapt to multiculturalism of virtual teams and dim career prospects in Europe. These apart, these techies are to 'negotiate the quagmire of immigration laws and rules (which are often humiliating) to maintain themselves in Europe and have to chew the common images of immigrant workers, diluted with racism, held by local people' (Upadhya 2006). They too struggle for an identity of a professional/knowledge worker as different from unskilled working class immigrants (from other small poor countries). As if these were not enough, the Indian techies have to withstand the anti-outsourcing sentiments in Europe and USA and a consequent fear of loss of job. Their isolation and social seclusion add to their woes. Thus, the Indian techie struggles hard not only to acquire the European work culture, multiculturalism, etc., but also engages himself in a reconstruction of his identity and self to relate to a foreign society.

ICT Turn of the Revolution

Sometime in late 1994, Health Scribe India, a firm, was set up at Bangalore by the Indian-American doctors and hospitals. The Health Scribe had set up a system that turned the American doctors touch-tone phone into a dictation machine and a PC would digitize doctor's voice. It would be transmitted to Bangalore (India), which would be transcribed by a student or so in two hours and would zip it back by the satellite as a text file that could be part of the US hospitals' computer system. So, where the doctor is sleeping in the night in USA the transcribed file gets ready quickly in India and in the morning doctor finds it there. This was a major breakthrough, as it could safely, legally and securely transcribe medical records, lab reports and doctor's diagnosis from Bangalore. Hence, lot of other industries thought about sending some of their back room jobs to be done in India as well. And, they did so but in a limited scale as the handling capacity of the satellite was limited (Friedman 2006: 130).

India had reached the peak of IT revolution by late 1990s with the Y2K bug solution and dot com boom. With the Y2K bug handling, Indian techies left their foot prints world over and Indian IT Industry started dating with that of the USA. Outsourcing from US to India as a new form of collaboration almost exploded. By the early 2000, the Y2K work was closed but a new business called 'e-commerce' had emerged. The fibre-optic lines turned out to be the magic strings. The laying of the fibre-optic lines across the ocean connected the main frames in USA to Indian IT companies like Wipro, Infosys, TCS, etc., and enabled managing American e-commerce. With the dot com boom, India had benefited. And, the boom laid the cables that connected India with the world. The fibre-optic bubble inflated the business links between the USA/UK and India. More than the boom the dot com burst brought enormous benefits to India, as it reduced the costs of communication drastically and made transfer of voluminous data from US firms to India possible. This allowed many American firms to outsource Indian knowledge (ibid.: 133). The dot com burst further encouraged many Indian engineers to return home, as the techies could find American assignments sitting at Bangalore/Bombay/Hyderabad. The big Indian IT firms also came with innovations and value-added proposals to sell their own new products in software and consultancies. They had graduated from maintenance to products. Their interaction with US firms became deeper and deeper and slowly through business process outsourcing they started to run the back room of US firms.

The post-Y2K recessionary trends in USA pushed US companies toward outsourcing, particularly the offshore type. This outsourcing trend was of course confined to the peripheral tasks of business, what is otherwise known as back room office jobs. This too created opportunities for Indian IT industry. The Indian IT sector then created within itself a new business sector known as ITES. Thus, it seems that recession in US turned out to be a saving grace for Indian IT industry. Apart from the economic downturn in the US, the other factors that were responsible for the growth of offshore outsourcing business in India were: its geographical location by which it stands several hours behind its markets in the west, its telecom liberalization policy during 1990s that reduced the cost of telephones drastically, its English educated and highly motivated manpower and lastly its low cost manpower. The most important of the above was the availability of cheap manpower that allowed the American companies to save 40 to 50 per cent costs (*The Economist*, 13 May 2003).

Notwithstanding the backlash in the US and the UK against offshoring, the companies continued to outsource from India. They did so not only because of the great cost saving but also because of the high quality services they received. Better quality services were imparted by Indian agents compared to their American counterparts, because in India the call centre employees/agents were not part-timers but full-timers, better educated, mostly graduates even sometimes post-graduates but not college drop outs. The Indian agents outperformed their American counterparts again because Indians treated these as careers. Of course, the Indian BPO industry has a retention problem, it has, however, kept the attrition rate below 30 per cent. Of late, large BPO companies are offering opportunities both laterally—allowing employees to move off the call centre to HR, marketing, accounts and quality control—and horizontally from team leaders to customer, operation and call centre managers (Greenspan 2005: 96). Thus, it is not just a temporary job but rather a career.

By 2003, the electronic back office had become the booming sector. Apart from the MNCs, big Fortune 500 companies had entered India's BPO sector, and the Indian IT big players like Infosys, Wipro, Satyam, also launched some form of BPO services (ibid.: 94).

Types of Investments in Indian ITES-BPO Sector

The ITES-BPO sector received investment from various sources and of various nature. The heterogeneity of the Indian BPO sector reveals several types of investment patterns and their corresponding organizational structures and management systems. Following are the three major types of investments that came through to India:

1. *Captives:* Those are essentially in-house service providers of global MNCs (e.g., HSBC, Dell, Hewlett Packard, Prudential, GE, etc.) that directly own and control their own offshore operations. These continue to dominate the Indian BPO sector. Captives could be of further two types: (i) Branch office: it is a representative office only for software development and not for marketing/selling products and services in India. (ii) 100 per cent subsidiary: it has a local management, but otherwise the parent MNC does everything else. Usually these operate from the software technology parks or export processing zones.
2. *Joint ventures:* In this case the MNC works with an Indian partner in India. It allows both the partner firms to benefit

from the collaboration and the MNC retains the option of switching it to a 100 per cent subsidiary if certain conditions are met. It could be of two types: (i) Third party MNCs: It means a global MNC operates from India with an Indian partner to provide services to client firms in other countries. (ii) Indian third party service provider: It means the Indian partner only provides for the services to the clients (category called as pure plays) and not anything else.

3. *Domestic sector:* (i) These are mostly the ITES-BPO arms of Indian IT firms (e.g., Wipro and Infosys). These are also service providers to clients abroad. (ii) Of late there developed a new sub-sector within the domestic sector which consists of purely Indian and exclusively ITES-BPO firms (not the arms of any IT firm). The principal location for Indian ITES-BPO industry remains the Tier-1 cities, namely, New Delhi and NCR, Mumbai, Bangalore, Chennai and Hyderabad. However, Tier-2 and Tier-3 cities in India have also experienced growth of ITES-BPO business, e.g., Pune (Convergys, WNS, Progeo, EXL & Mphasis), Vishakhapatnam (Satyam, Wipro, TCS, HSBC, etc.), Madurai (Honey Well), Nagpur (Krishna group), Chandigarh (Infosys, IBM-Daksh), Jaipur (GE), Thiruvananthapuram (Infosys), etc.

Nature of Work in ITES-BPO Industry

Based on available evidence, Taylor and Bain (2006: 48–49) maintained that it would be reasonable to conclude that voice services account for 60 to 65 per cent of sectoral employment and the various back office activities for 35 to 40 per cent. Bulk of these offshored services are low-end, encompassing voice services and simple transactional business processes which are highly standardized and routinized. The major types of services rendered by Indian ITES-BPO sector are: (a) finance and accounting (activities such as, general accounting, transaction management, corporate finance, compliance management and statutory reporting), (b) customer interaction services (CIS) (all forms of IT-enabled customer contacts such as in-bound/out-bound, voice or non voice based support used to provide customer services), and (c) human resource administration services (such as payroll and benefits, administration, travel and expense processing, talent acquisition and talent management services, employee and manager self-service delivery services, employee communication design and accounts, etc.). If the finance and accounts services account for 40 per cent of Indian ITES-BPO revenues, the CIS accounts for nearly 46 per cent and HR accounts for 3 per cent of the ITES-BPO revenues. Thus, these three types of services account for 89 per cent of the industry revenues. If their services are highly standardized and routinized, the jobs of the KPOs are highly customized (Noronha and D'Cruz 2009).

Cyber-Coolies

The word 'cyber-coolie' refers to that growing workforce which comes under the IT-enabled services like, call centres, medical transcription and business process outsourcing. This workforce emerged out of the policy of 'offshore outsourcing' of services followed mainly by a few developed countries like, USA, UK and Japan. European powers like France and Germany also do this, but their scales of outsourcing of services are very limited. And, India being an English-speaking country is favourably placed to be at the receiving end of this international outsourcing of services from USA and UK. As mentioned earlier, 'techno-coolie' is a term referring to IT workers in USA, Canada and UK who are essentially immigrants—may be Indians, Chinese, Philippinos or Hispanic—engaged in low-end technical jobs (mostly programming). Similarly the word 'cyber coolie' is a contemptuous word attributed to the knowledge workers of India in the ITES-BPO sector. Like the techno-coolies, the cyber-coolies are also a grossly underpaid lot. When a 'cyber coolie' delivers his/her offshore services through Internet being present in his/her home country, the 'techno-coolie' delivers his/her services abroad right on the cite of the client being present there. Usually, a techno-coolie is hired through a practice called as 'body shopping' from the developing countries because of the international sub-contracting practices followed by large corporations in these developed countries to keep their costs low.

Both techno-coolies and cyber-coolies are a class of knowledge workers that has been an off-shoot of international sub-contracting by large MNCs to developing countries. If in the 1960s-70s the large MNCs in the manufacturing sector outsourced their raw materials and sometimes value-added products from the developing countries and in the 1970s–80s these again outsourced their components and semi-finished products from developing countries (and sometimes even shifted their manufacturing units to escape rising costs and pollution), in the 1990s and 21st century the large corporations in the manufacturing as well as service sector in those industrial countries are outsourcing their technical services from the developing countries. This is the consequence of the cut-throat competition among MNCs in the west and their drastic efforts to reduce costs.

The word 'coolie' (whether techno-coolie or cyber-coolie) has certainly a contemptuous meaning and is used in a derogatory sense. Coolie meaning 'aka', a poor fellow, dressed in red, scurrying after us carrying our heavy luggage on his head as we board a train, all for a few pennies. It is indeed difficult to trace the exact origin of the word cyber-coolie/techno-coolie. But certainly the words were coined by the Indian left-wing intellectuals who have been against free trade. It is also true that the leftist have been trying to trade unionize this growing workforce which the workforce itself has not entertained. Hence, this contemptuous attribution. The other source of the word 'cyber-coolie' is the British critics of the phenomenon who are yet to free themselves from the 'Raj' hangover. British economy today, being more of a service economy, deals more with financing, banking and insurance than with manufacturing proper. Hence, it needs 'back-up services' in these areas which they outsource from its ex-colony, India which is also English speaking. And, this is also true that Unionists in Britain do consider these outsourced low-end jobs to Indians as job snatching. Therefore, this envious contempt.

These knowledge workers emerging as a distinct occupational category in India is of very recent origin, may be a direct consequence of India's globalization. As a distinct occupational category, it has certain distinct characteristic features and it is fast developing a sub-culture for itself. Most of my formulations here are based on information/publications in the Internet (secondary data). I also borrow the findings of a study conducted by Babu P. Ramesh (2004: 492–493) on the BPO workers of India. The empirical study was conducted among a sample of 277 custom-care agents from six call centres in Noida, New Delhi capital region. The BPO industry in India alone employed little more than 2.23 million according to NASSCOM (2009) (BPO industry includes the employees of the call centres who work over phones and business process offices and those who work over webs). Figure 1 below gives the fact sheet for the growth of manpower in Indian IT industry:

Figure 1
Indian IT Employment Figures—ITES-BPO Sector (in millions)

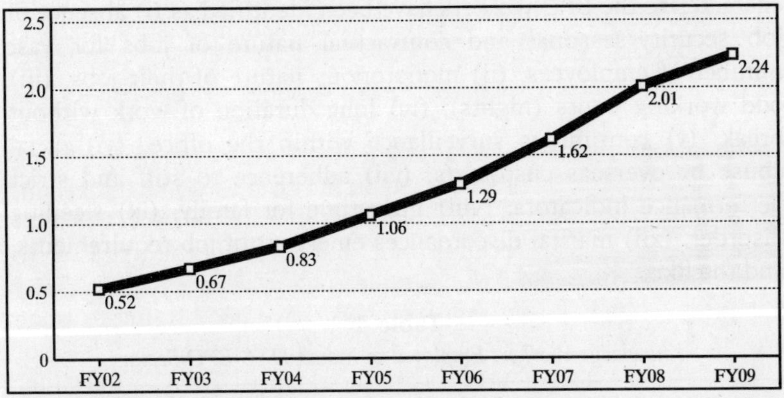

Figures do not include employees in the hardware sector.
Source: NASSCOM, Indian IT-BPO Industry, Fact Sheet, 2009.

These knowledge workers are all young, educated and mostly converted Indians who work in call centres and outsourced business processing offices to cater to American and British multinationals. They work through the nights, for good reasons that night in India is daytime for their clients in USA. Since they work through the nights, Harish Trivedi (2004) even calls them a *'chowkidar'* a derogatory word meaning night guard. They work through cyber phones and cyber webs to deal with their overseas clients. They speak in an American accent which they have painfully cultivated.

As their Indian accent is neutralized, their personality, biological clock and identity also have been neutralized. Because they are to conceal their real names and country of residence while dealing with their overseas clients, often they have to introduce themselves as Pete/Greg/Jane from Atlanta/Ohio etc. Thus, they are faceless workers with pretentious identities (from Hari to Harry or from Shalini to Shelly) who deal with invisible customers/clients located on the other side of the globe.

Many of these BPO workers not only work for very long hours but also at odd hours. Many find that they have little social life left, as they work during nights when their families and friends are at home. Some develop long-term sleep disorders, some take so much verbal abuse, day after day, from irate and racist Americans that they actually need psychological help, which now some call centres have learnt to provide for. The sources of their heavy stress that characterize the BPO workers have been identified as (i) absence of job security/seasonal and contractual nature of jobs for vast number of employees, (ii) monotonous nature of their jobs, (iii) odd working hours (nights), (iv) long duration of work without break, (v) continuous surveillance within the office, (vi) racial abuse by overseas customers, (vii) adherence to stiff and strict performance indicators, (viii) little time for family, (ix) sleeping disorder, (xii) marital discordances emergent of job requirements, and the like.

Table 1

Knowledge Workers Employed in Indian ITES-BPO Sector

	FY 2002	*FY 2003*	*FY 2004*	*FY 2005*	*FY 2006*	*FY 2007*	*FY 2008*	*FY 2009*
IT Exports and Services Exports	170,000	205,000	296,000	390,000	513,000	690,000	860,000	946,809
BPO Exports	106,000	180,000	216,000	316,000	415,000	553,000	700,000	789,806
Domestic Market	246,250	285,000	318,000	352,000	365,000	378,000	450,000	500,000
Total	522,250	670,000	830,000	1,058,000	1,293,000	1,621,000	2,010,000	2,236,614

Figures do not include employees in the hardware sector.

Source: NASSCOM, Indian BPO Industry, Fact Sheet, 2009.

The BPO employee survey (2004) by Data Quest presented here in Figure 2 shows that the worst stress factors (as reported by the percentage of BPO employees) are their long working hours (39.4%), odd working hours (38.6%), heavy workload (37.4%), repetitive nature of the work (37.2%), pressure to perform on matrices (36.1%) and insufficient holidays (36.6%). This, of course, is indicative of the exploitative nature of the BPO industry. However, BPO industry then was in its nascent form in India.

Today, BPO industry is much better placed in terms of alleviating its employee stress.

These young people are the scions of lower middle/middle class urban parents, mostly graduates, computer savvy, educated in convents or public schools from where they have acquired a fluency in English and sometimes possess a technical or science degrees but all of them long for an exposure to western popular culture. This workforce, in spite of its long hours of work, even at odd hours, also works in the weekends. But this is a grossly underpaid lot. This is why India is seen as an outsourcing threat. The cost of an Indian BPO employee is seven to ten times lesser than his American counterpart in ITES business. It is true that in India there exists a large pool of English-speaking low-skilled manpower. And, this makes India a western corporate attraction. The key is low wages.

Figure 2

Indian BPO Industry: Stress Factors

Percentage of employees who named these as the most important reasons for workplace stress. (Multi-coded responses, so total will be greater than 100 per cent)

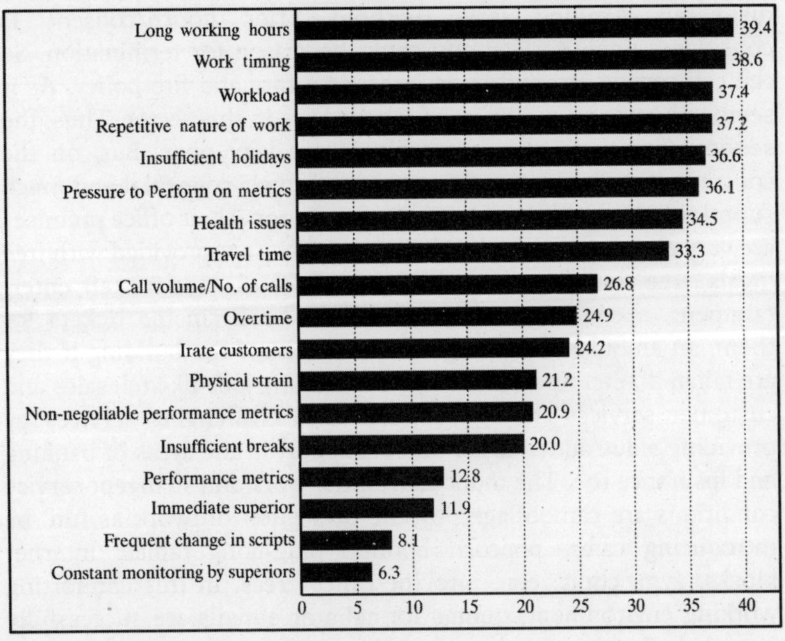

Source: BPO Employee Survey 2004. Data Quest

The organizational structure of call centres is basically dualistic, consisting of a core/permanent set of employees and the periphery/temporary workers. All call centre agents are periphery workers, who are substitutable, while team leaders and managers make the core group. The long-term career prospects are bleak/not so attractive. The dualistic workforce model allows the firm to regulate the workforce and nip in the bud any sign of trade unionism. Trade union is a strange word for this workforce. The labour practices that call centres follow are even much older. Because work is monitored on the spot and even after working hours with the help of specially designed software, computer network and closed circuit cameras. All interactions of these employees in the office are continuously recorded or taped and randomly checked by the manager. Most of the surveillance recorded at work is even comparable with situations of 19th century prisons.

Mistakes at work lead to immediate warnings and those are recorded in 'warning cards' that form part of the daily ratings of agents. If an agent commits three errors in a day he/she gets a zero rating. Three consecutive zeros lead to counselling or even dismissal. Availing leave without prior notice/consent is considered unauthorized and could be reason for termination. So the call centres, by and large, practice a hire and fire policy. As it seems, there is no modicum of labour laws in this sector. Thus, the service conditions of this workforce are very poor. But, on the contrary, its working conditions are extremely congenial and much superior to those in the manufacturing sector. Their office premises are very clean and fully air-conditioned. They are provided with free meals, free transport (car pick-up and drop), regular staff entertainment, a concierge service that will book cinema tickets for them, an ambulance waiting at the bottom of the building if they are fallen ill, etc. Apart from less challenging jobs like telesales and customer services they do render more challenging services by providing value added 'back office' support in the areas of banking and insurance too. The monotony of the work and stringent service conditions are camouflaged by the projection of 'work as fun' by introducing cafes, popcorn booths, ping-pong tables, internet kiosks, gym, clinic, etc., into the office areas. In this comforting working environment, quotas for calls or e-mails are successfully attended. Besides this working environment, a reasonably good salary (₹ 10,000 to 20,000 to 25,000 per month, which is of course not higher than skilled workers of the Indian manufacturing sector), use of latest technologies, young and educated peers, all make these knowledge workers believe that the job they are doing is of an executive/professional.

Emerging New Subculture

Employment in the BPO sector made a bigger impact in India as it turned out to be cultural and social too. It employed graduates from any stream not necessarily from engineering only. When the engineering and the software sector has predominantly male employees, employment of women come close to 50 per cent in the BPO sector. A culturally reserved Indian society where women lived sheltered lives within the bounds of traditions are bound to experience cultural and economic impact when they went out of home during nights to workplace.

This class of knowledge workers is a highly disciplined and young workforce. And, because of its education and predominantly lower middle/middle class origin, it turned out to be a docile work- force with high level of efficiency. But unfortunately, this highly productively docile workforce is bereft of labour rights and job security. As a distinct and new occupational category, this workforce is fast developing a subculture of its own. A recent study by Georgina Thomas (2008) among the call centre employees in the Indian city of Mumbai has referred to the emergence of such a sub-culture among these young elite workers, of course because of their changing lifestyles. This subculture is said to have two aspects: (i) Consumerism accompanied by other leisure time activities by both male and female employees, like smoking, drinking, frequent partying and movie going, mall shopping, etc. They relish the mall culture. The English they write is of a different variety, more of American-spoken English type (with abbreviated forms of expressions) like the nature and the types of products they market or products they do value addition. They represent a subculture that emphasizes traits like, low cost, instant satisfaction, use and throw, take it or forget it, minimum-quality assured, go cool, chill out, one night stand, etc. They change their jobs as frequently as they change their boyfriends/girlfriends. (ii) The other vital aspect of the subculture refers more gloomy traits like leading a self-centred life, living life in one's own terms and conditions, moving away from community and/family life, indulging in frequent pre-marital sex, extramarital affairs and divorces in the name of what is called as 'one night stand', etc. These traits certainly imply choosing life without commitment/bonds and without certain moral values that augur a free life of primitive type. These are new trends and do make a highly significant component of the subculture. This subculture emerging among BPO workers is of course anchored on the process of a separate identity formation among them, i.e., (i) different work culture (highly routinized, stressful, odd working hours, etc.), leading to (ii) a different lifestyle, leading to (iii) acquiring new cultural traits, leading to (iv) different perception of their social position and culture by others (including family members), leading to (v) formation of a different self, leading to (vi) a different cultural identity of the employees.

Conflicting Perceptions of Identity

Left-wing politics in India has been desperately trying to penetrate its trade unionism into this sector for last several years. But, surprisingly, in spite of the poor service conditions, routinized nature of their jobs with emotional hazards, this workforce holds sheer disrespect for the trade unions and the unionists. It is their own perceptions of being professionals/executives that holds back these elite knowledge workers from forming trade unions. Another important reason why these workers are found to be disinterested with trade unionism is that its nearly 30 per cent volatile (attrition) segment does not intend to continue in these jobs as a career, rather they consider this to be a stop gap arrangement to migrate or shift to better jobs. This kind of job perception by the ambitious young workforce finds the notion of unionism incompatible with itself.

A few Internet-based articles on 'cyber-coolie' by Harish Trivedi (2004), Prafulla Bidwai (2003), and Ranabir Ray Choudhury (2003) and Arundhati Roy, etc., have provoked strong reactions from among this workforce. A frustrated Narayan Ram Hegde of Union Network International (a global alliance of 900 unions) when miserably failed in his effort to induct a few of the knowledge workers into their trade union framework, noted that 'these young people have a negative image about unions. But they are more like cyber-coolies. Hopefully, they will be convinced over time'. The debate had certainly created some heat in the Internet. These young and educated workers claimed themselves to be 'cool professionals' against the attribution of being cyber-coolies. In the debate they too displayed their contempt for left-wing trade unionists. Here are some of their responses:

> Cyber-coolies, the term trade unionists and leftist types use condescendingly to describe outsourcing professionals only reveal their contempt for the dignity of labour. And for those claiming to represent the cause of labour that is already a major disqualification.
>
> The cyber-coolies argument is a load of crap, plain and simple. Working conditions as a rule are already better than what exists in other offices ... further most of the top software/BPO companies have a very good feedback system in place. Hence what is the need to go on strike, or have a bunch of gangsters speak on your behalf, when you can always just quit and join a competitor? At this point it is an employee's market, not employers and software companies are aware of it. The amount of begging my boss did in an attempt to prevent me from leaving to go do my MBA was almost shameful. There is no difference between unionists and a bunch of gangsters .... (TTG on 26 September 2005, at 13: 09 hrs)
>
> The left wing intellectuals who coined the term cyber-coolie were certainly not keen on free trade. But they do not mind selling their silly novels and (*contemptuous*) social analysis of Indian society in western market but have an issue with people making a decent living while performing support work for MNCs. It is widely known what unions have done to slow down economic reforms keeping India in perpetual under performance mode for the past decades. This is just another step in trying to curb the fast growing BPO market. (Chandra Dulam on 27 September 2005 at 00: 50 hrs)
>
> First of all a 'cyber-coolie' has a job and puts food on the table, so that ain't a bad thing. Secondly, he actually works (gasps!), something that the union idiots have never done their entire lives .... (Guru on 2 October 2005 at 14:50 hrs). (The Acron 2005)

In a website entitled 'Dancing with Dogs: Interesting debate' (18 August 2004) carrying this debate one finds some of these cool young professionals loosing their cool. Not only they did heavy left bashing but also literally lead a counter offensive against these left-wing Indian intellectuals for their contemptuous writings. Even a popular columnist like Gurucharan Das noted that 'Trivedi's depictions are truly bizarre. What he sees as exploitation by MNCs, the young people on the contrary see it as an exciting chance to make a career in global economy .... The minds of these 'cyber coolies' seem to be decolonized whereas poor Trivedi is stuck in a post-colonial past'. Thus, there exists a perceptual difference between those of the left-wing intellectuals and those of the elite knowledge workers. This workforce with 'professionalism as their lived experience' not only abhorred the terms like 'cyber coolies' and 'slaves on Roman ships' (Ramesh 2004) attributed to them by the left-wing intellectuals and rebutted back in the Internet but also firmly resisted the efforts of left-wing activists to unionize their workforce. The larger story needs to be told here in nutshell.

The early efforts to unionize Indian IT workforce was made by the International Federation of Commercial, Clerical, Professional and Technical Employees (FIET), a founding member of the Union Network International (UNI). Subsequently, in November 2000, the Information Technology Professional's Forum (ITPF) was formed at Hyderabad and Bangalore. It was led by Unionists from telecom sector. The offices were opened formally by UNI delegation to India and the financial assistance was extended by the Swedish Union for Clerical and Technical Employees in Industry (SIF) . In the opening ceremony the IT-based knowledge workers highlighted that as professionals they collectively wanted to work towards the furtherance of their careers and to fight their employers as victims of work exploitation. They recognized the fact that the interest of Indian IT-based knowledge workers need to be protected and the UNI was to act as their international guardian. 'Thus, a professional association with nuance, very much different from the conventional Indian trade unions, was envisaged' (Noronha and D'Cruz 2009: 113). It was to evolve as a new type of organization like Wash Tech in the USA, Alliance of IT workers in Australia and Syndicate in Switzerland. The ITPF was to serve as a model for knowledge workers in technology clusters in developing countries like Singapore, Malaysia, Taiwan, Argentina, Brazil and the Eastern European countries. Bulk of the IT employees attending the meetings were convinced of forming a trade union with nuance. They chose not to call their organization, ITPF, a trade union but reiterated its position as a forum for furthering IT professionals' goals. In the meanwhile there was a sudden explosion of employees in the ICT sector as the ITES-BPO sector employed more as a growing sector.

It went up from a modest 1,06,000 in 2001–2002 to 3,48,000 in 2004–05 (NASSCOM 2005). Hence, left with little choice, this workforce had to engage the ITPF.

Majority of knowledge workers still opined that ITES-BPO sector should keep away from unions, as their presence will cause decline in productivity, resistance to further expansion, drying-up of FDI flow, etc. Being professionals they do not require collective bargainings for their interests. These knowledge workers of course had a sense of 'professionalism as lived experiences' which meant to them: putting organizational interest first, giving optimum performance at work, their emotions, subjectivity and relationships are accorded secondary to work, keeping personal biases, grudges, favouritism and affective issues away from work situations, being formally dressed, maintaining behavioural etiquettes and mannerisms, collegial informal relationship between superiors and subordinates and the like. These actually may mean nothing more than cultivating a good work culture. Having smelt the mood of the knowledge workers the ITPF responded emphatically saying that it is not a union (Hirschfeld 2005) and is a knowledge forum of IT and ITES-BPO professionals to facilitate suitable legislation and enforcement of existing legislations for the employees. As it looked, it was a self-styled professional organization and hence in functioning it bore little resemblance to any full-fledged professional association which necessitates an educational criteria for membership, adopts codes of ethics for practitioners, protects members from competition from unqualified quacks, engages in activities to get licensing and educational requirements, etc. May be under pressure, the ITPF continued to behave like an association and provide information for professional development and networking services. It also had got an understanding with the Association of Professional Engineers, Scientists and Managers Australia (APESMA) for its services and information. Thus, ITPF developed dual identity as a professional forum as well as a trade union with UNI affiliation. The internal conflict manifested as it was pointed out that ITPF was receiving financial support from UNI-Asia Pacific Regional Office (UNI-APRO) as a union but claiming to be a forum of professionals. Because of this emergent rift within, a sizeable section of its members walked out to establish a separate union body named Centre for BPO Professionals (CBPOP) under the agies of UNI-APRO in July 2004. It had two service centres, one at Hyderabad and the other at Bangalore. The purpose was to mobilize larger ITES-BPO workforce by convincing them about the need for collective representation through a trade union and finally to consolidate this network of so-called professionals into a trade union. Soon it also opened chapters in New Delhi, Mumbai and Chennai. By March 2005, it had got a modest membership of 2,000 employees. On the other hand, ITPF hardened its stand on not being a trade union. In 2007, ITPF clarified that it has no relation with CBPOP and the UNI. It is another professional association like the Bangalore Management Association and it is registered under the Society's Registration Act of India and not under the Trade Union Act of India.

Soon, CBPOP faced serious challenges of membership as the number of knowledge workers contacted by them expressed dismay at the word 'trade' union and considered it to be strange and alien to them. The employees expressed a professional/managerial class consciousness and pointed out their different social class origins coupled with professional identity. Even they were candid enough to say that unions are for the blue collared factory workers, where working conditions are precarious. The acts of slogan shouting, marching in streets, picketing before their organization is matter of iconoclasm to professionals like them (Noronha and D'Cruz 2009: 118). They turned out to be believers of individualism and merit. Those young knowledge workers feared that the presence of unions would bring in levelling effect on merit and their career progress as the unions would protect the less capables, compress salary differentials and equalize their pay packages. Hence, unionization would be a regressive move. Besides reflecting their professional and class consciousness, the knowledge workers have spoken the language of their employers, that unionization would threaten the flow of FDI to BPO sector in India and it would be detrimental for a nascent industry. Surprisingly, following the line of the management's thinking, these employees also expressed the empathetic concern that the MNCs in USA, UK, etc., that are investing in India's BPO sector and those outsourcing from India via offshore arrangements are themselves facing backlash/criticism in their own countries for giving employment opportunities to Indians. Hence, it would spell disaster for the ITES-BPO industry in India to unionize it. The other aspect of the story is also equally true, that neither the NASSCOM nor the ITES-BPO companies were tolerant about the presence of unions among their knowledge workers. Hence, this so-called professional consciousness among the employees was coupled with a deep-rooted fear factor. Fear of being fired by the management also refrained these knowledge workers from joining any union.

They vindicated the position of NASSCOM that unions are irrelevant to ITES-BPO sector as the employers are providing exceptionally good work environments and salaries. Even the grievances are directly met by their CEOs and these companies have deployed better HRM practices.

To the bad luck of unionist, even after holding the first convention for the formation of a union during 18–19 September 2005, the CBPOP was denied of its registration as a trade union at national level. The unionists had come up with the initial name of the union as UNITES (Union for ITES Employees). But, the very word 'Union' was not acceptable to the workforce. Hence CBPOP maintained that unionism and professionalism are not incompatible and produced counter-examples of Indian Pilots Association, Bank Officers Association, etc., that are functioning like trade unions. But, the word 'Professional' was added to UNITES later on to satisfy the knowledge workers. The clever trade unionists even tried to manipulate the young knowledge workers' minds saying that the pseudo-professional hangover of theirs is nothing but an illusion infused by their managements for their own convenience. The unionists underscored that terms like, professionals, executives, etc., are only used to circumvent the law and strip employees of job security and even their occupational status. By soft-peddling these bourgeoning ideas the managements are taking away many stipulated rights of this workforce. The managements have been cleverly redesigning and redesignating occupations to suit flexibilization programmes. Accordingly, the earlier 'office clerk' is now designated as 'junior management executive', 'supervisors' as 'production executives', 'technical workers/operators' as 'knowledge technologists', and so on. But this argument probably could cut no ice with the ITES-BPO employees.

Again, the professionalism and class consciousness among the ITES-BPO employees came in the way, as they declined to share the floor with the other ITES-BPO workers (otherwise categorized as Class IV) in the allied/support services such as, transport, cafeteria, cleaning and the like. It was indicated that the allied supporting staff are not professionals. Thus, the idea of Indian ITES-BPO-based trade union was shelved.

The unionists finally understood that the idea of being professionals has already become part of the employees identity. Hence, UNITES Professionals felt the need of having dialogue with NASSCOM and were rightly advised to work more like partners to the managements and contribute to good governance of the industry, instead of posing as adversaries. But UNITES Professionals' leaders maintained that engaging constructively with industry did not amount to being co-opted by the industry.

Therefore, they would continue to champion the cause of the knowledge workers (rights, justice, fairness, etc.) and would represent their grievances against employers. UNITES Professionals, thereafter, emphasized its members' safety (as those are night workers) and even succeeded in negotiating four collective bargaining agreements in Small and Medium Enterprises (SMEs) of domestic sector (e.g., Excel Outsourcing Services, e-Merge Business Processing, Info-point and Transact Solutions) (ibid.: 128). But, at the same time, in view of the preponderance of professionalism among the knowledge workers, UNITES Professionals also behaved like a forum and took onboard some of the ethos and orientation of ITPF, e.g., to provide for educational and training services along with information and advices. Apart from envisaging services like, psychiatric support, counselling, yoga/fitness, group health insurance, placement consultation, legal support, etc., UNITES Professionals were to establish a core certification programme with leading IT educational institutions like NIIT and APTECH. To enhance its credibility as a professional society UNITES Professionals was interacting with other professional bodies like, HR Fora, The Computer Society of India, The Manufacturing Association of India, etc. Thus, the role of a professional association and trade union both seem to be converging with UNITES Professionals.

At the end, I may wrap it up by saying that the so-called professionalism of the ITES-BPO workforce is a matter of mere self-perception and conscious identity construction. This identity as so-called professionals, partly might have been systematically fomented by their managements during their training period and partly be resultant of their class consciousness. Otherwise, their professionalism in the true sense is highly contestable.

Of course, there prevails an ambiguity with regard to the objective conditions of work of these knowledge workers. The objective conditions that are goading an intellectual to perceive the knowledge workers as 'coolies' are countered by another set of objective conditions that go neither against the left-wing intellectuals' perception nor in favour of the agents' perception of themselves as 'cool professionals'. May be it is a new class of elite workforce which by its objective conditions make a class in-itself, but in order to make a class-for-itself it needs to possess a subjective consciousness of its being. Thus, an objective class is yet to be matched by a subjective consciousness or an objective class is yet to be converted into a subjective class. Therefore, unless and until a class in itself becomes a class for itself, it would be difficult to treat them as cyber-coolies. On the contrary, there exists a hiatus between their objective conditions (i.e., an elite workforce, with much better working conditions and strong work culture, but routinized low-end jobs) and their subjective consciousness (i.e., being professionals/executives). Thus, the knowledge workers have a class consciousness that does not match their objective conditions or vice versa. Thus, it is abundantly clear that the workforce has developed a 'false consciousness'. As in the early stage of industrialization, the sociological problems of industrial workers were, inadequate wages, long hours of work (bringing surplus value), poor work environment, job insecurity, etc., and in a later stage the same got changed to alienation (loss of skill and self), technologically deterministic human behaviour, industrial accidents/health hazards, unionization, collective bargaining and subsequently to participatory management and the like, with the advent of post-industrial society (part of the economy is knowledge-based), the sociological perception of the problems of the knowledge-based workers is bound to be different as the very nature of work has undergone change. This new subclass of elite workforce is an offshoot of the India's recent IT-ICT revolution which is still evolving fast. As these knowledge workers are slowly coming under the fold of trade unions, their service conditions and salaries are improving. BPO as a phenomenon in India is going to stay; it is not a very transitory phenomenon. Rather, it is fast expanding and once stabilized as a feature of Indian economy, the career prospects in BPO industry are going to be brighter like that of their prosperous cousins in the software sector. It must be kept in mind that this Indian workforce is today envied in the USA and UK as job snatchers.

In view of the noteworthy finding that there exists a hiatus between the objective conditions of work and the class consciousness of the knowledge workers, it deserves an explanation. Any serious attempt to explain away this phenomenon would fetch J.H. Goldthorpe's (1963) thesis of embourgeoisement as one pertinent concept in this context. As it looks, this class of knowledge workers has undergone a process of embourgeoisement of a slightly different kind. Because this workforce looks to be enriched with capitals of more cultural type (values). To explicate this capital of cultural type that have resulted in the embourgeoisement of knowledge workers, one could readily point out couple of points that these: (i) are college graduates, English educated when English is not the language of Indian working class, (ii) have acquired a distinct consumption habit as they relish the mall culture, (iii) have acquired a dress sense, etiquettes and mannerisms (all anglicized), (iv) have acquired a tremendous sense of self-esteem, and (v) have acquired some managerial values, e.g., (a) driven by a strong work culture, they serve their employers first and themselves later, (b) a sense of competitiveness among the members of the subclass itself, (c) the practice of informal collegial relationship among the knowledge workers and their bosses (which in fact underplays subordination in office), and (d) optimum performance at work. With a high level of embourgeoisement it is not surprising that these knowledge workers are averse to the idea of trade union.

In fact, the more enviable job snatchers are another new budding class of highly paid employees engaged in the knowledge-based outsourcing industry of India. These are today known as KPO (knowledge process outsourcing) professionals. These are true professionals like, graduate engineers (in areas of CAD, Biotech/Pharma.), MBAs, Chartered Accountants, economists, etc. They are engaged in offshoring knowledge, intensive business processes that require specialized domain expertise. Their jobs involve high-end processes like, computer-aided simulations, valuation research and analysis, data integration, investment research, patent filing, legal/insurance claims, and management consulting, etc. KPO industry is also export-oriented like the BPO industry. But, unlike the BPO industry that mainly provides the IT-enabled services, the KPO industry provides domain-based processes and business expertise that are more challenging and requires professional as well as technical expertise on the part of employees. The KPO industry in India is slowly growing to reach an export value estimated to be $12 billion by the end of year 2010 (UNI 2005). This industry is making use of the vast pool of highly qualified but unemployed/underemployed Indian manpower. This too is a new and growing sub-class of Indian professionals emergent of the ICT revolution.

Conclusion

In this context, the phenomenon of embourgeoisement again reinforces the bourgeois values among the knowledge workers and thereby successfully checked the unionization of the ITES-BPO sector and the spread of working class consciousness and ideology. Embourgeoisement thus has a blinding effect on the knowledge workers. By soft-peddling the managerial values, it has greatly undermined the working class solidarity in the ITES-BPO industry. Having allured the knowledge workers, it has allowed them to be co-opted by the managements to a certain extent to work in cooperation with them. It might have denied the knowledge workers certain rights, but on the other hand it has ensured a better future to the knowledge workers by benefiting this nascent industry in a developing economy. At the same time, it has kept open the democratic participatory apparatus of the workforce for negotiation and consultation.

To speak from the larger sociological perspective of social stratification, these newer technologies (ICT) have created newer sub-classes of workers and added to the existing pattern of social stratifications. If it introduced changes with structural relevance it is bound to bring changes in the culture, as culture too is dependent upon the social structure. The emergent culture is, of course, to reinforces the given structural patterns or at least may continue to be structurally evasive, as it found to be the case among the ICT workforce.

REFERENCES

Bidwai, Praful. 2003. 'IT Experts or Cyber Coolies?', July 11. Retrieved on 15 December 2006. http://www.rediff. com///news/2003/jul/11praful.html

Dataquest. 2004. 'BPO Employee Survey 2004: Industry Stress Factors', http://www.dqindia.com/content/dqtop202k4/empSurvey2004/2004/104110816.asp

Friedman, Thomas L. 2006. *The World is Flat: The Globalized World in Twenty-First Century*, Updated and Expanded, London: Penguin Books, p. 660.

Gentleman, Amelia. 2005. 'Painful Truth of the Call Centre Cyber Coolies', *The Observer International*, Guardian Unlimited, Sunday, October 30. Retrieved on 18 December 2006. http://observer.guardian.co.uk/international/story/0,6903,1604664,00,html

Greenspan, Anna. 2005. *India and the IT Revolution: Networks of Global Culture*, Palgrave: Macmillan, p. 224.

Hirschfeld, K. 2005. *IT Professionals' Forum in India: Organizations at a Crossroad*, Report on a Visit to IT Professionals Forum, February 2005. Available online at http://www.uniglobalunion.org/UNIsite/groups/pms/publications/ITPFIndia-En.pdf

Kumar, Nagesh. 2001. 'Indian Software Development: International and National Perspective', *Economic and Political Weekly*, 36 (45): 4278–90.

Lateef, Asma. 1996. *Linking Up with the Global Economy: A Case Study of the Bangalore Software Industry*, International Institute for Labour Studies, ILO, Geneva.

NASSCOM. 2005. 'Executive Summary' (India BPO Study). Available online at www.bpo.nasscom.org/artdisplay.aspx?cat_id=619 (Downloaded on 19 August 2009).

——. 2006. *Strategic Review 2006*, New Delhi.

——. 2008. 'Indian IT/ITES Industry: Impacting Economy and Society, 2007–08, p. 18. Retrieved on 17 February 2010. http://www.nasscom.in/Nasscom/templates/ NormalPage.aspx?id=53649.

——. 2009. *Indian BPO Industry, Fact Sheet*.

Noronha, E. and P. D'Cruz, 2009. *Employee Identity in Indian Call Centres*, New Delhi: Response Books, p. 184.

Ramesh, B. 2004. 'Cyber Coolies in BPOs', *Economic and Political Weekly*, 39 (5): 492–97.

Ray Choudhury, Ranabir. 2003. 'The "Cyber Coolie" is Here', *Business Line*, Internet Edition, Financial Daily from The Hindu Group of Publications, Monday, December 8. Retrieved on 15 December 2006. http://www.thehindubusinessline.co/bline/2003/12/08/stories/2003120800360800.htm

Saxenian, AnnaLee. 2002. 'The Silicon Valley Connection: Transnational Networks and Regional Development in Taiwan, China and India', *Science, Technology and Society*, 7 (1): 117–49.

Taylor, Philip and Peter Bain. 2006. *An Investigation into the Offshoring of Financial Services Business Processes*. Glasgow: University of Strathclyde.

The Acron. 2005. *Cool Professionals, Not Professional Coolies*, September 26, pp. 1–3, http://acron. nationainterest.in/?p=1625

Thomas, Georgina J. 2008. 'Working in Information and Communication Technology: A Sociological Study of Call Centres in Mumbai', An unpublished Ph.D. thesis in Sociology (Chapter IV), Institute of Indian Culture, Mumbai: University of Mumbai, pp. 127–70.

Trivedi, Harish. 2004. 'Cyber Coolies, Call Centre Workers are the New Slave Labourers of 21st Century', *Little India*, October. Retrieved on 18 December 2006. http://www.littleindia.com/october2004/CyberCoolies.htm

UNI. 2005. *300,000 KPO Jobs Coming to India*, rediff.com, December 26, 16: 36 IST. Retrieved on 27 November 2007. http://www.rediff.com/cms/print.jsp?docpath=/money/2005/dec/26bpo1.htm

Upadhya, Carol. 2004. 'A New Transnational Capitalist Class? Capital Flows, Business Networks and Entrepreneurs in the Indian Software Industry', *Economic and Political Weekly*, 39 (48) (November 27–December 3): 5141–51.

——. 2006. *The Global Indian Software Labour Force: IT Professionals in Europe*, Working Paper Series No. 1, National Institute of Advanced Studies, Bangalore, IDPAD (2003–2006).

Index